Corporate Governance and Development

THE CRC SERIES ON COMPETITION, REGULATION AND DEVELOPMENT

Series Editors: Paul Cook, *Professor of Economics and Development Policy, Institute for Development Policy and Management, Director of the Centre on Regulation and Competition (CRC) and Director, Competition Research Programme in the CRC, University of Manchester, UK* and Martin Minogue, *Senior Research Fellow, Institute for Development Policy and Management and Director of the Regulatory Governance Research Programme, CRC, University of Manchester, UK*

Titles in the series include:

Corporate Governance and Development

Reform, Financial Systems and Legal Frameworks

Edited by

Thankom Gopinath Arun

Reader in International Finance, Lancashire Business School, The University of Central Lancashire and Honorary Senior Fellow, School of Environment and Development, The University of Manchester, UK

John Turner

Professor of Finance, Queen's University Management School, Belfast, UK

THE CRC SERIES ON COMPETITION, REGULATION AND DEVELOPMENT

Edward Elgar

Cheltenham, UK • Northampton, MA, USA

Published by
Edward Elgar Publishing Limited
The Lypiatts
15 Lansdown Road
Cheltenham
Glos GL50 2JA
UK

Edward Elgar Publishing, Inc.
William Pratt House
9 Dewey Court
Northampton
Massachusetts 01060
USA

A catalogue record for this book
is available from the British Library

Library of Congress Control Number: 200992273

Mixed Sources
Product group from well-managed
forests and other controlled sources
www.fsc.org Cert no. SA-COC-1565
© 1996 Forest Stewardship Council

FSC

ISBN 978 1 84844 420 1

Printed and bound by MPG Books Group, UK

To my parents and Shoba
To Karen and Jack

Contents

Figures

Tables

Contributors

Thankom Gopinath Arun is a Reader in International Finance at the University of Central Lancashire and Honorary Senior Fellow at the University of Manchester.

Omar O. Chisari is Director, Center for Advanced Research, Universidad Argentina de la Empresa.

Blanaid Clarke is a Professor of Corporate Law, University College Dublin.

Gustavo Ferro is a Professor of Economics, Universidad Argentina de la Empresa.

Michel Goyer is an Assistant Professor of Industrial Relations and Organisational Behaviour, University of Warwick.

Royston Gustavson is a Lecturer in the School of Management, Marketing and International Business, Australian National University.

Faizul Haque is a Lecturer in Finance, Heriott-Watt University.

Nicholas Ndegwa Kimani is a doctoral student in the School of Management, Marketing and International Business, Australian National University.

Priya P. Lele is a Senior Associate at Ashurst LLP and a Research Associate at the Centre for Business Research, University of Cambridge.

Sumit K. Majumdar is a Professor of Technology Strategy, Information Systems and Operations Management, University of Texas at Dallas.

Donald Atieno Ouma is Head of Research and Policy Analysis, Nairobi Stock Exchange.

M. Masrur Reaz is a Private Sector Adviser, Department for International Development(DfID), Bangladesh.

Kunal Sen is a Professor of Development Economics, University of Manchester.

Mathias M. Siems is a Reader in the School of Law, University of Edinburgh.

Dalvinder Singh is an Associate Professor, School of Law, University of Warwick.

John Turner is a Professor of Financial Economics, Queen's University, Belfast.

Rocío Valdivielso del Real is a doctoral student at Birbeck College, University of London.

Preface

The subject of corporate governance is concerned with assuring providers of capital (shareholders, creditors and employees) that their investment will not be misused or misappropriated by corporate insiders such as large shareholders or managers. This book analyses the complex relationship between corporate governance and economic development by mainly focusing on the reform of corporate governance, the role of the legal system in corporate governance, and the interconnections between corporate governance and the financial system.

Economic liberalization has increased the economic power of many firms, which may have had a negative impact both on the welfare of society and economic efficiency. Consequently, this has enhanced the need for an appropriate legal and regulatory framework, which would help to protect capital providers and safeguard consumers. Financial market liberalization, an integral part of economic reform, has opened up a renewed focus on the issue of regulation, corporate governance and development. However, research and policy dialogue on the interrelationship between these three themes have been quite compartmentalized both in terms of disciplinary and thematic boundaries. This has minimized the scope of the discussions as to what extent regulation and corporate governance are instrumental in safeguarding investments, both financial and human, and leads to wider questions on international development both in terms of stability and sustainability.

The initial idea for this book emerged from a one-day multi-disciplinary conference entitled 'Competition, Regulation and Development' organized by the Centre on Regulation and Competition at the University of Manchester in November 2007. The conference explored the role of corporate governance in economic development in general and the interrelationship between regulatory shortcomings and corporate governance in particular.

The selected papers from the conference have been revised based on editorial comments and in line with the main themes presented in the volume. This volume offers a one-stop reference guide for practitioners, academics, researchers, donor agencies and to those who are interested in understanding the multi-dimensional/disciplinary aspects of corporate governance. We are greatly indebted to the contributing authors for making their work available to us and their cooperation in revising their drafts. The chapters in the book cover the key issues in corporate governance and the broad thrust of the various contributions to this edited volume is that the subject of corporate governance must become a growing priority for policymakers in developing nations. Poor governance can result in lower investment in long-term projects, having a detrimental effect on social welfare. In addition, major corporate failures remind us that poor corporate governance can seriously affect the lives of thousands of people – investors, savers, creditors, retirees, employees, suppliers, and consumers.

Finally, we must express our gratitude to those publishers of two original papers in the volume. We are especially thankful to Paul Cook and Martin Minogue for their support in listing the book in the CRC Book series.

Thankom Gopinath Arun
Preston/Manchester
August 2008

John Turner
Belfast
August 2008

Acknowledgements

We would like to express our thanks to the publishers for allowing us to reproduce the following articles:

Mathias M. Siems and Priya Lele, 'Shareholder protection: a leximetric approach' *Journal of Corporate Law Studies*, **17**, 17–50, 2007, (Hart Publishing).

T. G. Arun and J. D. Turner, 'Corporate governance of banks in developing economies: concepts and issues', *Corporate Governance: An International Review*, **12** (3), 371–7, 2004, (Blackwell Publishing).

1. Corporate governance and development: reform, financial systems and legal framework – an overview

Thankom Gopinath Arun and John Turner

INTRODUCTION

The initial idea for this book emerged from a conference entitled *Competition, Regulation and Development* organized by the Centre on Regulation and Competition at the University of Manchester in November 2007. The selected papers from the conference have been revised based on editorial comments and in line with the main themes presented in the volume. We are greatly indebted to the contributing authors for making their work available to us and their cooperation in revising their drafts.

Since the genesis of the corporation (or company), there has been a concern with what we now term corporate governance. Notably, even Adam Smith (1999) in *The Wealth of Nations* alludes to governance problems in early corporations. This book analyses the complex relationship between corporate governance and economic development by focusing on the reform of corporate governance, the role of the legal system in corporate governance, and the interconnections between corporate governance and the financial system. Although economists have typically viewed corporate governance as the ways by which investors assure themselves of getting a return on their investment, this book takes a broader view on the topic by developing a multi-dimensional perspective from disparate disciplines such as development studies, law, economics and finance.

In the finance and economics literature, there has been considerable debate as to whether finance ultimately matters for economic growth (Levine, 2004). Adherents of the Modigliani-Miller school argue that it is real investments which matter, not how they are financed. For example, Lucas (1988) argues that finance doesn't matter for economic growth. Taken to its logical conclusion, this perspective implies that how businesses are organized, governed and financed does not affect their value, and hence the performance of the overall economy. An alternative view, going back to Schumpeter (1912), is that finance is an important engine of economic growth. This view was given impetus by the seminal works of Goldsmith (1969), Shaw (1973) and McKinnon (1973). Since the late 1980s there has been a plethora of empirical studies examining the impact of finance on growth. On the whole, the empirical evidence suggests that the impact of financial development on growth is positive (King and Levine, 1993a, 1993b; Levine, 1997; Levine and Zervos, 1998; Beck and Levine, 2004; Levine, 2004). Indeed, the growing consensus is that finance does matter for development, and as a result, policy-makers have been paying closer attention to the structure and organization of financial systems. In particular, strenuous attempts have been made to strengthen the financial systems of developing economies (e.g. Arun and Turner, 2002).

If finance matters for economic development, then corporate govern-ance must also affect economic development for at least two reasons. First, corporate governance affects how and at what cost firms finance their real investments. Poor corporate governance can have a detrimental impact on a firm's performance, and if it is an endemic problem in a country, it will undoubtedly have a major impact on economic growth. Secondly, the quality and nature of corporate governance can affect the structure of the financial system. If shareholders are poorly protected and companies are poorly governed, then one would not expect to see a thriving market for publicly-traded equity. Instead, most external business finance will be provided by banks.

The broad thrust of the various contributions to this edited volume is that the subject of corporate governance must become a growing prior-ity for policymakers in developing nations. Poor governance can result in lower investment in long-term projects, having a detrimental effect on social welfare and affect the lives of many.

Financial crises in South-East Asia, Russia and Brazil have alerted poli-cymakers to the problems of poor quality of corporate governance in devel-oping countries. The seminal work by OECD in this regard clarifies the importance of corporate governance from a long-term development per-spective, by analysing the institutional conditions and actual functioning/ malfunctioning of corporate governance (Lin, 2001; Malherbe and Segal, 2001; Oman, 2001). The findings of this work emphasize that the quality of corporate governance matters significantly for developing countries in contributing to a country's ability to achieve sustained productivity growth and lasting democratic political institutions, both of which are crucial for long-term national development.

Corporate governance has a significant role to increase the flow and lower the cost of the financial capital and the importance of this role is likely to continue to grow as the needs of corporations for extra-firm finance have grown when the capacity of traditional sources of such finance has greatly diminished (Oman, 2001). This study has further argued out the potential benefits of improved corporate governance for achieving productivity growth in the real economy of many developing countries.

CORPORATE GOVERNANCE REFORM

Both in developed and developing economies, corporate governance systems have been undergoing reform. In developed economies, following the well-publicized collapses of Enron, WorldCom and Parmalat, governments and securities regulators have been attempting to strengthen corporate governance systems through a variety of reforms. In developing nations, pressure from international bodies and the increased competition arising from globalization have resulted in developing nations reforming their financial systems by adopting Anglo-Saxon corporate governance norms. Thus, given the importance of this issue, Chapters 2, 3 and 4 of this book looks at corporate governance reform. The chapters examine corporate governance reform in developed, developing and emerging economies.

In Chapter 2, Chisari and Ferro use a general equilibrium perspective to evaluate the net gains of implementing new standards of corporate governance in Argentina in relation to the attitudes of societies to the adoption of stricter rules and costs involved in the implementation. Their study takes account of the potential gains in terms of the capital market workings, along with the scarcity of resources and structural characteristics of the economy. The authors suggest that the costs of reform could impinge upon consumers, and not necessarily on shareholders alone. Indeed, Chisari and Ferro provide a warning that the net gains of corporate governance reform could be significantly negative.

In Chapter 3, Gustavson, Kimani and Ouma, in their chapter, question the wisdom of replicating the Anglo-American model of corporate governance in sub-Saharan Africa. Based on the experiences of Botswana, Kenya and Zambia, the authors argue that changes to the Anglo-American model need to be made in order to increase its fit to different cultures on a culture-by-culture basis. The chapter further argues that the changes are necessary only if they do not undermine the entire system, and the overall costs to society of change are less than the costs to society of not changing.

Goyer and Rocío analyse the impact of the reform associated with ownership structure, voting rights and the system of corporate law in the electricity sectors of Britain and Spain. The institutions of corporate governance are mediated by their interaction with the wider institutional framework in which they are embedded. The chapter illustrates the prominence of national institutions of corporate governance and suggests that differences between Britain and Spain largely account for the divergence in the transformation of the profile of the electricity sector in the two countries. The chapter further argues that the institutions of corporate governance matter, due to their interaction with national regulatory policies.

CORPORATE GOVERNANCE AND THE FINANCIAL SYSTEM

Capital markets have steadily become more sophisticated in developing economies, and these markets may play an important role in disciplining firms to act in an efficient manner. However, in developing economies, banks are typically the main source of business finance. Consequently, banks may play an important role in governance of firms via their lending. Given the dominance of banks in the financial systems of developing economies, close attention needs to be paid to the governance of these institutions. These issues are all addressed in the Chapters 5, 6, 7 and 8 of this book.

Using a dataset on a cross-section of Indian firms, Majumdar and Sen provide an analysis of the effects of the different types of corporate borrowing on firms' performance. The chapter argues that institutional borrowing has a strong negative effect on profitability for poorly performing firms, which highlights the need to take into account institutional differences and firm heterogeneity in the analysis of capital structure on firms' performance.

Arun and Turner discuss the corporate governance of banking institutions in developing economies. They take a conceptual approach to the corporate governance of banks, suggesting that banking and governance reforms can only be fully implemented once a prudential regulatory system is in place. The chapter further argues that corporate governance reforms may be a prerequisite for the successful divestiture of government ownership.

The previous chapter, by Haque, investigates the influence of firm-level corporate governance on the firm's cost of equity capital and capital market development in Bangladesh. Using an index for corporate governance, Haque suggests that capital markets provide incentives for better governance of firms. Reaz, in his chapter on the banking sector in Bangladesh, investigates the impact of corporate governance measures on banking sector performance and provides evidence of the abuse of control by majority shareholders and management boards. These two chapters on Bangladesh recognize the need for strong legal and regulatory institutions in order to bolster the disciplining function of the capital market and to protect minority shareholders, creditors and depositors.

CORPORATE GOVERNANCE AND THE LEGAL FRAMEWORK

The recent law and finance literature which has emanated from Andrei Shleifer and his co-authors has highlighted the important role of well-defined and protected property rights and legal protection for investors (La Porta et al., 1998, 1999, 2000). The legal system constrains and restrains the behaviour of managers and, as a consequence, protects shareholders and creditors. The most controversial aspect of this body of work is the claim that common law systems provide investor protection that is superior to that provided by civil law systems. This controversial issue, as well as the less controversial aspects of this body of work, are the focus of the final three chapters of this book.

Clarke examines the legal and regulatory framework in Ireland and the EU which regulates the advice given by the board of a target company to its shareholders during a takeover bid. She suggests that the nature of takeovers is not covered in general corporate governance regulation, nor is it covered adequately by specific takeover regulation. The study finds that although the rules do not attempt to set out all the circumstances in which a conflict arises, they do set out a number of circumstances in which conflict will exist.

Lele and Siems develop a shareholder protection index for five countries, providing interesting possibilities for comparing variations across time and legal systems. The study finds that shareholder protection has been improving over the last three decades. It also suggests that major differences in shareholder protection do not exist between common law and civil law countries.

Finally, Singh focuses on the corporate legal framework, based on the experience of the UK Financial Services Authority. It is important to highlight how corporate law provides limited safeguards to protect the interests of depositors, requiring some form of public regulation. This chapter analyses the interplay between general corporate law and banking regulation and supervision, explores the position of depositors as stakeholders in banks and delineates the duty the bank has towards them as unsecured creditors and the limited powers depositors have to respond collectively.

REFERENCES

Arun, T. G. and J. D. Turner (2002), 'Financial sector reforms: the Indian experience', *The World Economy*, **25**, 429–45.

Beck, T. and R. Levine (2004), 'Stock markets, banks and growth: panel evidence', *Journal of Banking and Finance*, **28**, 423–442.

Goldsmith, R. W. (1969), *Financial Structure and Development*, New Haven, CT: Yale University Press.

King, R. G. and R. Levine (1993a), 'Finance and growth: Schumpeter might be right', *Quarterly Journal of Economics*, **108**, 717–37.

King, R. G. and R. Levine (1993b), 'Finance, entrepreneurship and growth: theory and evidence', *Journal of Monetary Economics*, **32**, 513–42.

La Porta, R., F. López de Silanes, and A. Shleifer (1999), 'Corporate ownership around the world', *Journal of Finance*, **54**, 471–517.

La Porta, R., F. López de Silanes, A. Shleifer and R.W. Vishny (1998), 'Law and finance', *Journal of Political Economy*, **106**, 1113–55.

La Porta, R., F. López de Silanes, A. Shleifer and R.W. Vishny (2000), 'Investor protection and corporate governance', *Journal of Financial Economics*, **58**, 3–27.

Levine, R. (1997), 'Financial development and economic growth: views and agenda', *Journal of Economic Literature*, **35**, 688–726.

Levine, R. (2004), 'Finance and growth: theory and evidence', *NBER Working Paper Series*, no. 10766.

Levine, R. and S. Zervos (1998), 'Stock markets, banks, and economic growth', *American Economic Review*, **88**, 537–88.

Lin, C. (2001), 'Private vices in public places: challenges in corporate governance development in China', *OECD Development Centre Discussion Paper*.

Lucas, R. E. (1988), 'On the mechanics of economic development', *Journal of Monetary Economics*, **22**, 3–42.

Malherbe, S. and N. Segal (2001), 'Corporate governance in South Africa', *OECD Development Centre Discussion Paper*.

McKinnon, R. I. (1973), *Money and Capital in Economic Development*, Washington, DC: Brookings Institution.

Oman, C. P. (2001), 'Corporate governance and national development', *OECD Development Centre Technical Papers*, no. 180.

Schumpeter, J. A. (1912), *Theorie der Wirtschaftlichen Entwicklung*, Leipzig: Dunker und Humboldt.

Shaw, E. S. (1973), *Financial Deepening in Economic Development*, New York: Oxford University Press.

Smith, A. (1999) [1776], *The Wealth of Nations*, London: Penguin Books.

2. Gains and losses of adopting new standards of corporate governance: a CGE analysis of Argentina

Omar O. Chisari and Gustavo Ferro

INTRODUCTION

Practices of corporate governance in use at the international level, and in particular in the USA, have been presented as methods to facilitate access of less developed countries to the world savings supply. It is expected that by obtaining said access, welfare will be improved, particularly via higher growth rates. Cross-country econometric studies are the evidence habitually used to support this view.

This chapter presents an alternative approach, a Computable General Equilibrium (CGE) cost/benefit evaluation for Argentina. This perspective is interesting because it focuses not only on the conjectural gains of higher standards of corporate governance, but also on endowment of factors of an economy and on its structural characteristics. Not all economies are able to provide the resources needed to reach higher standards of corporate governance in unlimited quantities at a reasonable price. Moreover, the benefits and increasing costs of auditing cannot be evenly distributed after taking into account relative price interactions that influence factor rewards and social welfare.

For a small economy, open to both trade and capital flows, the cost of capital has an important exogenous component, depending on the rest of the world's evaluation of its economic and financial health. Therefore, there are two relevant questions. First, what are the general equilibrium net results of extending more demanding corporate governance practices of a given cost to a subset of firms in a given economy? Second, what is the reduction in the cost of capital that is necessary to compensate for those additional costs?

It is known that the costs of actions and policies are passed through to the economy via the inter-industrial chain. Goods 'intensive in corporate governance' will have higher prices, and they will impinge upon the

7

costs of industries that use them as inputs. Consumers will see different prices of consumption goods for their endowments of production factors. Expansion and contraction of industries will also modify their intensity in the demand of capital and labour. Elasticities of substitution, mobility of factors and international prices will become key parameters for the determination of the final result on aggregated and individual welfare. Moreover, the public sector itself will see different levels of revenue from taxation.

Corporate governance costs in our CGE framework are treated as an expense in an intermediate input. If an additional demand for audit services is mandatory and required by regulation, it can be modelled as an increase in the corresponding input coefficient for every industry (analogous to a loss of efficiency in the use of an intermediate good). An expansion of demand for those services will have to be matched with an increase of quantity supplied by the auditing industry; the elasticity of supply of that industry will therefore become a relevant parameter for the final impact on total costs. Then the availability of resources and the elasticity of supply of factors that that sector uses (in particular educated labour) will be relevant for the overall result, and structural differences between economies will also become relevant to explain total net benefits and their distribution, and to understand why some societies are more enthusiastic than others to adopt stricter standards.

The present chapter is organized as follows. Following this introduction, the next section discusses the definitions of corporate governance, and summarizes recent developments in the world and in Argentina. The third section presents the CGE model in use and its rationale. The fourth section reports the empirical results. Finally, the fifth section focuses on the conclusions of the analysis.

DEFINITIONS OF CORPORATE GOVERNANCE AND RECENT DEVELOPMENTS IN ARGENTINA

There are several definitions of corporate governance in the literature, but still there is not much clarity on what 'good' corporate governance is. We think it is helpful to distinguish between the set of 'available practices and standards' and a subset of 'good practices and standards'. The second one should include those practices that help to maximize (static or dynamic) welfare.

For OECD economies, corporate governance is the system of practices that controls and manages business corporations. Corporate governance practices as a system make specific the distribution of rights and responsibilities between stakeholders. They detail rules and procedures for the decision process, and provide a framework for the determination of the objectives of a company (CEF, 2005).

Gutiérrez-Urtiaga (2004) defines corporate governance as the set of institutions that determines how the residual claims are distributed between those who have participated in the generation of profits. Shleifer and Vishny (1996), in their survey, argue that corporate governance is the form in which stakeholders make sure they will obtain a return of their investment. On the other hand, Fremond and Capaul (2002) emphasize that good corporate governance practices reduce the ex-post expropriation risk; thus the ex-ante cost of capital is also lowered. CEF (2005) emphasizes the agency perspective, stressing that corporate governance is the mechanism which sets the incentives for the company's operation, in order to protect the interests, assets, rights and liabilities of the different participants.

Our definition, however, tries to reconcile all the previous concepts, which are not mutually exclusive. Hence, we view corporate governance as the available system of institutions or mechanisms that induce incentives in listed business firms, so as to distribute benefits between stakeholders, restricting discretion on such distribution (in a context of asymmetric information and incomplete contracts).[1] Those institutions and mechanisms are structured to solve conflicts of interests, and if this process is successful, the risk faced by investors and creditors of the firm will be lower. 'Good' corporate governance is defined as the subset of those practices that are welfare enhancing for the economy.

The gains of good corporate governance have been analysed in econometric studies of cross-sectional data or simple models of partial equilibrium. In the first case, a regression imputes causalities and orients qualitative reforms. In the second case, the various sectors and principal-agent relationships are examined, without appreciating the shocks that spill over to other related sectors. In contrast, a general equilibrium perspective allows us to see how the gains and losses of different corporate governance standards spread via the habitual interchange relations.

The international view of regulatory reforms on corporative governance issues is not uniform and can be grouped into two classes: the 'Soft Law'[2] approach and the 'stricter legislative reforms'[3] point of view. With respect to soft law, the more remarkable issues for emerging economies are the 'Principles' and the 'Regional Round Tables' of the OECD (OECD, 2003, 2004). Regarding stricter legislative reforms, the most influential norm at international level has been the Sarbanes-Oxley Act (SOX for brief), enacted in the USA after significant corporate scandals at the beginning of the millennium. Its goal is to protect investors and to improve the exactitude and trustworthiness of the information that listed firms are forced to disclose. SOX demands more and better quality information, and it intensifies penalties for wrongdoers. However, the costs of implementation could be very high. A growing literature attempts to assess the cost of SOX: Wallison (2005), Bergen (2005), Zhang (2005), Gifford and Howe (2004) and CRA International (2006).

Apreda (2001) characterizes corporate governance in Argentina before 1991 as follows:

1. During the twentieth century, the main domestic groups had been family controlled firms. The financial resources were obtained from own banks or public banks.
2. Only directors belonging to the controlling families were designated on boards. The CEO usually came from the founder family.
3. Almost all firms established clauses in their charters in order to favour the control groups regarding their directors. Many familiar firms stopped quoting, affecting interests of minority shareholders. The takeovers were friendly most of the times. Few in-cash dividends were paid.
4. No firms issued bonds in capital markets during the whole period 1913–90. They financed from internal sources, by loans and occasionally by new IPO. Of 550 quoted firms in 1960, only 103 are quoted today. In most cases, the number of independent directors coincides with the minimum required by regulation.

An important change has been going on in Argentina over the past decade or so. Large companies, which used to be family contolled, now belong to foreign groups, and minority participation is in the hands of institutional investors (mainly pension funds). During the 1990s, Argentina adopted norms of corporate governance from common law countries. Since 2000, reforms have centred on the legislation of securities markets. The legal context only imposed general aspects, delegating the statutory details to the regulator (CNV, Comisión Nacional de Valores). Decree 677/01 incorporated important changes: it gave new responsibilities to directors, enacted provisions about the independence of directors and external auditors, and established penalties. The composition of the Audit Committee was also regulated. Three or more board members must be on it, and the board of the issuing society should define its designation. The Committee's members must have experience in accountancy, finance and business topics (Marsili *et al.*, 2003). Apart from IDEA (2004) and Reina (2005), the body of literature on estimates of corporate governance costs is scarce. However, in this chapter we attempt to estimate the costs of adopting these new corporate governance standards in Argentina.

COMPUTABLE GENERAL EQUILIBRIUM MODEL AND SOCIAL ACCOUNTING MATRIX

A Computable General Equilibrium Model (CGE) is a numeric representation of the conditions of equilibrium of the economy. Consumers are endowed with factors and goods, and their preferences are represented with CES utility functions; producers maximize profits, hiring factors from consumers, and use their available technology to supply goods.

The CGE model uses a Social Accounting Matrix (SAM) as its database. The SAM is the most natural tool to present observed transactions for a defined period, since it represents all income and expenditure flows of aggregated agents considered in the model (Pyatt and Round, 1985). The model considered in this chapter is Walrasian in its logic, and it follows the general structure presented in Chisari *et al.* (1999).

The solution of the model is obtained using the general equilibrium representation, and the mixed complementary approach. Ferris and Pang (1997) summarize applications to economies and firms. The model is constructed in a GAMS/MPSGE environment, following the developments of Tom Rutherford. Brooke *et al.* (1992) developed GAMS, and Rutherford (1999) discusses MPSGE (Mathematical Programming System for General Equilibrium Analysis). Rutherford's MPSGE software is based on Mathiesen (1985), which suggests that CGE models can be seen as complementary problems. They involve duality conditions between excess demand and prices, on the one hand; and net benefits per unit and activity levels, on the other hand.

In the model used in the simulations, households decide on consumption, investment, labour supply (labour/leisure decision) and portfolio composition. Those decisions are a result of utility maximization.

Expenses are distributed into national, imported and investment goods. It is assumed that there is imperfect substitution between imported and national consumption goods. In tradable goods there is perfect substitution and in non-tradable goods there is imperfect substitution. Agents' budget constraints reflect total expenditure in goods and services, direct and indirect taxes and transfers between agents. Sources of income include labour income, capital payments and government transfers (unemployment subsidies, pensions and so on).

The government maximizes a general welfare utility function, which includes as its arguments the production of goods (public or private but of public provision), employment and pensions. Pensions, servicing of the debt, investments and operating expenses are assumed to be a constant proportion of government income; tax revenues and bond issues (net of capital and interest repayment) finance the government budget.

Argentina is considered a small country with respect to the rest of the world. The production of goods and services in the rest of the world is obtained from a production possibility frontier, with a constant marginal rate of substitution (there is only one scarce factor abroad). The rest of the world is therefore represented with this production sector and with a consumer who accrues all of the foreign factor.

The current account deficit (or surplus) is compensated with financial capital movements, represented as purchases or sales of bonds of domestic and foreign agents.

Unemployment is admitted; real wages are indexed to the CPI of the economy. We distinguish two types of labour: formal and informal. The first group represents the registered labour (normally more educated), and the second corresponds to less educated workers. In this model, an inelastic supply of labour is assumed.

Physical capital is specific for each one of the sectors. Financial capital is perfectly mobile but has a very low substitution with the rest of the capital factors. New capital goods are not incorporated in current capital in use, and the analysis is then for the short run.

The CGE model is based on the Social Accounting Matrix for Argentina as of 2003. The model comprises 29 productive sectors, ten income deciles/groups of consumers, the government sector and the rest of the world. There is an effort to integrate with the national accounts of the economy. The Central Bank and the pension system are explicitly modelled as producers. Sector 27 includes the industry that produces 'audit services'.

The participation of each decile in the consumption of the different goods and services, along with the compatibility of the SAM's sector, allowed the distribution of the consumption vector of the households, national as well as imported, between the different deciles. The government expenses are wages and salaries paid to government employees, purchases of goods and services, transfer payments and public debt services. This is all mainly financed by taxes, charged on firms and families. The deficit or surplus is the net saving of the public sector, which is covered with net bonds issued.

To understand how the additional costs of auditing are incorporated, let us consider the case of only one domestic agent with a utility function that depends on domestic goods and imported good consumption: $u(c, m)$. Equation 2.1 corresponds to the optimal condition of marginal rate of substitution equalized to relative prices, given by the price of the domestic good at international prices p^* and prices of imports p_m^*. Equation 2.2 is the budget constraint of the domestic agent, where w stands for wages, L^0 the endowment of labour, π and π_a for profits in the industry that produces the domestic good and in the industry that produces auditing services.

$$u_c/u_m = p^*/p_m \tag{2.1}$$

$$p^* c + p^*_m m = w L^0 + \pi + \pi_a \tag{2.2}$$

Equation 2.3 gives the production of domestic goods for consumption c or for exports x in terms of employment and capital (assumed in hands only of the rest of the world in this simplification, but not in the general model).

$$x + c = F(L, K) \tag{2.3}$$

Profits in the industry of consumption goods are given by:

$$\pi = p^* (x + c) - w L - r^* K - p_a a^d \tag{2.4}$$

Where r^* indicates the international rate of interest and $p_a a^d$ are the expenses in auditing services, assumed to be in fixed coefficients α with total value added:

$$a^d = \alpha F(L, K) \tag{2.5}$$

Profits maximization requires:[4]

$$(p^* - \alpha p_a) F_k - r^* = 0 \tag{2.6}$$

$$(p^* - \alpha p_a) F_L - w = 0 \tag{2.7}$$

when levels of capital and labour used in production are determined optimally.

At the level of the industry that produces audit services, the corresponding equations of profit definition, optimal conditions and production function are:

$$\pi_a = p_a G(L_a) - w L_a \tag{2.8}$$

$$a^s = G(L_a) \tag{2.9}$$

$$p_a G'(L_a) - w = 0 \tag{2.10}$$

Notice that it is assumed that the sector only uses labour to produce its services. In the general model we assume that there are different kinds of labour and that the sector uses qualified labour more intensively. Moreover, the elasticity of substitution between factors is used as a parameter to explore sensitivity to different assumptions on the supply of auditing services and scarcity of human capital.

We have also the familiar conditions of equilibrium in the labour market and in the auditing services market:

$$L_a + L = L^0 \tag{2.11}$$

$$a^d - a^s = 0 \tag{2.12}$$

From the former system, the current account equilibrium is obtained:

$$p^x x = p^*_m m + r^* K \tag{2.13}$$

The general equilibrium model then explores the effect on domestic welfare of increasing α, and then how r^* should be reduced to obtain positive results in terms of GDP, rate of profit of domestic producers or welfare of individual deciles. It is also seen that profit rates of industries change in relative terms, which means that the incentives to invest in those sectors will change too.

So, for the macroeconomic experiments of compensation we use the following assumption:

$$r^* = f(\alpha; \mathbf{v})$$

$$f'(\alpha) < 0$$

That is, the cost of capital to the economy is sensitive to the expenses in audit services. The cost of capital depends also on a vector $\mathbf{v}$ of exogenous parameters.

It is interesting to think that companies could have already selected an optimal level of expenses in audit services (for example to control managers by shareholders or to give a signal to capital markets). In that case, the level would have been obtained by maximizing profits with respect to α:

$$- dr^*/d\alpha - p_a F(L, K) = 0 \tag{2.14}$$

However, the regulatory authorities could consider that level insufficient, given spillover and macroeconomic effects and (as in the case of liquidity constraints for banks) could impose a minimum level higher than the one chosen by companies.

SIMULATIONS

In order to conduct simulations, first, firms in the economy are classified as Public Firms (PUF) or Private Firms (PRF). Shares of PUF are quoted in local or multinational markets, where strict standard requirements of corporate governance are mandatory. A PRF has softer legal and regulatory obligations regarding information disclosure and auditing. The PUF group is different from the PRF in the following aspects:

1. PUF use more intensive auditing services.
2. PUF have a more intensive use of financial capital.
3. Presumably, PUF have a greater degree of tax formality.

PUF are more intensive users of auditing services (internal and external) per unit of produced goods than are PRF. Such auditing services will be used as a proxy of the greater costs that originated from the fulfilment of corporate governance standards. In our simulations, these higher costs were approximated by estimating the additional expense that large and medium size firms have to incur because of the requirements of an Audit Committee, an obligation that PRF do not face. This cost is possibly the minimum of the differential expenditure requests to the PUF, but it is a quantifiable number based on public information.

PUF have a more intensive use of financial capital per unit of produced goods than PRF, and their major gain of adopting good corporate governance practices will be a capital cost decrease, or improved ways of access to credit.

The impact of the addition of more demanding standards of corporate governance was explored constructing a sample of Argentine companies susceptible to adopting the said practices, becoming PUF after the reform. Nowadays, only slightly more than 100 firms are PUF in the Argentine capital market and an important proportion of them are already listed in foreign markets. If the ownership of the companies is tracked, one half is family owned companies and the other half multinationals; there are no atomized companies in the Argentine market (Bebczuk, 2005).

For the simulations, we selected two kinds of firm that could afford higher costs of auditing:

1. Large firms: those with annual profits greater than AR$50 million (US$16 million).

2.   Medium sized firms: those with annual profits between AR$10 and 50 million (US$3.3 to 16 million).

Then, they were classified according to the SAM's activities. An audited cost of AR$0.6 annual millions (US$0.2 millions) was attributed to large firms, whereas for medium sized firms, this cost is AR$ 0.3 annual million (US$ 0.1 million). These amounts were obtained from personal communication with Argentine experts, and can be considered as highly reliable. They give a good proxy of the costs of an Auditing Committee populated by three independent internal directors in the company. The same sources made notice that additional costs of corporate governance improvement, such as those of an external auditing, have not had price increases after the implementation of Decree 677/01, which modified the regulation of corporate governance in Argentina. The costs of listing, determined by the Buenos Aires Stock Exchange, have a component almost totally fixed and an initial incidence at the beginning of quotation, so they were not considered. Finally, the indemnity insurance to directors is relatively cheap, since the coverage is low: in the Argentine case, it does not cover bad faith, wilful misconduct or serious damage. The local sentences for financial malfeasance do not have the severity of those in the USA.

We considered three scenarios. The difference between them is the quantity of firms that hypothetically will become PUF. All three scenarios include 415 large firms and a variable number of medium sized firms: 1000 (Scenario 1), 2500 (Scenario 2) and 4000 (Scenario 3).

Table 2.1 shows the increase of auditing costs, measured as a percentage increase of the auditing services, with respect to the initial participation within the costs of the respective sector (the producer of auditing services uses a sector specific factor; the idea was to reflect the specificity of the human capital dedicated to this task). The imputation by sector was made including the number of companies detected in each scenario and multiplying them by the unit cost of the increased auditing services when passing from PRF to PUF.

In some sectors, large firms are the rule, whereas in others there are many medium sized firms. The cost increases in auditing are therefore different for each sector, depending on the average size of a firm and the number of firms. There are also sectors that by their objective (such as Public Administration), or by the negligible importance of the higher costs in its intermediate consumption, do not have sizable impacts.

Table 2.2 presents the results of simulations from Scenario 2, considered the more plausible because of the number of firms involved. Two cases are studied: one with high elasticity of substitution between productive factors at the auditing sector, and the other with low elasticity of substitution. The

Table 2.1   Percentage increase in audit costs by sector and by scenario

	Scenario 1	Scenario 2	Scenario 3
Agriculture, farming, fishing, hunting and forestry	4.34	8.89	13.51
Natural gas extraction	4.05	6.07	8.50
Petroleum, mines and quarries	0.00	0.00	0.00
Non-intensive industry energy	4.19	7.59	11.02
Intensive industry energy	3.50	6.35	9.25
Electricity generation	0.00	0.00	0.00
Electricity transport and distribution	10.10	14.04	18.23
Gas transport and distribution	6.53	6.53	6.53
Water	0.00	0.00	0.00
Construction	1.81	4.14	6.47
Commerce, restaurants and hotels	0.69	1.13	1.57
Transport, storage and communications	1.04	2.01	2.99
Financial intermediation, real estate and services to companies	1.47	2.66	3.84
Public administration publish and defence	0.00	0.00	0.00
Education, social and health services and other services	0.30	0.47	0.64

objective was to appraise the potential impact of the relative scarcity of skilled labour, of which 'Financial' (sector 27) is an intensive user.

As we mentioned above, our exercise is analogous to an efficiency loss of all sectors in the use of sector 27's input. The general result is that GDP reduction is in the range of 0.23 to 0.39 per cent depending on the assumptions on elasticity of substitution of factors in sector 27 and on the conditions in the labour market (unemployment or full employment). Even though audit expenses are paid to domestic factors, there are still significant losses.

We have included an indicator of government welfare, similar to the Equivalent Variation for private households. Changes in level of activity and in relative prices affect government welfare. In turn, lower government revenue (linked to GDP) heavily influences the welfare of the poor included in the first deciles because they receive financial aid and social transfers. In contrast, the richest are concentrated in the last deciles and they are entitled to capital rewards, financial endowments and skilled labour income (intensively used by the auditing industry).

Firms' profits diminish (slightly) since they have to spend more on auditing services. The other face of the mirror is given by 'Financial' sector 27 since its profits grow, being the provider of auditing services.

Table 2.2　Aggregated results from simulations (Scenario 2), and exercises of compensation, shown as percentages

Variation in	Unemployment		Full Employment		Compensation Exercises (from D)		
	A	B	C	D	E	F	G
First decile welfare	−0.20	−0.33	−0.15	−0.15	−0.05	2.65	0.63
Second decile welfare	−0.25	−0.38	−0.21	−0.20	−0.11	2.29	0.49
Third decile welfare	−0.30	−0.43	−0.27	−0.25	−0.17	2.05	0.39
Fourth decile welfare	−0.27	−0.41	−0.25	−0.24	−0.16	1.86	0.34
Fifth decile welfare	−0.28	−0.42	−0.29	−0.26	−0.20	1.51	0.23
Sixth decile welfare	−0.25	−0.41	−0.29	−0.26	−0.21	1.22	0.15
Seventh decile welfare	−0.26	−0.42	−0.33	−0.29	−0.25	0.76	0.00
Eighth decile welfare	−0.20	−0.34	−0.27	−0.24	−0.20	0.63	0.01
Ninth decile welfare	−0.09	−0.17	−0.11	−0.11	−0.08	0.65	0.11
Tenth decile welfare	0.06	0.09	0.10	0.07	0.08	0.27	0.13
Government welfare	−0.16	−0.23	−0.03	−0.02	−0.01	0.33	0.08
Primary sector profit rate	−0.46	−0.37	−0.26	−0.20	−0.14	1.54	0.29
Secondary sector profit rate	−0.89	−0.77	−0.74	−0.64	−0.55	1.91	0.06
Tertiary sector profit rate	0.03	−0.002	0.22	0.15	0.29	4.15	1.25
Ratio investment/GDP	−0.07	−0.04	−0.01	−0.01	0.10	3.02	0.83
GDP	−0.29	−0.39	−0.25	−0.23	−0.22	0.00	−0.17
Compensatory reduction of cost of capital					1.14	26.7	7.94

Notes:　A, C = Low Elasticity (0.25), B, D = High Elasticity (1.25), E = Profit Rate of the Economy, F = GDP level at Constant Prices, G = Welfare of Most Affected Decile.

The simulations under unemployment are computed assuming constant wages in real terms. An increase in auditing costs also increases total average costs for firms. Under fixed real wages, unemployment is increased even further, and this explains why welfare levels are reduced more than under full employment or with flexibility of wages.

We can see that increasing the elasticity of substitution between factors of production does not necessarily reduce the impact of additional costs. Under unemployment, since the auditing industry is able to use more skilled labour to substitute for capital, it absorbs more resources from the rest of the economy, and hence the fall of GDP is higher.

It is noticeable that the burden of the reform does not affect welfare in an even pattern across deciles. In fact, it hurts the poorest deciles more and the richest much less, because there is a reduction in the unemployment of skilled labour (under unemployment) or an increase in skilled labour salaries (under full employment).

Notice that cost increases are permanent (to be paid every period) and therefore gains shall be compared at their present value too. To assess gains that can compensate for the additional costs, we consider three exercises of compensation using as a reference Scenario 2. We address only the case of full employment and high elasticity of substitution (Columns E, F and G in Table 2.2).

First of all, we compute the required reduction of the international rate of interest to restore the average profit rate in the economy to its level prior to the increase in auditing costs. However, it is not sufficient to recover initial welfare levels. Column E of Table 2.2 presents the results of simulating the cost increases of extending stricter corporate governance standards, coupled with the reduction in the international rate of interest already mentioned. In other words, if higher expenses in auditing services apply, and also the international rate of interest is diminished by 1.14 per cent of its previous level, then the profit rate of the economy will remain constant. The necessary compensation is modest and can be considered 'affordable' for the economy.

Second, the change in the international rate of interest required to restore the GDP (at constant prices) level prior to the introduction of stricter standards was investigated (Column F). Welfare levels grow substantially, basically because the costs are transferred abroad. The reduction in the effort necessary to compensate the current account reduces exports, which in turn reduces GDP, and this creates a 'multiplier effect' that further reduces the cost of capital to compensate for changes. That is why the necessary reduction in the rest of the world factor payments to restore the former level of GDP is very significant (it must fall to more than a quarter of its former level). This case does not seem plausible.

Third, we computed the compensation necessary to recover the welfare level of the most affected decile in Scenario 2. The seventh decile is in an intermediate situation, since it receives small amounts of transfers from the government and it does not have a significant endowment of skilled labour. Results are shown in Column G; we can see that it requires a fall in the cost of capital for the economy of 8 per cent with respect to its original level to restore the seventh decile welfare to its initial level. However the rest of the deciles obtain significant net gains.

CGE simulations are of course sensitive to changes in parameters, in assumptions on factor mobility and in rules of macroeconomic closure. However, our first results show that more demanding rules of corporate governance could have important effects on the allocation of resources, on welfare and income distribution. Those dimensions are habitually put aside in most studies, which tend to make their recommendations on the basis of industrial organization or partial equilibrium analyses.

CONCLUSION

Previously, the net gains of new standards of corporate governance have been analysed in quantitative terms using cross-sectional studies or partial equilibrium models. In this chapter, we show that a general equilibrium perspective could explain different attitudes of societies to the adoption of stricter rules. Direct and indirect costs, as well as the distribution of the burden, must be taken into account to understand evaluations of reforms.

We simulate the extension of more severe standards of corporate governance to a subset of firms in an Emerging Economy; in order to explore how the costs increase for the firms, how they spread into the economy, and which reduction in capital costs is needed to compensate those increased costs.

When we use the CGE model for the case of Argentina in 2003, we find that while the costly standards are set to a representative group of firms, there is a reduction in GDP that varies in the range of 0.23 to 0.39 per cent depending on the assumptions on elasticity of substitution of production functions at the auditing industry, and on the conditions in the labour market (unemployment or full employment). The required reduction in cost of capital to compensate those costs depends on the benchmark used but the model shows that even moderate reductions of the cost of capital could be enough to compensate for the costs of upgrading corporate governance. The problem is that those gains are conjectural, and that distribution of the burden of costs does not necessarily coincide with the distribution of gains.

There are some possible extensions to the model presented in this chapter. The first is straightforward: a more detailed consideration of the costs of corporate governance. It is not expected to yield a different qualitative result, but the data will be different. Second, to quote in a public market is costly in itself, in part because of direct expenses and in part due to higher 'exposure'. There is a strong presumption of more lax accomplishment of tax obligations in private firms with respect to public ones. This is an important factor taken into account by small firms in underdeveloped economies. Although this could improve the revenue of the government, the net effect is not clear if exit of firms is possible.

ACKNOWLEDGEMENTS

We thank the valuable research assistance provided by Andrés Blanco in developing the simulations, and by David Pacini in an initial draft, and an anonymous referee who made suggestions to improve the paper. Errors remaining are ours.

NOTES

1. Whereas the concept applies to firms listed in public markets, good practices extend to private business, or state owned corporations, even to non-profit organizations.
2. Codes of good practices of Corporate Governance, promoted by government or international organisms such as Cadbury Report in UK, Winter Report of the European Commission, Principles of the OECD, and so on.
3. Sarbanes-Oxley Act in the USA, Decree 677 in Argentina, and so on.
4. AR$3.10 = US$1, at the end of September 2006.

REFERENCES

Apreda, R. (2001). 'Corporate governance in Argentina: the outcome of economic freedom (1991–2000)', *Corporate Governance, An International Review*, **9** (4), 126–39

Bebczuk, R. (2005), 'Corporate governance and ownership: measurement and impact on corporate performance in Argentina', *Anales XLI Reunión Anual*, La Plata: Asociación Argentina de Economía Política (AAEP), 1–28.

Bergen, L. (2005), 'The Sarbanes-Oxley Act of 2002 and its effects on American business. Financial Services Forum', Mimeo, Boston, MA: College of Management, University of Massachusetts.

Brooke, A., D. Kendrick and A. Meeraus (1992), *GAMS: A User's Guide, Release 2.25*, San Francisco, CA: Scientific Press.

CEF (2005), 'El gobierno corporativo en Argentina', *Nota de Política no. 5*, Buenos Aires: CEF.

Chisari, O., A. Estache and C. Romero (1999), 'Winners and losers from the privatization and regulation of utilities: lessons from a General Equilibrium Model of Argentina', *World Bank Economic Review*, **13** (2), 357–78.

Chisari, O and G. Ferro (2007), 'A social welfare evaluation of adopting new standards of corporate governance: a CGE appraisal for the case of Argentina', *Revista Brasileira de Economia de Empresas*, **7** (1), 7–20.

CRA International (2006), *Sarbanes-Oxley Section 404 costs and implementation issues', Spring 2006 Survey Update*, Washington, DC: Charles Rivers Associates.

Ferris M. C. and J. S. Pang (1997), 'Engineering and economic applications of complementarities problems', *SIAM Review*, **39** (4), 669–713.

Fremond, O. and M. Capaul (2002), 'The state of corporate governance: experience from country assessment', *World Bank Policy Research Working Paper* 2828. Washington DC: World Bank.

Gifford, R. and H. Howe (2004), 'Regulation and unintended consequences: thoughts on Sarbanes Oxley', *The CPA Journal*, **74** (6), available at http://www.nyssapa.org/cpajournal/2004/604/perspectives/p6.htm.

Gutiérrez Urtiaga, M. (2004), 'El gobierno de las empresas desde la perspectiva del análisis económico', *Revista de Estabilidad Financiera*, Madrid: Banco de España, No. 4.

Holmstrom, B. and S. Kaplan (2003), 'The state of US corporate governance: what's right and what's wrong?' *Finance Working Paper* No. 23/2003. Brussels: European Corporate Governance Institute.

IDEA (2004), *Workshop sobre Comité de Auditoria*. Buenos Aires: Instituto para el Desarrollo Empresarial de la Argentina.

INDEC (2001), *Matriz de insumo producto para Argentina 1997*, Buenos Aires: Ministerio de Economía y Servicios Públicos, Argentina.

Kolstad C.D. and L. Mathiesen (1991). 'Computing Cournot-Nash Equilibria', *Operations Research*, **39** (5), 739–48.

La Porta, R., F. López de Silanes and A. Shleifer (1998). 'Corporate ownership around the world', *Working Paper* 6625. Cambridge, MA: National Bureau of Economic Research.

Marsili, M. C., M. Araya, D. Fabio de Montalbán, E. Bacqué, E. Peláez, R. J. Moffo y Gabriela Dall'Asta (2003), *Mercado de capital: régimen de las emisoras*, Adhesión al 50° aniversario de la CSA (1953–2003), Buenos Aires: UADE-CSA, Rubinzal-Culzoni Editores.

Mathiesen, L. (1985), 'Computational experience in solving equilibrium models by a sequence of linear complementarities problems', *Operations Research*, **33** (6), 1225–50.

Mohanram, P. and S. Sunder (2004), 'How has regulation fair disclosure affected the functioning of financial analysts?' *Contemporary Accounting Research*. **23**, 441–525.

Murphy, K. (1999), 'Executive Compensation', Mimeo, Chicago, IL: University of Chicago.

OECD (2003), *Survey of Corporate Governance Development in OECD Countries*, Paris: OECD.

OECD (2004), *Principles of Corporate Governance*, Paris: OECD.

Pyatt, G. and J. I. Round (1985), *Social Accounting Matrices: a Basis for Planning*, Washington DC: World Bank.

Reina, L. (2005), 'Mala praxis. Seguros: protección para altos ejecutivos'. *La Nación*, Buenos Aires, 3 April.

Rutherford T. (1999), 'Applied General Equilibrium Modelling with MPSGE as a GAMS subsystem: an overview of the modelling framework and syntax', *Computational Economics*, **14** (1/2), pp. 1–46.

Shleifer, A. and R. Vishny (1996), 'A survey in corporate governance', *Working Paper* 5554, Cambridge MA: National Bureau of Economic Research.

Shoven, J. B. and J. Whalley (1992), *Applying General Equilibrium*, New York: Cambridge University Press.

Wallison, P. (2005), 'Sarbanes-Oxley and the Ebbers Conviction', *Financial Services Outlook*, AEI Online, http://www.aei.org/publications/pubID.22648/pub_detail.asp, 10 June 2005.

Zhang, I.X. (2005), *Economic Consequences of the Sarbanes-Oxley Act of 2002*, Rochester NY: William E. Simon Graduate School of Business Administration, University of Rochester.

3. The Anglo-American model of corporate governance in sub-Saharan Africa: explanatory and normative dimensions

Royston Gustavson, Nicholas Ndegwa Kimani and Donald Atieno Ouma

INTRODUCTION

In sub-Saharan Africa, the corporate governance[1] model that has been adopted is the so-called 'Anglo-American' (that is, British and US) model. Although there has been much discussion in both the literature and amongst business leaders of this model, there is no precise definition of what Sub-Saharan Africans understand this term to mean, nor is there any consensus other than that it is a unitary board model. While it cannot be doubted that good corporate governance adds value to a corporation, the authors of this paper believe that corporate governance needs to be deconstructed (Gustavson et al., 2005).

We are aware that a substantial amount of work is being done in the area of establishing legal and institutional arrangements for corporate governance in Africa, especially by governments and regulatory agencies (Armstrong, 2003, 2006). We are also aware of the contributions of other sets of actors, such as the Kenya-based Centre for Corporate Governance (which operates throughout East Africa), or the Institute of Directors in Southern Africa under the auspices of which the King Committee on Corporate Governance was initiated. Corporate governance also plays an important role in the African Peer Review Mechanism, but although the purpose of corporate governance is given (NEPAD, 2004: 59),[2] there is no discussion of the model of corporate governance. While there has also been empirical research on how the model is being implemented within sub-Saharan African countries (see for example Goldsmith, 2003), with the notable exception of work being done in South Africa (especially King, 2002; Rossouw, 2005a, b), there is little evidence that the normative dimensions have been addressed, for example in terms of analysing the appropriateness of the Anglo-American corporate governance model as it is being championed by governments and regulatory agencies.

There is, admittedly, little evidence as to why the model was chosen; anecdotal evidence, which needs research support, suggests that it was either unreflective choice or as a result of pressure from organizations such as the World Bank and IMF. While corporate governance standards and practices ostensibly aim to promote positive social change through increased transparency and accountability, economic development and greater integration of the corporations of each country into the global financial community, it is important to note that the Anglo-American model of corporate governance does not always work well even in Anglo-American cultures. Therefore the central argument of this chapter is that there is no reason to assume that the Anglo-American model (whatever this is perceived to be) must be adapted *in toto*. It may well be that some aspects may be beneficial to sub-Saharan African economic and social development and so should be taken over, but other aspects may be damaging to social development and so the society must then question whether or not the economic benefits are worth the social damage (on this, see Reed, 2002). The need therefore arises to consider which of the constituent parts of the corporate governance model are essential and which can be modified to make them more in keeping with local cultural values.

This chapter is the first step in a research project that aims to develop an understanding of what the 'Anglo-American' model of corporate governance actually means in sub-Saharan Africa and how it works; using these data it then attempts to modify the model to make it more effective.[3] Here, we draw upon John Braithwaite's understandings of both 'explanatory theory' as a set of 'ordered propositions about the way the world is', and normative theory as 'a set of ordered propositions about the way the world ought to be' (Braithwaite, 2002: ix). The first part of this chapter outlines the theoretical frameworks used for analysing the empirical trends in corporate governance legislation: Donaldson and Dunfee's Integrative Social Contracts Theory (1999) and Hofstede and Hofstede's dimensions of national cultures (2005). This is followed by a comparison of principles of good corporate governance practices of listed companies as expressed in the relevant legislation or guidelines of three sub-Saharan African countries: Kenya, Botswana and Zambia.

THEORETICAL FRAMEWORKS

Social Contract Theory

One of the theoretical underpinnings of our work is Donaldson and Dunfee's Integrative Social Contracts Theory (1999; hereinafter ISCT), one of the most prominent theories in the field of business ethics. Social contract theory 'focuses on a community or group of rational, self-interested individuals who are presumed to consent to the terms of a hypothetical agreement because it is in their rational interest to do so' (Dunfee, 1997: 585). The idea of a contract is something with which businesspersons feel comfortable: they negotiate contracts and work with contracts throughout their business lives. ISCT differs from standard social contract theory. The standard theory produces a hypothetical contract: it is based purely on reasoned argument, and as such states what should be, ignoring what is. ISCT attempts to integrate a hypothetical contract with the actual ethical norms of a society. The part of the theory on which we would like to focus is the distinction between what ISCT calls hypernorms and what it calls microsocial contracts. Hypernorms 'are principles so fundamental that they constitute norms by which all other norms are to be judged. They are discernible in a convergence of religious, political, and philosophical thought' (Dunfee and Donaldson, 2005: 244). Microsocial contracts on the other hand are the ethical norms of particular communities; they are allowed to stand so long as they do not conflict with hypernorms, which invariably take precedence.

Our Variant of ISCT

In our research, we view hypernorms as being things that are fundamental to the system of corporate governance: things without which the system would at best not work very well, and at worst be undermined to, or beyond, the point of collapse. Unlike Donaldson and Dunfee, we view everything as a hypernorm unless we can argue that it should be a microsocial contract. We believe that this is essential as any divergence from commonly accepted standards of the international business community may have significant negative consequences for a society. The difficulties in deciding whether an issue is a hypernorm or a microsocial contract are clearly seen from the following argument by Elegido (1996: xv–xvi):[4]

> one still has to consider in detail the consequences which are likely to follow from refusing or accepting a request for a certain questionable payment. At this

level of analysis it is suggested that the answer could be very different depending on whether one is, say, a clearing agent in the port of Lagos or an investment banker in New York. This is not to say that clearing agents in Lagos are justified in surrendering to every attempt to extort money from them, or that there are no conceivable circumstances in which it would be ethical for an American investment banker to give in to extortion requests. The point is rather that the specific circumstances in which issues arise are relevant to the ethical assessment of the alternatives facing the actor, and that, generally speaking, there are many issues in which some ethically relevant circumstances tend to differ systematically between developed and developing countries.

We view microsocial contracts as being parts of a corporate governance model that may be adapted to each community using that community's norms as their basis; so long as the benefit to the community of adopting a microsocial contract outweighs the disadvantages to the community of adopting a contract which is at variance with the dominant multinational contracts (hypernorms). Note that we refer to the community, not shareholders. It is the community, through the legislative arm of government, that allows business to operate, and surely any rational community would only allow business to exist for the community's overall benefit.

Social Contracts and Cultures

If we are going to identify any microsocial contracts in the area of corporate governance, we would suggest looking for large-scale cultural influences, and so turn to the famous work of Geert Hofstede (Hofstede and Hofstede, 2005), who scored cultures in 74 countries and regions on four dimensions. As his work is based on actual cultures, it is clearly in the domain of extant contracts, all of which are therefore microsocial contracts and some of which may also be hypernorms. An advantage of using this framework is that we can increase the certainty of attributing particular findings from our analysis of corporate governance practices to cultural differences, rather than to other factors. Hofstede's work in Africa was published as the results for one country, South Africa (the sample was exclusively Caucasian), and two regions, West Africa (Ghana, Nigeria, and Sierra Leone) and East Africa (Kenya, Ethiopia, Tanzania, and Zambia). It should be pointed out that we are proceeding on the assumption that Hofstede's work reflects a generalized national culture, and so we will be looking for a best fit between the generalized national culture and the generalized social contracts that underpin corporate governance.[5]

The data in Table 3.1 show that the two countries after which the Anglo-American model is named, the United Kingdom and the United States,

Table 3.1   *Hofstede's cultural dimensions: scores for African and selected Anglo-American countries/regions*

Dimension	Power distance	Individualism/ collectivism	Masculinity/ femininity	Uncertainty avoidance
West Africa	77	20	46	54
East Africa	64	27	41	52
South Africa	49	65	63	49
United States	40	91	62	46
Australia	36	90	61	51
United Kingdom	35	89	66	35

Source: Hofstede and Hofstede (2005): 43–4, 78–9, 120, 169.

have similar scorings on these criteria, as does another country with a similar cultural background, Australia. On the first three of the dimensions, West Africa and East Africa have scores which are similar to each other but which are very different to those of the Anglo-American countries: their scores are the highest two or lowest two on each of the scales. South Africa sits somewhere in between, but is more 'Anglo-American' than 'African'; it should be remembered that Hofstede's sample (Hofstede and Hofstede, 2005: 27) consisted of white South Africans only.

Power distance

The first of Hofstede's dimensions is power distance, that is, 'the extent to which the less powerful members of institutions and organizations within a country expect and accept that power is distributed unequally', and it is noted that, in large power distance countries, 'subordinates are unlikely to approach and contradict their bosses directly' (Hofstede and Hofstede, 2005: 46). Anglo-American cultures score lower on this scale, indicating that there is lower acceptance of unequal power distribution: those at the top do not have unfettered power, and so are likely to be questioned. This would suggest that the board is aware that society will place restrictions on its power and that its decisions will be subject to justification and questioning. On the other hand, there is significant power distance in West and to a lesser extent East Africa suggesting, for example, that decision making will be concentrated at board level and that those decisions will not be directly queried even when they relate to management rather than governance, which may be to their organization's detriment; and that shareholders in West and East Africa may not be as activist as their British or American counterparts, which may also be to their society's detriment.

Individualism/collectivism

The second dimension is individualism/collectivism.

> Individualism *pertains to* societies in which the ties between individuals are loose: everyone is expected to look after himself or herself and his or her immediate family. Collectivism *as its opposite pertains to* societies in which people from birth onward are integrated into strong, cohesive in-groups, which throughout people's lifetimes continue to protect them in exchange for unquestioning loyalty. (Hofstede and Hofstede, 2005: 76)

Hofstede found that the three most individualistic cultures were Anglo-American, namely, the USA (score of 91), Australia (90), and the UK (89); indeed, these were the only three countries to score more than 80. We therefore expect to find their corporate governance model, the so-called Anglo-American model, to be appropriate for individualistic cultures. East Africa scored 27 and West Africa 20, indicating that in these cultures collectivism was culturally predominant. This suggests, for example, that we may expect to find more emphasis on value for individuals, and in particular individual shareholders, in the Anglo-American countries, but more emphasis on value for society, and in particular local stakeholders, in West African and East African countries. If the Anglo-American individualistic shareholder approach is forced on to the collectivist African cultures, we would expect to find tension.

Masculinity/femininity

The third dimension is masculinity/femininity. In masculine cultures,

> emotional gender roles are clearly distinct: men are supposed to be assertive, tough, and focused on material success, whereas women are supposed to be more modest, tender, and concerned with the quality of life. A society is called *feminine* when emotional gender roles overlap: both men and women are supposed to be modest, tender, and concerned with the quality of life. (Hofstede and Hofstede, 2005: 120)

Countries with a relatively high masculinity score include the UK (66), South Africa (63), the USA (62) and Australia (61). As such, we may expect to find their corporate governance model to be masculine (for example, focused on financial profit), which would appear to conflict with the more feminine culture in West Africa (46) and East Africa (41), where a more natural governance model may focus on the impact of the organization on the quality of people's lives. Interestingly, Hofstede also points out that 'unlike individualism, masculinity is unrelated to a country's degree of economic development' (Hofstede and Hofstede,

2005: 120), and so it cannot be assumed that the more feminine focus will naturally change to a more masculine one as these areas develop economically. This is important as it means that it cannot be argued that a 'masculine' model should be imposed in order to assist economic development.

Uncertainty avoidance

The fourth dimension is uncertainty avoidance, 'the extent to which the members of a culture feel threatened by ambiguous or unknown situations' (Hofstede and Hofstede, 2005:167). As the countries we are examining are clustered on this scale, we would not expect it to be significant for our study.

COMPARISON OF THE THREE COUNTRIES' LAWS

In comparing the expression of principles of good corporate governance practices of listed companies in the relevant legislation of sub-Saharan African countries, we consider three countries: Kenya, Botswana and Zambia. For Kenya, we chose its *Guidelines on Corporate Governance Practices by Public Listed Companies in Kenya* (Republic of Kenya, 2002; hereinafter Kenya's *Guidelines*)[6] which were issued pursuant to the Capital Markets Authority Act.[7] We use the respective Companies Acts (hereinafter CA) of Botswana[8] and Zambia,[9] as these countries do not presently possess guidelines on corporate governance practices similar to Kenya, where extent of disclosure (or non-disclosure) forms an essential part of disclosure obligations in corporate annual reports.

We used the Kenyan *Guidelines* as our framework for comparing the countries' legislation. We found some divergence, with some issues being explicitly stated in one country's legislation but not in others; on other issues, we found no significant differences. A qualitative assessment of reasons as to why this is the case may form the basis for determining which issues may be regarded as hypernorms and which may be regarded as microsocial contracts.

The Board and Board Committees

In Kenya, it is mandatory to establish an audit and nominating committee (s.2.1.1(ii)), and recommended that other committees be appointed as may be necessary (s.2.1.1(i)). Botswana's CA appears to be silent on this issue, but in Zambia directors 'may delegate any of their powers to a committee or committees of directors' (s.217(6)).

Directors' Remuneration

Kenya's *Guidelines* (s.2.1.2) states that 'remuneration should be sufficient to attract and retain directors'. For executive directors, remuneration should be 'competitively structured and linked to performance'; for non-executive directors, remuneration should be 'competitive in line with remuneration for other directors in competing sectors'. There should be a 'formal and transparent procedure for remuneration of directors, which should be approved by shareholders'. Botswanan and Zambian legislation is far less demanding. In Botswana, remuneration should be determined by the company in a general meeting (First schedule, table A, part I [hereinafter table A], art.75). In Zambia, the company must determine directors' remuneration by ordinary resolution (s.206(14)).

Supply and Disclosure of Information

Kenya's *Guidelines* attempts to bring together in one concise statement a number of ideas which are scattered in various sections of its CA. In Botswana and Zambia, the CA contains similar provisions regarding the supply and disclosure of information, but these are scattered in various sections of the legislation, making it difficult to draw them together in a concise manner. Kenya's *Guidelines* states that the board: 'should be supplied with relevant, accurate and timely information to enable the board [to] discharge its duties' (s.2.1.3(i)); should disclose in its annual report 'its policies for remuneration including incentives for the board and senior management' (s.2.3.1(ii)); and shall make public disclosure 'of any management or business agreements entered into between the Company and its related companies, which may result in a conflict of interest' (s.2.5.1). However, the meaning of 'public' in this context is not elaborated. Interestingly, neither Botswanan nor Zambian legislation makes such clear provision; at most, the requirement for disclosure is made in general terms.

Zambia's CA provides that 'directors may meet together for the despatch of business and adjourn and otherwise regulate their meetings as they think fit' (s.217(2)). However, it is silent if and how the board should be supplied with relevant accurate and timely information necessary to discharge its duties. It is, however, more explicit regarding remuneration including incentives for the board and senior management: it requires disclosure of payments for compensation for loss of office to members of the company and for such proposal to be 'approved by an ordinary resolution of the company' (s.222(1)); it imposes a prohibition on payments for 'transfer of the whole or any part of the undertaking or property of the company', unless disclosure of such particulars is first made to the members of the company and for such proposal to be approved by an ordinary resolution of the company (s.222(2)); and where payments are made to directors in connection with takeover bids, the director is required to 'take all reasonable steps to ensure that particulars of the relevant payment are included in or sent with any notice of the offer made for their shares which is given to any shareholders' (s.223(1)(b)). The register of directors and secretaries must show for each director the 'number, description and amount' of any shares or debentures held in the company (s.225(1)). Finally, directors are required to make disclosure of loans and receipts (s.169(1)).

In Botswana, supply and disclosure of information is handled with similar attention to detail. There is a requirement for a statutory meeting to be held between one and three months from the date the company is entitled to commence business (s.96(1)). A statutory report must be sent to all members of the company at least two weeks before the meeting (s.96(2)), which must contain information relating to shares allotted, and cash received with respect to the shares (s.96(3)). There must be a register of directors and secretaries (s.157), and particulars of directors must be given in trade catalogues, circulars and business letters (s.158). Other mandatory provisions include an obligation on directors to disclose any payments made to them for loss of office as a result of a takeover (s.150(1)), a requirement for a register of all directors' share holdings (s.152), a prohibition of allotment of shares to directors except on the same terms as to all members, and a restriction on sale of undertakings by directors (s.153); disclosure in a general meeting of particulars of accounts of directors' emoluments, pensions, and payments of any compensation for loss of office (s.154) and of loans to directors or officers (s.155); and disclosure by directors of interests in contracts (s.156 and table A, art.83).

Board Balance

We noted with interest that Kenya's *Guidelines* recommends the establishment 'of a balance of executive directors and non-executive directors (including at least one-third independent and non-executive directors) of diverse skills or expertise in order to ensure that no individual or small group of individuals can dominate the boards' decision-making processes' (s.2.1.4). By contrast, this issue is not raised in the CA of either Botswana or Zambia.

Appointments to the Board

The three countries' legislation covered the same broad issues regarding appointments to the board. Kenya's *Guidelines* recommends that 'There should be a formal and transparent procedure in the appointment of directors to the board and all persons offering themselves for appointment, as directors should disclose any potential area of conflict that may undermine their position or service as director' (s.2.1.5). Zambia's CA covers the same issues, although providing less clarity. In essence, it holds that companies should have at least two directors (s.204(1)), and that 'the number of directors of a company shall be the number of first directors named in the application for incorporation, or such other number as the company may decide by ordinary resolution' (s.206(1)). Botswana's CA requires the appointment of directors to be voted on individually (s.144). It came as a surprise to learn that conflicts of interest might arise: a director 'may act by himself or his firm in a professional capacity for the company, and he or his firm shall be entitled to remuneration for professional services as if he were not a director' (table A, art.83(5)).

Multiple Directorships

Kenya's *Guidelines* prohibits directors from holding directorships in more than five public listed companies, and alternate directorships are not permissible for more than three public listed companies (s.2.1.6). Zambia's CA is silent on this issue. In Botswana, there is no clear prohibition on multiple directorships: the CA permits a director to 'hold any other office or place of profit under the company (other than the office of auditor) in conjunction with his office of director for such period and on such terms as the directors may determine' (table A, art.83(3)).

Re-election of Directors

The legislation of the three countries appeared to broadly agree on the issue of re-election of directors. Kenya's *Guidelines* recommends that 'All directors except the managing director should be required to submit themselves for re-election at regular intervals or at least every three years' (s.2.1.7(a)); that 'Executive directors should have a fixed service contract not exceeding five years with a provision to renew subject to: (i) Regular performance appraisal; and (ii) Shareholders approval' (s.2.1.7(b)); and that 'Disclosure should be made to the shareholders at the annual general meeting and in the annual reports of all directors approaching their seventieth (70th) birthday that respective year' (s.2.1.7(c)).

Botswana and Zambia have a similar approach. In Botswana, directors are reappointed in general meetings (s.144). At the first annual general meeting, all directors are required to retire from office; in subsequent general meetings, the one-third of directors who have been longest in office are required to retire. However, retiring directors are eligible for re-election (table A, art.88–90). Zambia's CA makes similar provision regarding the reappointment of directors (s.206).

Resignation of Directors

A point of divergence between the three countries concerns the resignation of directors. Zambia's CA allows for a director to resign office by notice in writing to the company (s.210(1)). There is no requirement to provide reasons for the resignation. Similar provisions occur in Botswana (table A, art.87(e)). By contrast, Kenya's *Guidelines* recommends that 'Resignation by a serving director should be disclosed in the annual report together with the details of the circumstances necessitating the resignation' (s.2.1.8). However, we note that a disjuncture exists in practice, as this recommendation is usually not followed through; the notice usually states when the director resigned, but does not necessarily provide reasons for doing so.

Role of Chairman and Chief Executive

Disparities arose among the three countries regarding the positions of chairman and chief executive. In Kenya, the *Guidelines* states that the 'Chairperson of a public listed company shall not hold such position in more than two public listed companies' (s.2.2.2), and recommends that 'There should be a clear separation of the role and responsibilities of the chairman and chief executive . . . Where such roles are combined a rationale for the same should be disclosed to the shareholders in the annual report of the company' (s.2.2.1). In Botswana, however, the CA simply provides that directors may 'appoint one or more of their body to the office of managing director for such period and on such terms as they think fit' (table A, art.106), and that 'a managing director shall receive such remuneration . . . as the directors may determine' (table A, art.107). Zambia's CA contains similar provisions (ss.214(2) and (4)).

Approval of Major Decisions by Shareholders in Meetings

Although the three countries all require shareholders to participate in meetings, there are distinct differences as to how shareholder approval of major company decisions should be obtained. Kenya's *Guidelines* recommends that 'There should be shareholders participation in major decisions of the company' (s.2.3.1), and proceeds to give examples of such decisions: 'major disposal of the Company's assets, restructuring, takeovers, mergers, acquisitions or reorganization'. By contrast, Botswana's CA only lays out procedures for participation in general meetings (ss.96–110 and table A, arts 47–73), yet no clarification is given as regards the types of decision where shareholder participation is particularly recommended. A similar shortcoming is seen in Zambia's CA. Whilst procedures are given for shareholder participation in general meetings, no clarification is given as regards the types of decisions where shareholder participation is particularly recommended.

Annual General Meetings

There are differences between the three countries with regard to the actual conduct of annual general meetings. Kenya's *Guidelines* recommends that the board should 'provide to all its shareholders sufficient and timely information' pertaining to the AGM (s.2.3.2(i)), 'make shareholders' expenses and convenience primary criteria when selecting venue and location' of AGMs (s.2.3.2(ii)), and 'provide sufficient time for shareholders' questions on matters pertaining to the Company's performance' (s.2.3.2(iii)). In contrast, neither Botswana's nor Zambia's CA addresses these issues in similar detail.

Accountability and Audit

This is an issue on which the three countries are in full agreement. With regard to annual reports and accounts, Kenya's *Guidelines* recommends that 'The board should present an objective and understandable assessment of the Company's operating position and prospects' and 'ensure that accounts are presented in line with International Accounting Standards' (s.2.4.1). Similar requirements are seen in Botswana, where there is an obligation for the company to present to a general meeting a profit and loss account and a balance sheet which give a true and fair view of the company's state of affairs as at the end of its financial year (ss.111–13, 115–20 and table A, arts 122–6). Zambia's CA makes similar provision, requiring the company to keep such accounting records as will enable the preparation of true and fair accounts (s.162), and to present these before the company in general meeting (s.164).

Relationship with Auditors

The three countries appear broadly to agree upon the importance of having formal and transparent arrangements between the company and its auditors. However, whereas Botswana and Zambia provide the procedures, only Kenya makes clear and unambiguous statements as to what is required of the board and its shareholders. For example, Kenya's *Guidelines* recommends the establishment of 'a formal and transparent arrangement for shareholders to effect the appointment of independent auditors at each annual general meeting' (s.2.4.3), and that 'The board should establish a formal and transparent arrangement for maintaining a professional interaction with the Company's auditors' (s.2.4.4). Botswana's CA provides for the appointment and fixing of remuneration of auditors through the AGM (s.121), for the disqualification of directors for appointment as auditor (s.123), and for their right of access to books and to attend general meetings (s.125). Similar provisions are found in Zambia's CA (ss.162(5) and 171).

Professional Qualification of Company Officers

Not all of the three countries appear to recognize the importance of professional qualifications of certain key company officials. Kenya's *Guidelines* states that the 'Chief Financial Officers and persons heading the accounting department of every issuer shall be members of the Institute of Certified Public Accountants' (s.2.5.2(i)), and that where such persons are not yet registered members, they must register within 12 months from the date of appointment to such position' (s.2.5.2(ii)). Similarly, company secretaries must be members of the Institute of Certified Public Secretaries (s.2.5.3). In Botswana and Zambia, membership by secretaries or chief accounting officers of a professional association does not appear to be mandated by law, but company auditors must be, in Botswana, 'a member of a body of accountants' established under law, or a person authorized by the Minister (s.123), or in Zambia, a member of the Zambia Institute of Certified Accountants (s.172).

ANALYSIS OF FINDINGS ARISING FROM CROSS-COUNTRY COMPARISONS

When analysing these data in terms of hypernorms and microsocial contracts, we must also be looking for more than cultural explanations. For example, in Kenya there are restrictions on multiple directorships, but such restrictions would have little practical effect in the other countries examined: Zambia in 1995 (the year after its CA) had only two companies listed on the Lusaka Stock Exchange, a figure that had risen by 2005 to 13 (ASEA [2006]: 73); and Botswana in 2005 had 28 listed companies (ASEA [2006]: 37).

Hypernorms

Some of these issues clearly seem to be hypernorms. For example, if we look at auditing practices, including the appointment of auditors and the preparation of financial statements, we can see no reasons, cultural or otherwise, why there should not be international standards. As stated on pp. 25–6, we believe that microsocial contracts should only come into play when the community benefits from the move away from a hypernorm, and we believe that strong arguments can be put that internationally accepted auditing practices are essential for the attraction of foreign and even domestic capital, which is important to aid the development of these economies.[10] Another hypernorm, gender, is raised in the Kenyan *Guidelines* (s.3.1.3.viii). This concern for gender is probably driven by western values rather than the efficient functioning of Kenyan boardrooms. Is it what the authors of the *Guidelines* believe to be international best practice? Clearly, it is in a society's best interests to have the best possible pool of candidates for board positions, and to exclude women would be to exclude many potentially excellent candidates. Nevertheless, the global situation is that there are currently many more men than women who have the necessary qualifications and experience to be directors, and we must be careful lest positive discrimination results in less-than-ideal appointments. Here we think of the situation in Norway where legislation required that at least 40 per cent of the members of a board are women, and that 'if a company does not comply with this requirement by the end of 2008, the company may be dissolved'.[11] In some countries there would surely not be a large enough available pool of suitable women to be able to implement this policy within the given timeframe.

Microsocial Contracts

Director independence
Let us now turn to what may be microsocial contracts. Our first example is director independence. Increasingly, countries using the Anglo-American model state in their legislation or best practice guidelines that there should be a majority of independent directors. This is fine in individualistic cultures, but is it appropriate in collectivist cultures? Clearly, directors should be independent in that they are not involved with companies that are major suppliers or customers. But in determining the meaning of 'independent' within the context of non-executive directors, we identify two cultural issues which merit further empirical examination.

The first issue relates to tribalism or ethnicity. The 1989 Kenyan population census divided the population into 42 tribal or ethnic groupings

(Republic of Kenya, 1989); tribal data from the 1999 census was not released. Many people have a very strong bond with members of their own tribe, and a tribal identity which may be stronger than their identity as Kenyans. To what extent is it realistic for a director, under these circumstances, to be independent of her or his tribal affiliation (an issue raised in Gustavson *et al.*, 2005)? Kenya has a fairly collectivist culture (see 'East Africa' in Table 3.1), and it is reasonably conceivable that Kenya would take a more stakeholder-oriented view than, say, the United States.

The second issue relates to the role of family units and collective organizations among immigrant Indian capitalists, which has historical and cultural connotations. We suggest that these considerations might be relevant for directors of listed companies that were originally started by local Indian capitalists. These may feel a great bond to their community and family rather than remaining independent in the strict sense of the word. As David Himbara (1994: 35) points out:

> Immigrants from the Indian sub-continent played a determining role in the development of commerce and industry in East Africa. Beginning with coastal-based merchant activities before the colonial period, the commercial prominence they attained enabled them to remain the predominant force during the colonial period and after. This, in turn, provided them with a foundation for playing a similar role in industry, from the 1940s to the present.
>
> Some of the determining factors that distinguished the Indians from businessmen in other Kenyan communities were their commercial skills, as evidenced by an ability to survive in remote areas on modest resources and by sheer determination and hard work; their vision of the potential mass market and the patience to transform it into an actual market; their general efficiency and competitive edge; and the *role of family units and collective organizations in providing mechanisms to engender discipline and cohesion.* Not even the domination of politics and agriculture, through legislative means, of the white settlers, and later Kenya [*sic*] Africans, could offset or reduce the critical importance of local Indian capitalists in retail and wholesale trade, finance, and manufacturing. [emphasis added]

Among the prominent local Indian capitalists that he cites are the Chandaria family of Kenya and the Madhvani Group of Uganda who have extensive investments in commerce, manufacturing and the agricultural sectors of the respective countries. It is not clear how directors under these circumstances would be independent given, for example, the pressure on family members to join the family business as soon as they have completed their high school or university education, even if they are not the most highly skilled candidates. Anecdotal evidence made available to one of the Kenyan co-authors of this chapter clearly suggests that there is a strong expectation within elements of the Indian business class that family members should eventually contribute to the family business, notwithstanding their qualifications or other interests.

Given such circumstances, we question whether such non-independence is actually bad. For one thing, Himbara appears to suggest that the use of family units by Indian capitalists is deeply rooted in history, and it is how they have always operated in East Africa. Similarly, in instances where Indian businesses are set up to serve the needs of the Indian community, for example in banking and finance, it would seem that in giving that business a social licence to operate, the local community is entitled to say, 'you can set up among us but a member of our own has to be a director'. Presumably, this ensures that the voices of the community most directly affected by the business are heard.

For these two reasons, we would suggest that the jury is out on the question of whether director independence, in the context of tribe or family, should necessarily be interpreted in the same way as it would be interpreted in an individualist context.[12] Nevertheless, we appreciate that these cultural considerations in no way undermine the importance of conscientious attention to rules and details regarding directors' independence. But cultural considerations may require an attempt to modify the notion of director independence in a way that does not undermine the model of corporate governance.

Resignation of directors

A second example of a microsocial contract relates to resignation of directors. Kenya's *Guidelines* states that 'Resignation by a serving director should be disclosed in the annual report together with the details of the circumstances necessitating the resignation' (s.2.1.8). This implies that directors have broader obligations to society, as appropriate for a collectivist culture: resignation from a board of directors does not have purely personal implications. Such a requirement also makes good business sense. From annual reports, is appears that this provision is not strictly enforced in practice; this is an issue calling for empirical inquiry.

Annual general meetings

A third example relates to Kenya expecting that 'The board should make shareholders' expenses and convenience primary criteria when selecting venue and location of annual general meetings' (s.2.3.2(ii)). As the majority of Kenya's listed companies have a single dominant shareholder, this is essential if we are not to see expropriation of value from minority shareholders, treatment of whom is a major ethical issue for boards (Gustavson, 2007). As Reed has noted, one of the characteristics of corporate governance in developing countries is that the primary agency problem is often between majority and minority shareholders, rather than between owners and managers (Reed, 2002: 233).

CONCLUSION

The central argument of this chapter is that although essential corporate governance standards and practices should be global in order to ensure the integration of the corporations of each country into the global financial community, we need to consider which of the constituent parts of the corporate governance model are essential and which can be modified to make them more in keeping with local cultural values. This is important: the Anglo-American model of corporate governance does not always work well even in Anglo-American cultures. We should only make these changes, however, when we are confident that first, they will not undermine the entire system, and second, when the overall costs to society of doing so are less than the costs to society of not doing so. It is therefore submitted that a central component of a future research agenda should be a more comprehensive 'mapping' of both the empirical and normative dimensions of the Anglo-American corporate governance model, with the ultimate aims being twofold. First, there is the development of contemporary and comprehensive theory; and second, following on from this, the development of sound normative proposals in the form of new policies and practice.

ACKNOWLEDGEMENTS

An earlier, unpublished version of this chapter was read to the 6th BEN–Africa [Business Ethics Network Africa] Conference, Stellenbosch Business School, Belville, South Africa, 26 July 2006, under the title 'Perceptions of the Anglo-American Model of Corporate Governance in Sub-Saharan Africa I – The Commonwealth Affiliated Countries: A Pilot Study'. Royston Gustavson is grateful to Strathmore Business School, Strathmore University, Nairobi, Kenya, and above all to George Njenga, the School's director, for support during his sabbatical leave during which, amongst other things, the final version of this chapter was prepared.

NOTES

1. In this chapter we adopt the same definition of corporate governance as is stated in Kenya's *Guidelines*, namely, 'the process and structure used to direct and manage business affairs of the company towards enhancing prosperity and corporate accounting with the ultimate objective of realizing shareholders' long-term value while taking into account the interest of other stakeholders' (Republic of Kenya, 2002, s. 1.2).
2. There is a very different definition, and one that would appear to be much closer to

African values, in NEPAD, 2003 (p. 20), an earlier document relating to the African Peer Review Mechanism: 'Corporate Governance is concerned with the ethical principles, values and practices that facilitate holding the balance between economic and social goals and between individual and communal goals. The aim is to align as nearly as possible the interests of individuals, corporations and society within a framework of sound governance and common good.'

3. The research project is planned to include all current and former Commonwealth countries in Africa. Through a comparison of countries all of which have a common law heritage, and which in many cases are geographically contiguous, it becomes easier to identify which of the constituent parts of the corporate governance model are essential and which can be modified to make them more in keeping with local cultural values. The countries selected for this chapter are all current members of the Commonwealth, namely, Botswana, Kenya, and Zambia.

4. Elegido expands on this on pp. 245–58.

5. Cultures cross national boundaries, and more importantly each nation-state may have many distinct cultures. Nevertheless, in many countries, including each of those studied, the system of legislative acts, regulations and guidelines under which business operates exist at the level of the nation-state. To examine whether or not there is a generalized national culture which is reflected in its system of legislative acts, regulations, and guidelines is clearly far beyond the scope of this chapter.

6. These are not to be confused with the *Principles for Corporate Governance in Kenya and a Sample Code of Best Practice for Corporate Governance* issued in 1999 by the Private Sector Initiative for Corporate Governance and reprinted by the Private Sector Corporate Governance Trust (now the Centre for Corporate Governance).

7. Capital Markets Authority Act, Chapter 485A of the Laws of Kenya (online at http://www.kenyalaw.org/eKLR/). In the introduction, it is stated that Kenya's Capital Markets Authority 'has developed these guidelines for good corporate governance practices by public listed companies in Kenya in response to the growing importance of governance issues both in emerging and developing economies and for promoting growth in domestic and regional capital markets. It is also in recognition of the role of good governance in corporate performance, capital formation and maximization of shareholders' value as well as protection of investors' rights' (s.1.1). The *Guidelines* states that its purpose 'is to strengthen corporate governance practices by public listed companies in Kenya and to promote the standards of self-regulation so as to bring the level of governance in line with international trends' (s.1.4). Kenya's Capital Markets Authority, in developing the guidelines, 'adopted both a prescriptive and a non-prescriptive approach' (s.1.5) in that it requires that the extent of compliance (or non-compliance) with the *Guidelines* to form an essential part of disclosure obligations in corporate annual reports (s.1.7).

8. *Chapter 42.01 of the Laws of Botswana* is relatively old, having originally been enacted in 1959, but amendments have been made as recently as 1995. According to its short title, the Act 'consolidates and amends the laws relating to the constitution, incorporation, registration, [and] management [of companies] . . . and for other purposes incidental thereto'. (The Act was online from 4–14 May 2006 after which online access was withdrawn; see www.laws.gov.bw).

9. *Chapter 388 of the Laws of Zambia*, in its short title, indicates that its scope extends to far more than companies which are listed, as it provides, *inter alia*, for the formation, management, administration and winding-up of companies, and provides for matters connected with or incidental to the foregoing. It is a relatively new piece of legislation, having been enacted in 1994 (Republic of Zambia, 1994).

10. In a globalized environment, managers of capital (foreign or domestic) can use accounts prepared using international standards to allocate capital according to their risk return criteria, whether within the domestic economy or without.

11. See The Public Limited Companies Act section 6-11a, 20-6 and The Limited Liability Companies Act section 20-6 as cited in Noss, 2006: 6.

12. This is not the same as appointing someone to a board because they have strong links with senior government ministers; this is a practice found throughout the world. The nature of the link may be different (here tribal rather than 'old school tie') but the purpose and practice is global.

REFERENCES

Armstrong, P. (2003), 'Status report on corporate governance reform in Africa prepared on behalf of the Pan-African Consultative Forum on Corporate Governance', Nairobi: PAFCG, http://www.ifc.org/ifcext/cgf.nsf/AttachmentsByTitle/Pan_Africa_2003_Report_on_CG_in+Africa/$FILE/Status+Report+on+Corp+Gov+in+Africa.pdf, accessed 8 February 2006.

Armstrong, P. (2006), 'Conference report. Third Pan-African Consultative Forum on Corporate Governance. Dakar, Senegal, 8–10 November 2005', http://www.ifc.org/ifcext/cgf.nsf/AttachmentsByTitle/Pan_Africa_2005_Fi··nal+Report/$FILE/Final+Report1.doc, accessed 8 February 2006.

ASEA [2006], *African Securities Exchanges Association Yearbook 2005*, Cairo: CASE.

Braithwaite, J. (2002), *Restorative Justice and Responsive Regulation*, Oxford: Oxford University Press.

Donaldson, T. and T. Dunfee (1999), *Ties That Bind: A Social Contracts Theory Approach to Business Ethics*, Boston, MA: Harvard Business School Press.

Dunfee, T. W. (1997), 'Social contract theory', in P. H. Werhane and R. E. Freeman (eds), *The Blackwell Encyclopedic Dictionary of Business Ethics*, Oxford: Blackwell, pp. 585–9.

Dunfee, T. W. and T. J. Donaldson (2005), 'Integrative social contracts theory', in P. H. Werhane and R. E. Freeman (eds), *Business Ethics*, vol. 2 of *The Blackwell Encyclopedia of Management*, 2nd edn., Oxford: Blackwell, pp. 243–7.

Elegido, J.M. (1996), *Fundamentals of Business Ethics: A Developing Country Perspective*, Lagos Business School Management Series [1], Ibadan (Nigeria): Spectrum Books.

Goldsmith, A. A. (2003), 'Perceptions of governance in Africa: a survey of business and government leaders', *Journal of African Business* **4** (3), 25–54.

Gustavson, R. (2007), 'Minority shareholders', in R.W. Kolb (ed.), *Encyclopedia of Business Ethics and Society*, vol. 3, Thousand Oaks, CA: Sage Publications, pp. 1392–1393.

Gustavson, R., N. N. Kimani and D. A. Ouma (2005), 'The confluence of corporate governance and business ethics in Kenya: a preliminary investigation', paper to the 5th BEN–Africa Conference, Kasane, Botswana, 31 August.

Himbara, D. (1994), *Kenyan Capitalists, the State, and Development*, Nairobi: East African Educational Publishers.

Hofstede, G. and G.J. Hofstede (2005), *Cultures and Organizations: Software of the Mind*, revised and expanded 2nd edn., New York: McGraw-Hill.

King, M. (2002), *King Report for Corporate Governance in South Africa 2002*, Johannesburg: Institute of Directors in Southern Africa.

NEPAD (2003), 'Objectives, standards, criteria and indicators for the African Peer Review Mechanism *(The ARPM)*', NEPAD document NEPAD/HSGIC-03-

2003/APRM/Guideline/OSCI, 9 March, http://www.nepad.org/2005/files/documents/110.pdf , accessed 19 May 2006.
NEPAD (2004), 'Country self-assessment for the African Peer Review Mechanism', Midrand, South Africa: NEPAD and the African Union, http://www.nepad.org/2005/files/documents/156.pdf, accessed 19 May 2006.
Noss, C.O. (2006), *Gender Equality in Norway*, Strasbourg: European Commission for Democracy Through Law (Venice Commission), CDL-JU(2006)028.
Private Sector Corporate Governance Trust (1999), 'Principles for corporate governance in Kenya and a sample code of best practice for corporate governance', Nairobi: Private Sector Initiative for Corporate Governance; rpt. Nairobi: Private Sector Corporate Governance Trust, n.d., (This is also available online at www.ecgi.org/codes/documents/principles_2.pdf.)
Reed, D. (2002), 'Corporate governance reforms in developing countries', *Journal of Business Ethics,* 37, 223–47.
Republic of Botswana (2006 [1959]), Companies Act, Chapter 42:01 of the Laws of Botswana.
Republic of Kenya (1989), 'Code List for 1989 Population Census', http://international.ipums.org/international/world_census_forms/kenya_1989.pdf, accessed 23 May 2006.
Republic of Kenya (2002), 'Guidelines on corporate governance practices by public listed companies in Kenya', www.cma.or.ke/docs/CORPORATE%20GOVERNANCE%20GUIDELINES,%202002.pdf, accessed 23 August 2005.
Republic of Zambia (1994), 'The Companies Act: Chapter 388 of the Laws of Zambia', http://www.zamlii.ac.zm/media/news/viewnews.cgi?category=all&id=1059035960, accessed 12 January 2006
Rossouw, D. (2005a), 'Business ethics and corporate governance in Africa', *Business & Society* **44** (1), 94–106.
Rossouw, D. (2005b), 'Did King II put its money where its mouth is? The philosophical premises of the second King Report on corporate governance and the implications thereof', paper to the 5th BEN–Africa Conference, Kasane, Botswana, 31 August 2005.

4. Corporate governance and the transformation of the electricity sector in Britain and Spain: the interaction between national institutions and regulatory choices

Michel Goyer and Rocío Valdivielso del Real

INTRODUCTION

Privatization, liberalization, and deregulation have brought major changes in the legal and industry structure of utility companies in the European Union.[1] These developments have altered both the processes of policy making and the extent and forms of public control over suppliers. Nonetheless, these developments have failed to produce convergence among EU member states. We analyse in this chapter the transformation of the industrial profile of the electricity sector in Britain and Spain. The transformation of the electricity sector in Britain was characterized by a transition from a fragmented structure of domestic firms to one where a few foreign firms are the dominant players. The evolution of the structure of the Spanish electricity sector, in contrast, was marked by the consolidation of the market power of the established companies with a substantial control by domestic players.

The argument presented in this chapter highlights the importance of the differences in the national institutions of corporate governance found in the two countries. The adjustment process of electricity companies is best conceptualized as a set of constraints and opportunities faced by managers in the conduct of the business strategy of the firm. The institutions of corporate governance in Britain expose the firm to the pressures of financial markets and force management to seriously pay attention to the interests of minority shareholders. Takeovers have been prominent in the transformation of the sector. The Spanish system of corporate governance, in contrast, does not expose managers to the same extent to the pressures of the financial markets. The prevalence of takeovers as a mechanism of firm adjustment has been rather limited.

We argue that the integration of two theoretical perspectives – institutional-based Varieties of Capitalism (VoC) and regulation – best account in a complementary fashion for the diverging transformation of the electricity sector in the two countries. First, the constellation of domestic institutional frameworks acts as a mediator on the impact of new exogenous (and endogenous) developments. The Varieties of Capitalism theoretical perspective, in particular, has emphasized the critical importance of patterns of institutional complementarities among the various sub-spheres (finance and corporate governance, industrial relations, innovation system, and inter-firm relations) of the economy that lead to diverging forms of behaviour on the part of economic actors (Hall and Soskice, 2001; Soskice, 1999). The key insight is that the impact of an institution cannot be studied in isolation as it is mediated by its interaction with other features of the national institutional framework, therefore implying that different types of institutional fit are possible (Hall and Franseze, 1998). Therefore, the differences in the national institutions of corporate governance between Britain and Spain result in divergence in outcomes.

Second, we argue that regulation theories provide a key complement to the VoC perspective to account for the transformation of the industrial profile of the electricity sector in the two countries. For regulation researchers, privatization and liberalization of network utilities in Europe did not result in a simple retreat of the state, but rather in a redefinition of its role. The new capitalist order is mediated by regulation and the rise of the regulatory state (Jordana and Levi-Faur, 2004, 2005; Müller and Wright, 1994). The liberalization of network industries has demonstrated that freer markets require more rules to properly function (Vogel, 1996). The paradox of 'privatization and deregulation' testifies to a paradigm shift from the interventionist to the regulatory state (Majone, 1997). The main contribution of regulation approaches for the case study of the transformation of the electricity sector in Britain and Spain lies in the ability to capture the origins and political foundations of institutional frameworks. The choice of an institutional framework, often resulting from sectoral patterns of re-regulation, represents the choice of policy-makers exhibiting motivational multiplicity across national settings. Governments set the terms of market competition by favouring particular modes of re-regulation. The study of the transformation of the electricity sector in Britain and Spain requires a joint analysis of both regulation perspectives and institutional-based comparative political economy approaches. The combination of these two theoretical perspectives presents a strong case against a purely deregulatory economic environment.

We make a final methodological note. The process of liberalization of the electricity sector in Britain began in 1990 – earlier than in Spain (1996) and in the rest of the European Union. The golden share scheme for the electricity sector in Britain expired in March 1995. The expiration date for the golden share scheme in Spain was June 2007.[2] Is the empirical data presented in the chapter driven by an issue of timing? Is Spain condemned to follow the same path as Britain, the pioneer in the liberalization and re-regulation of the electricity sector in the European Union? The argument presented in this chapter is not contingent on the timing of the liberalization and re-regulation processes of the electricity sector in different countries. We highlight the importance of national institutions of corporate governance, institutions that were in place before liberalization and re-regulation and have remained largely stable since then. We also emphasize the importance of regulatory choices made by policy makers in the two countries. The differences in the transformation of the profile of the electricity sector in Britain and Spain are accounted for by the joint interaction between national institutions and regulatory choices. The presence of one without the other would have failed to produce the observed evolution of the sector in each country.

The rest of this chapter is divided into four sections. First, we present the broad patterns of transformation of the electricity sector in Britain and Spain. Second, we demonstrate how the differences between the two countries are best accounted for by their national institutions of corporate governance. Third, we argue that regulation perspectives serve as a key complement to institutional-based comparative political economy approaches. Fourth, the conclusion is presented.

THE TRANSFORMATION OF THE INDUSTRIAL PROFILE OF THE ELECTRICITY SECTOR IN BRITAIN AND SPAIN

This section documents the different patterns of evolution of the transformation of the industrial profile of the electricity sector in Britain and Spain. We summarize the main characteristics of the market structure and ownership of the electricity industries in the wake of privatization, liberalization and re-regulation. We operationalize the concept of the industrial profile of the electricity sector with the use of two indicators. First, we refer to the market structure of competition, namely whether a few firms dominate the industry or not. Second, we refer to the structure of private property. Are electricity firms independent entities owned by domestic shareholders or are they subsidiaries of other (foreign) companies?

The Reform of the Electricity Sector in Britain

Throughout the 1990s, the sets of policies known variously as privatization, liberalization, deregulation, and the 'British Model' dominated the political agenda for electricity utilities (Thomas, 2001). The aim of these reforms was a desire to transform the electricity industry from a monopoly into a competitive market: the creation of a spot market as the main price-setting arena for wholesale electricity sales; the creation of retail competition so that all consumers can choose their electricity supplier; the corporate separation of the activities that would remain long-term monopolies, essentially the operation of the network from activities that would be market-driven; and the corporate separation between generation and supply (see Thomas, 2005, 2006).

The electricity sector has experienced a huge amount of restructuring in the areas of distribution and retail supply since its privatization in 1990. Two key features characterize the transformation of the sector: the changing structure of industry and the prominence of takeovers. First, there has been a complete redrawing of the profile of the industry structure. In the wake of the privatization process, there were three main generators (National Power, Powergen and Nuclear Electric); and 12 regional distribution/retail supply companies. All were initially protected from unwanted takeover bids by the government's 'golden shares' scheme. This protection system ran out in 1995. The distribution companies were individually too small to have had an impact outside the UK and were taken over by foreign companies as soon as government protection from takeover was removed. The two more likely candidates to become world players were National Power and Powergen, the two privatized generation companies, which had between them a market share of about 80 per cent in 1990. These two companies, however, were shadows of the firms created a decade before, their market share in 1998 being about a third of what it had been in 1990. By 2001, National Power had had to split itself into a UK company (Innogy) and an international company (IPG) in order to ensure its survival. In March 2002, Innogy was itself taken over by RWE. Powergen, on the other hand, was taken over by E.ON in 2002.

Second, takeovers of British electricity companies by foreign rivals have been both prevalent and paramount (see Table 4.1). The regulatory system designed by Beesley and Littlechild (1983) was intended to provide a structure that allowed free entry in the market. Takeovers and mergers played a prominent role in this evolution as they were interpreted as a healthy sign of market discipline in competitive markets. Takeover and mergers were of little concern as long as the entry barriers were low enough to maintain a realistic threat of competition (Thomas, 2001, 2005).

Table 4.1 British Electricity companies: takeovers and mergers for the REC (Regional Electricity Company)

	1995	1996	1997	1998	1999	2000	2001	2002	Trade name	2005
National Power							Innogy	RWE	Innogy	RWE
Powergen								E.ON	Powergen	Powergen
ScottishPower									Scottish Power	Scottish Power
Scottish Hydro				SSE					SSE	SSE
Nacional Grid								N Grid Tra	N Grid Transco	National Grid
Eastern distrib	Hanson Trust		Energy Group	Texas Utils (Pacificorp)				EDF	24Seven	EDF
Eastern supply	Hanson Trust		Energy Group	Texas Utils (Pacificorp)				E.ON	Powergen	Powergen
EMidlanddistrib		Dominion		Powergen					E Midlands Elec	EMidlands Elec
EMidlandsupply		Dominion		Powergen				E.ON	Powergen	Powergen
London distrib		Entergy		EDF					24Seven	EDF
London supply		Entergy		EDF					London Electric	EDF
Manweb distrib	ScottishPower								SP Manweb	SPManweb
Manweb supply	ScottishPower								Scottish Power	Scottish Power
Midlands distrib		Avon Energy			GPU			Aquila	Aquila	EON
Midlands supply		Avon Energy		National Power			Innogy	RWE	NPower	RWE
Northern distrib		CalEnergy							Northern Electric	CEElectric
Northern supply		CalEnergy					Innogy		NPower	RWE

Table 4.1 (continued)

	1995	1996	1997	1998	1999	2000	2001	2002	Trade name	2005
Norweb distrib	NW Water								United Utilities	Utilities
Norweb supply	NW Water					Texas Utils (Pacificorp)		E.ON	Powergen	Powergen
Seeboard distrib	C&SW Corp					AEP		EDF	24Seven	EDF
Seeboard supply	C&SW Corp					AEP		EDF	Seeboard Energy	EDF
Southern distrib				SSE					SSE Power Dist	SSE
Southern supply				SSE					Southern Electric	SSE
SWALEC distrib.	Welsh Water					WPD			WPD	WPD
SWALEC supli	Welsh Water				British Energy	SSE			Swalec Electric	SSE
SWEB distrib	Southern Co				WPD				WPD	WPD
SWEB supply	Southern Co				EDF				SWEB	EDF
Yorkshiredistrib			Y'shire Holding				Mid American Energy		Y'E' Distrib	CEElectric
Yorkshiresupply			Y'shire Holding				Innogy	RWE	NPower	RWE

Source: Own elaboration based on data from annual reports.

Privatized electricity companies in Britain were initially protected from unwanted takeover bids by a government golden share scheme. The principle behind the scheme in each of the electricity companies was to allow time for the companies to adapt to changed circumstances, free from the threat of a hostile takeover. In effect, the golden share was a restriction on any one body from owning more than 15 per cent of the outstanding shares of an electricity company. Its expiry in March 1995 removed this restriction and opened up the possibility of predators securing control of the companies. This possibility was far from hypothetical since they offered the prospect of secure, if unspectacular, monopoly profits, good cash flows and access to what were widely perceived to be substantial capital assets. The government's attitude towards potential changes in ownership was also crucial (Deakin *et al.*, 2002). Once the first hostile takeover bid was announced there was considerable speculation as to the likelihood of the bid being referred to the Monopolies and Mergers Committee (MMC). The decision of the Secretary of State not to make such a reference therefore gave an effective green light to the acquiring ambitions of other companies.

Finally, it is important to point out that the ultimate outcome of the transformation of the industrial profile of the electricity sector in Britain diverges substantially from the original vision of Beesley and Littlechild. As noted by Thomas (2003: 339), 'the electricity companies in Britain were victims of the political and regulatory desire to be seen to be creating a competitive industry'. The evolution of the UK energy industry is noteworthy for the study of regulation since the centralized electricity incumbent (CEGB) was split up both horizontally and vertically by political design. The political authorities limited its reconfiguration for quite some time through strong policy against vertical integration. However, the ideal industrial structure, a full de-integrated structure with competitive generation and retail services, has only been partially achieved. The combination of structural split and liquid capital markets did render British companies ripe for being the recipients of takeover bids from foreign companies.

The Reform of the Electricity Sector in Spain

Electricity was first produced for public consumption in Spain in Barcelona in 1875. Numerous small companies centred in the major towns developed from that time until the end of the nineteenth century. At the beginning of the 1980s, the electricity sector consisted principally of ten vertically integrated (generation, distribution and retailing) regionally based companies with banks as substantial shareholders; and Endesa (Empresa Nacional de Electricidad) the large state-owned company formed in 1944. Endesa was initially only involved in generation. Private companies were obliged to buy all of the electricity that Endesa generated (Salmon, 1995: 153).

Reorganization of the electricity industry became necessary in the 1980s as the result of two factors: the fragmented pattern of production that arose from the historical evolution of the industry and the serious financial problems facing the industry in the early 1980s. Policy makers sponsored a series of mergers and asset swaps (including interests in power generation) between firms in the sector. For example, the three largest companies (Endesa, Hidrola and Iberduero) agreed in 1984 to take over smaller loss-making companies in exchange for government assistance. Fecsa (Fuerzas Eléctricas de Cataluña), one of the companies in most serious financial difficulties, was forced to sell some of its interests in property and minerals as well as in electricity. The process continued through the 1980s and into the 1990s.

The explicit support of the government strengthened the incentives of firms to merge with other Spanish companies. Both Endesa, still a public company at that time, and Iberduero (the predecessor of Iberdrola) embarked on an aggressive policy of acquisitions and takeovers of their small competitors (Crampes and Fabra, 2004; Arocena et al., 1999; Régibeau, 1999; Salmon, 1995). By the end of 1993, Endesa had acquired a myriad regional electricity companies (ENHER, Unelco, GESA, ERZ, Electra de Viesgo, Saltos del Nansa, and Sevillana de Electricidad). In 1992 Iberduero merged with Hidrola, and this in turn led to the creation of Iberdrola. By 1994 the only two companies outside these two groups were Hidrocantábrico and Unión Eléctrica-Fenosa.

The result was that the structure of the electricity sector was fundamentally transformed through a series of mergers and asset consolidation in anticipation of the future liberalization of the market. Out of these consolidations Endesa and Iberdrola emerged as the dominant firms in the industry, with Endesa becoming integrated in both distribution and generation activities. In 1995, as part of its plans to liberalize the industry, the Partido Popular (PP) government decided to privatize Endesa completely without any restructuring. Endesa reinforced its predominant position in the domestic market and became one of the biggest European companies after the above series of acquisitions. By 2002, the electricity sector had clustered into five groups that are all vertically integrated in both generation and distribution activities – in sharp contrast to the case of Britain when the privatization started in this country.[3] Of these consolidations, Endesa and Iberdrola emerged as the dominant firms in the industry, with the former making the transition from a pure generation to a fully vertically integrated (generation and supply) company. Moreover, the ownership structure of the three largest electricity companies (Endesa,

Table 4.2   Equity stake held by long-term shareholders' groups

	1996	1997	1998	1999	2000	2001	2002	2003	2004	2005
Endesa					10.1	12.6	10.1	12.6	10.1	9.0
Iberdrola					17.3	16.1	16.9	15.0	14.8	13.0
U.Fenosa	15.0	15.0	20.0	19.0	22.6	24.3	24.7	40.3	39.3	56.2

Source: Own elaboration based on data from annual reports and other investor information from companies in Spain.

Table 4.3   Key long-term shareholders of Spanish electricity companies

Endesa	Caja Madrid
	La Caixa
	BBVA
Iberdrola	BBVA
	BBK
Union Fenosa	BCH (BSCH)
	Banco Pastor
	Caixa Galicia
	Caixanova
	Caja del Mediterraneo
	ACS

Source: Own elaboration based on data from annual reports.

Iberdrola, and Unión Eléctrica-Fenosa) was itself characterized by ownership concentration (see Tables 4.2 and 4.3). Large domestic banks and non-financial corporations constituted the bulk of hard core, long-term shareholders for Spanish electricity companies.

NATIONAL INSTITUTIONS OF CORPORATE GOVERNANCE

The previous section documented the different patterns of the transformation of the industrial profile of the electricity sector in Britain and Spain in the wake of privatization and liberalization policies. The structure of private property in the electricity sector in Britain was characterized by an evolution from a substantial number of firms with domestic majority ownership to the current situation where the entire sector is composed of subsidiaries of foreign companies. The evolution of the structure of the

Table 4.4　Ownership structure: analysis by type of shareholders in Britain (%)

	Average Years	Institu- tional Investors	Private Investors	Foreign Investors	Govern- ment	Others
Eastern Electricity	(1991–95)	75.6	23.1		1.3	
East Midland Electricity	(1991–96)	67.7	17.2			15.1
London Electricity	(1993–95)	56.7	25.8	11.9		5.6
Midlands Electricity	(1991–95)	68.9	18.3		0.9	11.9
Northern Electricity	(1991–95)	79.6	19.4		1	
Norweb	(1992–96)	66.2	16.9			16.9
Seeboard	(1992–95)	57.7	25.3			17
Southern Electricity	(1991–98)	73.7	18.1			8.2
South Wales Electricity	(1991–95)	76.9	21.2			1.9
National Power	(1991–99)	73.6	21.3			5.1
Scottish Hydro- Electric (SSE)	(1991–2005)	60.2	24.1	5		10.7
Scottish Power	(1991–2005)	59.2	28.1		1.2	11.5

Source:　Own elaboration based on data from annual reports.

Spanish electricity sector, in contrast, was marked by the consolidation of the market power of the established companies, with substantial control by domestic players. The argument presented in this section is that the institutional arrangements of corporate governance of the two countries largely account for the differences in the transformation of the industrial profile of their electricity sectors. We identify two central dimensions of the national institutional arrangements of corporate governance: ownership structure of companies, and the system of corporate law and voting rights.

First, the ownership structure of companies constitutes the primary dimension of national systems of corporate governance. The opposition has traditionally been marked by a contrast between Anglo-Saxon economies where ownership is diffused (that is no single group or groups of shareholders owning a substantial percentage of equity capital) and the main owners are institutional investors; versus that of continental Europe and Japan where ownership is concentrated in the hands of a small number of 'strategic' players: family, banks, or non-financial corporations (Shleifer and Vishny, 1997). The ownership structure of British and Spanish electricity companies conforms to this dichotomy (see Tables 4.2 to 4.5).

The importance of the ownership structures of companies manifests itself

Table 4.5 Ownership structure: analysis by type of shareholders in Spain (%)

	Average Years	Spanish Financial	Institutional Investors	Private Investors	Foreign Investors
Endesa	(2000–2005)	17.3	13.8	24.5	44.4
Iberdrola	(2000–2005)	25.9	7	33	34.1
Unión Fenosa	(1996–2005)	33.9	7.1	29.7	29.3

Source: Own elaboration based on data from annual reports.

through their influence in shaping the preferences of the key shareholders (Mayer, 2000; Vitols, 2001). Institutional investors in Anglo-Saxon economies take a portfolio approach to risk management that, in turn, translates into their reluctance to become central players in the decision-making process of firms. Instead, their preferences lie in seeing portfolio companies achieving high rates of returns on their shares. This has sometimes led them to become active in pressuring firms to pursue strategies that would result in increased share price, but with a purely shareholder value maximization. Mutual and pension funds do not seek to substitute themselves as the managers for portfolio companies. In contrast, shareholders in concentrated ownership systems of corporate governance possess strategic and often multiple goals. For one thing, ownership is frequently embedded in a larger pattern of cross-share holdings whereby firms hold stocks in each other as part of a strategy to protect themselves against unwanted hostile takeover bids that would affect the capacities of managers to develop the strategy of a firm with a long-term perspective. Another motivation is that banks often view their equity stakes as a mechanism to maintain business relationships and protect their loans. A final motivation of large owners could be to extract private benefits from their control of the corporation at the expense of minority shareholders (Zingales, 1998).

The ownership structure of companies shapes the course taken by takeovers in their adjustment process. In countries characterized by ownership concentration, the occurrence of hostile (or unwanted) takeovers is a rarity (Mayer and Franks, 1997). The acquisition of a firm would require a potential bidder to secure the approval of the largest shareholder, or to convince the members of the shareholder group to sell their stakes. In contrast, the absence of ownership concentration entails the possibility of unwanted takeover bids. Managers possess serious incentives to pursue strategies that will increase the stock market capitalization of the firm which, in turn, make it more prohibitive for a potential bidder to acquire the company.

The ownership structure of companies in Britain and Spain constitutes the first dimension of the institutional arrangements of corporate governance that was influential in the respective transformation of the industrial profile of the electricity sector. Ownership diffusion in Britain was conducive to takeover bids and the presence of institutional investors interested in market capitalization gains reinforced this process. The presence of ownership concentration and of friendly, long-term shareholders in Spain made it less likely that a restructuring of the sector would take place through unwanted takeovers. However, the ownership structure of companies only constitutes a first-cut approach to account for the differences in the transformation of the sector in the two countries. For one thing, managers can enact a panoply of anti-takeover measures to protect themselves against unwanted takeover bids in diffused ownership systems of corporate governance. In addition, the degree of ownership concentration in the electricity sector in Spain is important (15–20 per cent of outstanding shares) but not insurmountable.[4] A committed bidder can focus on the acquisition of the remaining free floats (85 to 90 per cent).

The second crucial institutional arrangement of corporate governance that differentiates Britain and Spain is their system of corporate law and its associated voting rights for minority shareholders. Managers can protect themselves against unwanted takeover bids through anti-takeover measures and deviations from the one-share, one-vote principle. The issue of voting rights is related to the process by which equity holders, especially institutional investors as minority shareholders, translate their equity stake into voting power. Minority shareholders prefer systems of corporate governance with the fewest deviations from the one-share, one-vote standard. This standard is one of the best means by which minority investors can collectively achieve influence proportional to their stakes. Managers, in contrast, might prefer to stabilize the ownership structure of the company by giving more power to some shareholders, especially long-term owners.

There are two main deviations from the one-share, one-vote principle. The first falls under the category of unequal voting rights. The most common form of unequal voting rights is the award of multiple voting rights to certain shares by companies. Multiple voting rights are often justified by the desire of firms to reward long-term investors, thereby cultivating a loyal base of shareholders. But unequal voting rights can also be used by managers as a tool to provide hard-core shareholders with a disproportionate voting influence in comparison to their equity stakes. The second deviation from the one-share, one-vote principle is that of the voting rights ceiling that caps the amount of votes any investor may cast regardless of the total number of stocks held. Voting rights ceilings may be used by managers to protect themselves against the potential rise of a large investor in firms with no loyal group of hard-core shareholders.

The use of deviations from the one-share, one-vote standards is permitted in both Spain and the United Kingdom. However, the frequency of their use exhibits sharp divergence. For example, only one of the UK FT 100 index companies had an ownership ceiling, and none had unequal voting rights in 2002 (Davis Global Advisors, 2002: 68). For the specific case of the electricity sector, golden shares were initially introduced by the government. The golden share scheme acted as an impediment on take-overs since no shareholder was allowed to control more than 15 per cent of outstanding shares (Oxera, 2005). The first attempted takeover of a priva-tized electricity company took place in December 1994, shortly before the expiration of the golden share scheme in March 1995. Moreover, it is also worth noting that none of the privatized electricity companies had any mechanisms of protection in the form of deviations from the one-share, one-vote standard other than the golden share scheme, resulting in a surge of takeover activities after March 1995.

By contrast, the use of deviations from the one-share, one-vote standard is widespread in the electricity sector in Spain. First, the three major elec-tricity companies (Endesa, Iberdrola, and Unión Eléctrica-Fenosa) issue two classes of stock: voting and non-voting shares. The latter are used to raise capital without affecting the company's control structure since the holder is entitled to dividends but does not possess any voting rights. Second, the voting rights at the largest two firms exhibit a substantial deviation from the one-share, one-vote standard through the use of voting caps, as described in the annual reports of Endesa and Iberdrola for various years. No shareholder may cast a number of votes higher than that corresponding to 10 per cent of the total outstanding shares. This deviation significantly increases the influence of loyal, long-term shareholders.

NATIONAL INSTITUTIONS AND SECTOR-SPECIFIC REGULATION: THE SPECIFICATION OF THE INTERACTION

The different processes of the transformation of the industrial profiles of the electricity sectors in Britain and Spain testify to the importance of diversity in modern capitalism. Important studies have highlighted the central role of national institutions in creating and sustaining this diversity across capitalist economies (Hall and Soskice, 2001). The transformation can be conceptualized as a series of institutional stages in which managers seek protection from unwanted takeover bids. The first set of institutions is that of the ownership structure of the company. The presence of ownership concentration implies that takeovers are negotiated. A dispersed ownership structure, in contrast, leaves the firm open to unwanted takeover bids. The second set of institutions is related to the national system of corporate law and its associated rules governing voting rights. National systems of corporate governance that protect the voting rights of minority shareholders are more likely to experience a flurry of takeovers acting as a restructuring mechanism. By contrast, national systems of corporate governance that enable management to implement substantial deviations from the one-share, one-vote standard imply a reduced role for financial market pressures in the process of adjustment of firms.

The national institutional arrangements of corporate governance in Britain and Spain exhibit strong variation on these two dimensions which, in turn, shapes the transformation of the industrial profile of their domestic electricity sector. The importance of national-level institutional arrangements highlights the explanatory value of the institution-based comparative approach for the study of the transformation of the electricity sector. We adopted a one-sector, two-nation research design whereby variation in the institutional arrangements of corporate governance of the two countries (IV) is matched with variation in the transformation of the industrial profile of the electricity sector (DV).

The central role of institutional frameworks in explaining cross-country variation, however, does not necessarily imply the irrelevance of sector-based theoretical approaches to regulation (Levi-Faur, 2006). The regulation of the electricity sector in Britain and Spain provide ample examples and instances of sector-based differences that are not driven by national institutions of corporate governance. The British model is characterized by the establishment of new regulatory bodies with a substantial degree of autonomy and discretion, and transparency in the decision-making process (Coen, 2005). Policy-makers constrained their future course of potential actions by providing independent regulatory authorities with substantial powers. Moreover, the political authorities have limited the reconfiguration of the electricity industry through strong policy against vertical integration and by the breaking-up of the sector into many smaller companies (Thomas, 2003). The transformation of the Spanish electricity sector, by contrast, has displayed diametrically opposite characteristics: the absence of strongly independent regulatory institutions; the integration of generation, distribution, and retail activities; and the consolidation of the sector in a small number of large companies (Arocena, 2003; Régibeau, 1999; Salmon, 1995).

The above paragraph highlights the presence of substantial variations between the regulatory policies adopted in the electricity sectors in Britain and Spain. It should be read in conjunction with the discussion in the previous section where we presented significant differences in the systems of corporate governance of the two countries. In other words, an account of the divergence of the transformation of the profile of the electricity sector in Britain and Spain is confronted with a double variation: in the national institutions of corporate governance, as well as in the regulatory choices of policy makers. Therefore, the task consists in specifying the context in which the importance of one type of variation matters for outcomes. We argue that an account of the nationally specific transformation of the profile of the electricity sector is best explained by a process of conjunctural causation requiring the joint interaction between institutions' corporate governance and national patterns of regulation.[5] The main insights of the institution-based Varieties of Capitalism perspective lie in highlighting the role of institutions in the coordination of the activities of the firm, and their effects on the degrees of freedom of actors. The degree to which financial markets constrain the behaviour of management constitutes a good example of the constraining effects of institutional frameworks. However, the focus of the VoC perspective is not an account of the origins and political foundations of institutional frameworks; institutions could be set up as a rational solution to some coordination problems, but they could also be the products of political agendas and actions that emerge from conflict between societal groups (Morgan, 2005). In other words, the choice of an institutional framework represents the choice of policymakers who exhibit motivational multiplicity across and within national settings. The main insight of regulation theories is precisely that the settings of rules and functions in newly liberalized industries reflect the preferences of policy-makers with substantial observed differences across advanced capitalist economies (Jordana and Levi-Faur, 2005; Vogel, 1996).

The issue of regulation is also seen as important by scholars working within an institution-based comparative political economy framework. For example, Hall and Soskice (2001) recognize the importance of regulation in sustaining modes of economic coordination. The German coordinated market economy, for example, is characterized by the importance of rigid labour markets and compulsory training requirements as key elements in the ability of firms to succeed in the areas of incremental innovation. Otherwise, unconstrained managers might be tempted to rely on dismissals to adjust to market fluctuations which, in turn, could seriously deter employees from developing firm-specific skills. The focus of theoretical perspectives highlighting the importance of national institutional frameworks is on economic coordination, not regulation. This focus obscures two issues. First, advanced capitalist economies have experienced a flurry of rapid regulatory changes over the last two decades

(Jordana and Levi-Faur, 2004, 2005; Müller and Wright, 1994). The liberalization of electricity markets at the European level has destroyed the old order of publicly-owned monopolies. There is a potential mismatch between the numerous changes that took place in the regulatory sphere and the apparent stability in the mode of economic coordination. The task becomes one of identifying which types of regulatory changes sustain the existing mode of coordination of firms, as opposed to those that undermine it (Hall and Thelen, 2005). Second, the issue of regulatory choices raises the salience of the political dimension of institutional arrangements in capitalist economies (Morgan, 2005). The analysis of institutional formation and complementarity is not simply about increased economic returns, but raises issues of conflict prevalent between societal groups. Institution-based comparative political economy scholars recognize the importance of history and contingency (Hall, 1986). The institution-based Varieties of Capitalism theoretical perspective distinguishes between two different issues: the effects of institutions on the presence of complementarities, and the basis for the institutional origins of these complementarities. Institutional complementarities refer to the enhancing effects of one institution upon others; their origins, on the other hand, might be driven by many different factors (Hall, 2005). The next step consists of highlighting the importance of the motivational multiplicity of policy makers pursuing more than one goal, or conceptualising a similar goal through different means. The incorporation of the role of politics in regulatory choices complements the focus of the VoC perspective on coordination and provides the basis for a comparison between Britain and Spain in the analysis of the evolution of the electricity sector: the policy of market 'deregulation' without attempts by the state to promote the emergence of large domestic firms versus the policy of building national champions.

Regulatory Choices in Britain

Throughout the 1980s and 1990s, the set of policies known as privatization, liberalization and deregulation constituted the hallmarks of the 'British Model' and dominated the political agenda for electricity utilities (Thomas, 2001). At the heart of these reforms was a desire to transform the electricity industry from a monopoly into a competitive market so that electricity could be bought and sold like other commodities and products. The process of privatization constitutes the starting point of the transformation of the electricity sector in Britain since deregulation preceded European directives. As in many other countries, privatization was motivated by the desire of policymakers to increase government revenues. However, the story of the privatization of the UK economy is not simply one of generating revenue. Many countries proceeded to privatize large firms without the introduction of full-scale deregulation. Other dimensions characterized the process of privatization under the administrations of Thatcher and Major. The Thatcher government pursued the goal of encouraging a wider share of ownership, or so-called 'popular capitalism' (Veljanovski, 1987; Vickers and Yarrow, 1991). The public flotation of utility companies such as British Telecom (1984) and British Gas (1986) included the sale of a significant proportion of the shares to the general public rather than relying on friendly companies that could act as long-term shareholders.

Another consideration inherent in the process of privatization in Britain was the war on organized labour. A series of new industrial relations legislation enabled the Thatcher government to triumph over the National Union of Miners in 1984–5 and, more generally, to reduce the powers of militant trade unions (Davies and Freedland, 1993; Taylor, 1993). In Britain, much of the power of the trade union movement lay in public-owned utilities. Since these had monopoly powers over important public services, any strike action would quickly have a powerful impact on the general public and the national economy. The process of privatization under Thatcher, which invariably involved the breaking up of these large companies and the introduction of competition, was bound to have an impact on trade union power.

Thus, the privatization of the electricity sector not only involved a transfer of ownership from the public to the private sector, but was also accompanied by the dispersion of ownership and the fragmentation of the sector into many smaller firms. The position of two influential scholars in the process of privatization in Britain – Michael Beesley and Stephen Littlechild – is highly illustrative. These scholars were sceptical about the need for extensive regulation of competitive markets. Nevertheless, they recommended that a highly fragmented market be created rather than waiting for the market to develop by itself. There was little suggestion that once established, markets would need regulatory oversight.

The implication of Beesley and Littlechild's prescriptions on competition, namely that the priority was to provide a structure that allowed free entry to the market, was that takeovers and mergers played a prominent role in the evolution of the industrial profile of the sector since they were interpreted as a healthy sign of market discipline in competitive markets. The electricity sector in Britain has experienced a huge amount of restructuring since its privatization in 1990, especially in the distribution and retail supply, and takeovers were of little concern as long the entry barriers were low enough to maintain a realistic threat of competition (Thomas, 2001, 2005). However, the pressure of competition as a mechanism for increasing the competitiveness of domestic firms never materialized. As pointed out by Thomas (2003: 339), 'the electricity companies in Britain were victims of the political and regulatory desire to be seen to be creating a competitive industry'. The evolution of the electricity sector in Britain is best characterized by increasing concentration resulting from takeovers by foreign companies rather than heightened competition through the entry of new firms in the industry.

Regulatory Choices in Spain

The reforms of the Spanish electricity sector, in contrast, have developed in a policy context where industrial policies and the security of supplies have played a prominent role. The process of privatization in Spain, as in other countries, was motivated by the desire of policymakers to generate revenue. In contrast to the Thatcher experiment, the privatization programme reflects the government's goal of procuring as large a financial contribution as possible to the budget at the expense of market restructuring and, consequently, of a more rapid and effective liberalization of the market. Indeed, more money can be extracted from a sale if the prospects of market rivalry are low and entry difficult since these would translate into higher profit expectations. This decision stood in sharp contrast to practices and policies adopted in the UK. According to the privatization consulting commission, the Consejo Consultivo de Privatizaciones (CCP), the state raised a total of 45 per cent of its total profits from the partial sales of the capital of the energy sector companies during the period 1996–2005 (*La Razón,* 2006).

Another consideration of Spanish policymakers is related to the claims that in a time of 'globalization' firms have to be large in order to effectively compete on world markets. The notion of economies of scale stands paramount in this logic of size under globalization. The claim that generators have to be large at a national level to be viable competitors in global markets has often been complemented by the argument that such national concentration would not lead to an increase in market power (Thomas, 2003).

This preference for building national champions able to compete in European markets led policymakers repeatedly to declare their desire to see that privatized firms should remain in Spanish hands (Cano, 1998). They used two mechanisms to achieve this goal. First, the Spanish electricity sector, under the guidance and regulatory powers of the state, was consolidated from over two hundred to five vertically integrated (generation, distribution and retailing) companies with substantial holdings by the banking sector (Salmon, 1995: 153). The aim of this consolidation was to eliminate smaller companies who were seen as being unable to compete in the liberalized European electricity markets.

Second, Spanish policymakers provide strong incentives for companies to merge in order to grow in size. Both Endesa and Iberdrola proceeded to an impressive shopping spree of their small competitors in the late 1980s and early 1990s (Crampes and Fabra, 2004; Arocena *et al.*, 1999; Régibeau, 1999; Salmon, 1995). By 1994 the only two companies outside these two groups were Hidrocantábrico and Unión Eléctrica-Fenosa. The Spanish electricity industry is therefore characterized by a high degree of horizontal concentration in generation, as well as a high degree of vertical integration between generation, distribution and retailing. The process of mergers, acquisitions, and alliances did not end after the change in the regulatory regime (Arocena, 2003). In fact, successive Spanish governments have advocated since the early 1980s the creation of large Spanish groups in order to compete with large international rivals.[6]

CONCLUSION

The advent of liberalization has neither induced convergence between national models of capitalism nor eliminated sectoral regulation. The analysis of the cases of the British and Spanish electricity sector performed in this chapter illustrates quite well the prominence of national institutions of corporate governance and the centrality of patterns of re-regulation. The institution-based Varieties of Capitalism theoretical perspective and regulation theories share scepticism about the notion that liberalization results in a race towards the bottom of the lowest standards. But each would be individually incomplete in fully accounting for the specific nature of the transformation of the profile of the electricity sector in Britain and Spain. The VoC literature has provided essential insights into understanding the viability of economic divergence in an age of greater economic integration. The coordination of the activities of the firm requires the presence of regulation, even in liberal market economies where market signals constitute primary mechanisms of adjustment. However, the insights provided by the VoC theoretical perspective need to be complemented with perspectives that stress the importance of patterns of re-regulation, and the role of policy makers in this processes.

The institutions of corporate governance are mediated by their interaction with the wider institutional framework in which they are embedded. In particular, it is within their interaction with national regulatory policies that the institutions of corporate governance matter, not by themselves.

Finally, the insights associated with a conjuncturally based causal process invites further inquiries. The presence of different types of business system and the divergence in regulatory orientation of policymakers in many transition and developing economies should be associated with nationally-specific patterns of transformation. Regulatory choices are not neutral given the importance of coordination; but a purely functionalist account of the origins of these choices would fail to capture the importance of the preferences of actors.

NOTES

1. A previous version of the chapter was presented at the Corporate Governance and Regulation Workshop, University of Manchester, 17 November 2006. We would like to thank Reinhard Bachmann, Klaus Nielsen, and the participants of the workshop for their comments on the paper.
2. However, the Zapatero government abolished this scheme in November 2005 in part due to pressures from the European Commission. (*Wall Street Journal,* 28 November 2005: 6).
3. Endesa, Iberdrola, Unión Fenosa, Hidrocantábrico and Electra de Viesgo.
4. The aggregate stake for the largest four friendly shareholders was 17 per cent Endesa (2000–5); 32 per cent Iberdrola (2000–5); 26 per cent Unión Fenosa (1996–2005). *Source*: Own calculation from annual reports.
5. Conjunctural causation refers to a situation whereby only the combination of multiple conditions will produce a specific outcome: X1 and X2 produce Y (see Ragin, 1987). The impact of one institution or variable depends on the presence of others, that is a single variable by itself will not lead to the desired/predicted outcome.
6. Although space does not enable us to adequately analyse the episode, the attempt by E.ON to acquire Endesa testifies to the preference of Spanish policy makers for national champions. The actions of the Zapatero administration were essential in thwarting the ambitions of E.ON. First, the Spanish government increased the supervisory powers of the national energy regulator (Comisión Nacional de Energía or CNE) over which it wields substantial influence. The immediate consequence was that the energy regulator imposed a number of severe conditions on the proposed E.ON takeover which were seen as a dissuasive ploy. Second, the Zapatero administration orchestrated the arrival of Acciona (one of Spain's largest construction companies) into the capital of Endesa. The former quickly acquired over 20 per cent of Endesa. The incursion of Acciona pointed to a concerted effort to disrupt E.ON's bid with government officials nudging their friends in industry to block foreign firms. The concerted actions between Spanish policy makers and a construction company were not accidental. The decision of Acciona is part of a trend among construction companies that are looking to invest the wealth accumulated in the decades of the long building boom that is now coming to an end, as well as constituting a strategic move being carried out on behalf of Spain's ruling elite anxious to protect its sources of energy.

REFERENCES

Arocena, P., K. Kühn, and P. Régibeau (1999), 'Regulatory reform in the Spanish electricity industry: a missed opportunity for competition', *Energy Policy,* **27**, 387–99.

Arocena, P. (2003), 'The reform of the utilities sector in Spain', in C. Ugaz and C.W. Price (eds), *Utility Privatization and Regulation: a Fair Deal for Consumers*, Aldershot and Brookfield, VT: Edward Elgar, 125–48.

Beesley, M. and S. Littlechild (1983), 'Privatisation: principles, problems and priorities', *Lloyds Bank Review*, **149**, 1–20.

Cano, S. D. (1998), *Políticas de Privatización: Aproximación Teórica. Experiencias Prácticas y Propuestas para España*, Madrid: Consejo Económico y Social.

Coen, D. (2005), 'Business-regulatory relations: learning to play regulatory games in European utility markets', *Governance*, **18** (3), 375–98.

Crampes, C. and N. Fabra (2004), 'The Spanish electricity industry: plus ça change . . .', CMI Working Paper. Cambridge: University of Cambridge, Department of Applied Economics and Cambridge, MA: MIT, Center for Energy and Environmental Policy Research.

Davis Global Advisors (2002), *Leading Corporate Governance Indicators*, Newton, MA: Davis Global Advisors.

Davies, P. and M. Freedland (1993), *Labour Legislation and Public Policy*, Oxford: Oxford University Press.

Deakin, S., R. Hobbs, D. Nash, and G. Slinger (2002), 'Implicit contracts, takeovers, and corporate governance: in the shadow of the City Code', *Working Paper no. 254*, ESCR Centre for Business Research, University of Cambridge.

Hall, P. (1986), *Governing the Economy: the Politics of State Intervention in Britain and France*, New York: Oxford University Press.

Hall, P. (2005), 'Institutional complementarity: causes and effects', *Socio-Economic Review*, **3** (2), 373–7.

Hall, P. and R. Franzese (1998), 'Mixed signals: central bank independence, coordinated wage bargaining and European monetary union', *International Organization*, **52** (3), 505–36.

Hall, P. and D. Soskice (eds) (2001), *Varieties of Capitalism: the Institutional Foundations of Comparative Advantage*, Oxford: Oxford University Press.

Hall, P. and K. Thelen (2005), 'Institutional change and the varieties of capitalism', unpublished paper Presented at the Annual Meeting of the American Political Science Association, Washington, DC, 1 September.

Jordana, J. and D. Levi-Faur (2004), 'Towards a Latin America regulatory state? The diffusion of autonomous regulatory agencies across countries and sectors', in D. Levi-Faur and E. Vigoda-Gadot (eds) *International Public Policy and Management: Policy Learning and Political Boundaries*, New York and Basel: Marcel Dekker, 155–88.

Jordana, J. and D. Levi-Faur (2005), 'The diffusion of regulatory capitalism in Latin America: sectoral and national channels in the making of new order', *The Annals of the American Academy of Political and Social Science*, 598, 102–24.

La Razón, 2006. 'El Sector Energético Representa la Mitad de los Ingresos Procedentes de Privatizaciones', Saturday 22 April, p. 59.

Levi-Faur, D. (2006), 'Varieties of regulatory capitalism: getting the most out of the comparative method', *Governance*, **19** (3), 367–82.

Majone, G. (1997), 'From the positive to the regulatory state: causes and consequences of changes in the mode of governance', *Journal of Public Policy*, **17**, 139–67.

Mayer, C. (2000), 'Corporate governance is relevant', in T. Dickson (ed.), *Financial Times: Mastering Strategy*, London: Pearson Education.

Mayer, C. and J. Franks (1997), 'Corporate ownership and control in the UK,

Germany, and France', *Bank of America Journal of Applied Corporate Finance*, **9** (4), 30–45.

Morgan, G. (2005), 'Institutional complementarities, path dependency, and the dynamics of firms', in G. Morgan, R. Whitley and E. Moen (eds) *Changing Capitalisms? Internationalization, Institutional Change, and Systems of Economic Organization*, Oxford: Oxford University Press.

Müller, W. and V. Wright (eds) (1994), *The State in Western Europe: Retreat or Redefinition?*, London: Frank Cass Publishers.

Oxera (2005), 'Special rights of public authorities in privatized EU companies: the microeconomic impact', *Report Prepared for the European Commission*, Oxford: Oxera.

Ragin, C. (1987), *The Comparative Method: Moving Beyond Qualitative and Quantitative Strategies*, Berkeley: University of California Press.

REE (1997), *Explotación del Sistema Eléctrico. Informe 1996*, Madrid: Red Eléctrica de España.

Régibeau, P. (1999), 'Regulatory reform in the Spanish electricity industry: Same as it ever was?', in R. Vaitilingam (ed.), *A European Market for Electricity?*, London: Centre for Economic Policy Research.

Salmon, K. (1995), *The Modern Spanish Economy: Transformation and Integration into Europe*, London: Pinter.

Shleifer, A. and R. Vishny (1997), 'A survey of corporate governance', *Journal of Finance*, **52**, 737–84.

Soskice, D. (1999), 'Divergent production regimes: coordinated and uncoordinated market economies in the 1990s', in H. Kitschelt, P. Lange, G. Marks and J. Stephens (eds), *Continuity and Change in Contemporary Capitalism*, New York: Cambridge University Press.

Taylor, R. (1993), *The Trade Union Question in British Politics, 1945–1992*, Oxford: Basil Blackwell.

Thomas, S. (2001), 'Theory and practice of governance of the British electricity industry', *International Journal of Regulation and Governance*, **1** (1), 1–24.

Thomas, S. (2003), 'The seven brothers', *Energy Policy*, **31**, 393–403.

Thomas, S. (2005), 'Experience of electricity liberalisation in Britain', unpublished paper presented at the Korean Development Conference, Seoul, 20 June.

Thomas, S. (2006), 'The British model in Britain: failing slowly', *Energy Policy*, **34**, 583–600.

Veljanovski, C. (1987), *Selling the State: Privatisation in Britain*, London: Weidenfeld and Nicolson.

Vickers, J. L. and G. Yarrow (1991), 'Economic perspectives on privatization', *Journal of Economic Perspectives*, **5**, 111–32.

Vitols, S. (2001), 'Varieties of corporate governance: comparing Germany and the UK', in P. Hall and D. Soskice (eds), *Varieties of Capitalism: The Institutional Foundations of Comparative Advantage*, Oxford: Oxford University Press.

Vogel, S. (1996), *Freer Markets, More Rules: Regulatory Reform in Advance Industrial Countries*, Ithaca: Cornell University Press.

Zingales, L. (1998), 'Why it's worth being in control?' in G. Bickerstaffe (ed.), *Financial Times: Mastering Finance*, London: Pearson Education.

5. The relationship between debt structure and firm performance in India

Sumit K. Majumdar and Kunal Sen

INTRODUCTION

A central issue in corporate governance is the nature of the relationship between suppliers of finance and managers of firms. In particular, the literature asks the question: how do suppliers of finance ensure that the managers of firms do not steal the funds they supply and invest in bad projects? Much of the discussion on how suppliers of finance monitor managers has been confined to the more advanced economies (Mayer, 1990; Singh, 1995; Shleifer and Vishny, 1997). There is relatively little knowledge of financier-manager relationship in developing countries. Moreover, much of the discussion of this relationship has focused on suppliers of equity, rather than on suppliers of debt (Barton and Gordon, 1988; Bettis, 1983; Bradley *et al.*, 1980; Hoskisson and Hitt, 1994; Majumdar and Chhibber, 1999; Titman and Wessels, 1988).

In this chapter, we study the implications of debt structure for firms' performance in India. Firms in India are very highly leveraged, with the mean debt equity ratio of the firms evaluated exceeding two times or 200 per cent of the nominal equity values. This phenomenon is a function of the soft-budget constraints that have been perpetrated in Indian industry over several decades (Majumdar, 1998). The large presence of debt in the capital structure of Indian firms indicates that the extent of the influence debt holders in India have on firms' performance is particularly relevant in the Indian context.

The rest of the chapter is in four parts. The next part provides an exposition of the key theoretical issues relating to the relationship between debt structure and firms' performance. The third section describes the Indian debt structure. The fourth section summarizes the findings of the empirical analysis. The final section concludes.

DEBT STRUCTURE AND FIRM PERFORMANCE: THE CONCEPTUAL LINKS

Firms usually borrow using two principal types of debt instruments: loans from banks and other financial intermediaries, and the issuance of bonds such as mutual funds to financial institutions, to individuals and to other firms. In the corporate finance literature, two theoretical perspectives have emerged to explain why different types of debt may have different implications for the performance of the firm. The first, the information cost view, argues that financial markets are characterized by asymmetric information between lenders and borrowers as lenders cannot distinguish between good borrowers and bad borrowers (Stiglitz and Weiss, 1983). Given that lenders face significant information asymmetries that create possibilities for opportunism by better-informed firms, banks and other financial intermediaries can play an important role in financing and governing banks (Chirinko and Elston, 2006).

Such financial intermediaries can access non-publicly available information about the firms they lend to, and by obtaining such information can reduce the information costs associated with lending (Leland and Pyle, 1977; Fama, 1985). In contrast, arm's length lenders, such as bondholders, will have to rely on publicly available information or expend significant resources to obtain privately held information about the firm. According to the 'information cost' view, arm's length debt is associated with higher information costs than debt held by financial intermediaries, usually termed monitored or informed debt in the literature. Since lower information costs incurred by lenders will translate into lower costs of financing, firms that rely more on monitored debt are expected to be more profitable than those who rely less on monitored debt.

The 'information cost' view also makes a distinction between short-term debt and long-term debt. The renewal process associated with short-term borrowing triggers periodic evaluation of the firm's ability to meet its debt payments, and hence is a more effective monitoring mechanism than long-term debt where such periodic evaluations of the firm's performance does not occur (Fama, 1985). Short-term debt has other benefits to the firm: this renewal of bank loans serves as a positive signal to other lenders who then need not undertake similar costly evaluation of their claims (James, 1987; Lummer and McConnell, 1989). Thus, short-term borrowing is expected to exert a greater positive effect on the firm's performance, due both to the lower costs of financing that the firm faces, and the regular monitoring that occurs in the periodic evaluations of the firm.

An alternative theoretical perspective, the property rights view, takes as its starting point the separation between ownership and control in modern corporations (Berle and Means, 1932).[1] There are two ways that the property rights view is relevant to our discussion of the strategic implications of different types of corporate borrowing on firms' performance. First, the distinction between state and private ownership is important. While, in theory, state-owned firms are owned by the public, the *de facto* control rights belong to the state. Thus, although agents of the state, the bureaucrats, have concentrated control rights, they have no significant cash flow rights because these are effectively dispersed amongst the tax payers of the country (Shleifer and Vishny, 1997).

Moreover, bureaucrats controlling the firm have other objectives that are dictated by their political interests and have less of an interest in maximizing the value of the firm. Thus, the property rights view suggests that state-owned lenders would be less interested in the monitoring of firms they lend to or in recovering the funds that they lend.[2] For these reasons, firms that borrow more from such sources would not be under as much pressure to perform better as firms who borrow more from private sources.

A second insight that the property rights view can provide us on the strategic implications of corporate borrowing, is with respect to the difference between secured and unsecured debt. Secured creditors provide funds against collateral, which can be claimed in the event that the firm defaults on the borrowing. Unsecured creditors, on the other hand, cannot do so. More important, if the firm were to become bankrupt, secured creditors have higher-order priority on claims over the firm's assets over unsecured creditors. Thus, for unsecured creditors, the incentive to monitor a firm and to ensure that it remains profitable and in business is significantly greater than for secured creditors. From a property rights perspective, we would expect that firms which borrow from unsecured creditors are more likely to perform better than firms that borrow from secured creditors.[3]

DEBT STRUCTURE IN INDIA

In India, firms borrow using five types of debt instruments. These are: (a) short-term borrowing from commercial banks; (b) long-term borrowing from term-lending institutions, which we will call institutional borrowing; (c) borrowing in the form of debentures which are corporate bonds that in some, but not all, cases are converted to shares after a specific lock-in period; (d) fixed deposits, which are deposits that yield a specified rate of interest over a given period of time from the market; and (e) a residual category called 'other borrowing' which includes trade credit and other funds accessed from the inter-corporate market.

Table 5.1   A typology of corporate borrowing and its likely impact on firm performance

	Informed or Arm's-Length?	Short-term or Long-term?	Private or State-Owned?	Secured or Unsecured?	Predicted impact on profitability from an 'information cost' perspective	Predicted impact on profitability from a 'property rights' perspective
Bank borrowing	Informed	Short-term	Both	Unsecured	+	?
Institutional borrowing	Informed	Long-term	State-Owned	Secured	+	−
Debentures	Arm's Length	Long-term	Private	Secured	−	?
Fixed Deposits	Arm's Length	Long-term	Private	Unsecured	−	+
Other borrowing	Both	Both	Both	Both	?	?

Note: +: Positive; -: Negative; ?: Uncertain.

In Table 5.1, we classify these five debt instruments according to whether these instruments are monitored or arm's length, short-term or long-term, private or state-owned and unsecured or secured. Much of the classification is self-explanatory, except the classification of banks as both state-owned and privately-owned and term-lending institutions as being wholly state-owned. In 1969, several commercial banks, making short-term working capital loans to industry, were almost fully nationalized and continue to remain under state ownership.

In 1991, barriers to the entry of private banks in India were relaxed and there was significant entry of such banks, especially of domestically owned private banks (Sen and Vaidya, 1997). Several foreign banks expanded their scale of operations with the relaxation of branch licensing policies. Thus, there is currently a mix of ownership among commercial banks, with all three types of ownership, state, private domestic and foreign, present in varying degrees. With respect to institutional borrowing, financial institutions making long-term loans were established, *de novo*, by the government after independence. For example, the Industrial Finance Corporation of India was set up in 1948, and the Industrial Development Bank of India in 1964. These are the two major suppliers of long-term loans to Indian industry. There are also a number of specialized long-term lenders, all owned by the government, such as the Industrial Reconstruction Bank of

India, the Small Industries Development Bank of India and the Shipping Credit and Investment Corporation of India.[4]

Apart from these central government-owned financial institutions, almost every major Indian state, there being 28 states in India's federal structure, has a State Financial Corporation and a State Industrial Investment Corporation. These corporations are also major long-term debt suppliers to industry. The only major private-sector financial institution in India is the Industrial Credit and Investment Corporation of India; however, on its board of directors the government has a noticeable presence and for practical purposes it behaves like a state-owned enterprise.[5] Thus, unlike in advanced market economies, long-term loans to Indian firms are provide by state-owned financial institutions.

There is one other institutional feature in India that deserves special mention. The role of unsecured creditors in monitoring firms' performance becomes even more important if the bankruptcy procedure is costly and inefficient, since the unsecured creditor comes last among debtors in the order of priority on claims over the firm's assets (White, 1989). In India, bankruptcy laws are weak and exit procedures for firms extremely cumbersome (Anant *et al.*, 1992). The bankruptcy procedure is governed by the Sick Industrial Companies Act 1985 (amended in 1992). Under this act, firms which have accumulated losses in excess of net worth for over ten years are referred to the Board of Industrial and Financial Reconstruction (BIFR). The BIFR typically uses a consensus approach to approve a suggested rehabilitation package that needs to meet with approval from the firm's managers, workers, creditors and share-holders. Very rarely are firms shut down and the whole process is extremely time-consuming; during this period, production is stopped and workers and creditors are not paid.

There are significant legal barriers to exit in India. The Industrial Disputes Act 1947 does not allow large industrial units to retrench workers or shut down without government approval. The Urban Land Ceiling and Regulation Act 1976 does not allow firms to sell land without permission of the relevant local government. In summary, while for all creditors, the Indian bankruptcy and exit procedures are costly, it is even more so for unsecured creditors, so that these creditors have the greater incentive to ensure that the firms they lend to do not become financially unviable.

In the last two columns of Table 5.1, we also provide the predictions of these theories on the possible impact of each type of borrowing on firm profitability using the insights from the two theories that we discussed earlier. We expect monitored debt from such bank and institutional borrowing to have a positive impact (and conversely, debentures and fixed deposits, a negative impact) on firms' performance under the information cost perspective, and within monitored debt, for bank borrowing to have a stronger impact than institutional borrowing as the former is short term and the latter long term.

With respect to the property rights view, we expect that fixed deposits, which are private and unsecured, will have a positive effect and, conversely, institutional borrowings, which are from state-owned enterprises and secured, a negative effect, on firms' performance. However, it is not clear whether bank borrowing will have a positive or negative effect; while it is unsecured, it is provided by both state- and privately-owned banks. A similar argument applies to debentures which are private but a secured form of debt that firms have access to.

THE RELATIONSHIP BETWEEN DEBT STRUCTURE AND FIRMS' PERFORMANCE

We used firm-level data for 1026 Indian manufacturing firms listed on the Bombay Stock Exchange for the period 1988–93. The borrowing data are extracted from the balance sheets of individual firms. Ownership data are for the proportion of shares held by foreign investors, the government, directors, financial institutions which are principally government-owned, individual blockholders and the general public. The data also include information extracted from the profit and loss accounts of the sample firms. The data were collected from multiple sources. The Center for the Monitoring of the Indian Economy (CMIE) provided initial data. Thereafter, details on ownership and aspects of firms' behaviour and performance were collected from the Bombay Stock Exchange and the office of the Registrar of Companies of the Government of India.

The principal limiting factor was the availability of data on ownership, which were not readily available for all firms. In conjunction with the guidance provided to us by officials of the Department of Statistical Analysis and Computer Services of the Reserve Bank of India, we were able to collect ownership data for the sample of firms included in the study. The data collected are cross-sectional and not time-series because of difficulties associated with obtaining ownership patterns.

Measure of Performance

Firms' performance is measured using return on sales, in common with similar work studying the impact of ownership on firms' performance (Boardman and Vining, 1989). This accounting-data based measure is used for all our observations; hence, there is consistency in measurement within the sample. Previous research (Kay and Mayer, 1986) has established that accounting ratios have significant correlation with economic rates of return. A number of studies in the industrial organization field (Bain, 1951; Cowling and Waterson, 1976) and in the strategic management field (Capon *et al.*, 1990) have employed such measures.

Control Variables

We also introduced several control variables that may have an impact on a firm's performance. The most important among these is the nature of ownership of the firm. There are three principal owners in the Indian context: the state, foreign investors, and the domestic corporate sector. Firms with a higher degree of state ownership may be expected to perform poorly as compared to privately owned firms, given that the cash-flow rights of these firms ultimately accrue to the public, who have neither the ability nor the incentive to monitor them (Shleifer and Vishny, 1994; Chhibber and Majumdar, 1998). The opposite would be true for privately owned firms, whether foreign or domestically owned (Boardman *et al.*, 1997; Chhibber and Majumdar, 1999).

We introduce two other control variables for ownership: directors' share in equity and the ownership of the shares of the top 50 shareholders. According to the property rights view of equity structure in the corporate governance literature, the greater the cash flow rights of the manager in a particular firm, the more likely is it that the managers will not divert the firm's assets to their own ends, and will be interested in maximizing the value of the firm. Concentrated ownership in the form of higher equity ownership among the top 50 shareholders would fulfil the same objective, as large shareholders can engage in concerted action to discipline managers, and have the incentive to do so (Shleifer and Vishny, 1997).

Firms' size is an important determinant of performance. Larger firms have a greater variety of capabilities and enjoy economies of scale; these can positively impact performance (Penrose, 1959). Additionally, larger firms can exploit market power (Shepherd, 1986), both in product markets as well as in factor markets, an issue particularly germane in India where institutional factors have fostered rent seeking (Bardhan, 1984; Bhagwati, 1993) and are able to earn greater profits. Conversely, larger firms have problems of coordination which can negatively influence performance (Williamson, 1967). Nevertheless, given the Indian institutional scene, it is likely that market power arguments with respect to size are likely to dominate over coordination failure issues, and size and profitability are expected to display a positive relationship (Majumdar, 1997). We introduced firm size as an additional control variable.

In the Indian context a number of firms are owned by a common industrial house (Mohan and Aggarwal, 1990). Such common ownership can lead to the spillover of firm-specific capabilities among all members of the group, with an impact on the performance of each member (Amsden, 1989). Moreover, by building up a brand name and a reputation for fair dealing, business groups can reduce transactions costs for affiliated firms to access finance, technology and management talent (Khanna and Palepu, 2000). If this is the case, group affiliated firms are expected to be more profitable than unaffiliated firms.

However, a number of these business groupings are family controlled and in such firms, tunnelling may occur; that is, resources may be transferred out of profitable companies to the controlling shareholders, the members of the family in this case, or to unprofitable companies in the group. Group affiliated firms may also be sheltered from competition, both internal and external, by virtue of the coordinated political lobbying that the group can exert on their behalf. Thus, it is not clear *a priori* whether group affiliated would necessarily perform better than unaffiliated firms. We introduced a variable that captures whether a firm is a member of a business group or not.

Finally, we introduced a liberalization year dummy which takes the value of unity for all observations which occur in the post-1991 period; zero otherwise. The year 1991 is considered to be a watershed in the evolution of economic policies in India. That year, a comprehensive set of economic reforms were initiated, the most important of these being the dismantling of the licensing regime for large corporate firms along with the removal of quotas on most capital and intermediate goods (Ganesh-Kumar *et al.*, 2003). The liberalization year dummy was introduced to capture the possible beneficial effects of the reforms on firm performance.

Key Findings

Among the principal explanatory variables, except for fixed deposits, all other variables that capture the structure of debt were found to be statistically insignificant. Bank borrowing, institutional borrowing and debentures exerted no significant influence on firms' performance. In contrast, fixed deposits had a strong positive effect. The lack of significance of bank and institutional borrowing suggested that an 'information-cost' perspective on the role of banks and other financial intermediaries in monitoring firms' performance in India does not seem to find empirical support.

In contrast, the results provided support for the 'property rights' perspective on the strategic implications of corporate borrowing in the Indian context. The key finding here was that creditors that are unsecured and private exerted the strongest control on firms' performance, and neither secured creditors such as institutional lenders or bond-holders, nor unsecured public creditors such as banks, exerted any significant influence at all. Insecure property rights on the firm's assets in the event of bankruptcy combined with control rights that belong to the public rather than with bureaucrats implied that private unsecured creditors have clear incentives to monitor firms' performance, and do so in the Indian context.

With respect to variables that capture firms' ownership, only state ownership mattered in determining firms' performance and it has a significant negative effect on the latter. No other ownership, whether to do with the ownership of the firm, foreign, private corporate, or the concentration of ownership among certain shareholders, directors or the top 50 shareholders, mattered in determining firm performance.[6] The lack of significance of the foreign ownership variable may be due to the fact that it is not ownership, per se, but the property rights that accrue at different levels of ownership that matters in determining performance outcomes for foreign-owned firms operating in India. Foreign firms perform better when property rights devolve unambiguously to foreign shareholders, in terms of majority ownership, in contrast to situations when foreign shareholders cannot exercise effective control (Chhibber and Majumdar, 1999).

The lack of significance of the domestic corporate and concentrated ownership variables are counter-intuitive findings and their explanation may lie in institutional factors unique to India. Indian industrialists, even with relatively small shareholdings, have treated the public companies they have controlled and managed as sources of personal and family wealth enhancement (Bardhan, 1984). The widespread presence of tunnelling in India has been empirically established, particularly among business groups (Bertrand *et al.*, 2002). Lax enforcement of corporate laws has also contributed to the expropriation of firms by owners and managers at the cost of outside shareholders. Also, family-owned firms are often not well managed if the owners are themselves the managers (Burkart *et al.*, 2003). Thus, directors' share in equity may be proxying for family-run firms, which are not expected to be the most profitable in the Indian context.

The lack of significance of four debt structure variables, bank borrowing, institutional borrowing, debentures and other borrowing, was surprising and needs to be explored further. It may be that the impact of these variables on profitability differs across firms with different levels of profitability, and thus, the aggregate effect masked these sub-aggregate effects. In order to examine this possibility, we estimated quantile regressions for our sample of firms, with return to sales as the dependent variable, and

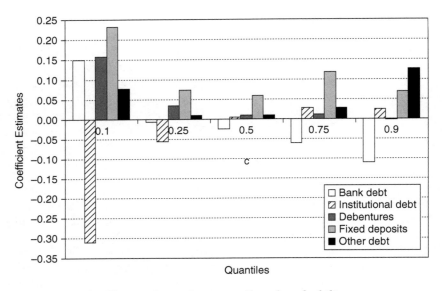

Figure 5.1   Coefficients for various quantiles of profitability

each of the five borrowing variables entered separately and in turn as independent variables.

The quantile regression is richer than least squares estimation as it takes into account the heterogeneity of firms, and the possibility that both the magnitude and the nature of the relationships between the debt structure variables and performance may differ across firms (Koenker and Bassett, 1978; Koenker and D'Orey, 1987). Standard regression estimates denote changes at the mean of the dependent variables for a unit change in the independent variables. Standard ordinary least squares estimation assumes that conditional distribution of the profitability variable will be homogeneous, implying that whatever point on the conditional distribution is analysed, the estimates of the debt structure variables, and the other variables as well, are the same. If, instead, the relative importance of the debt variables at different points of the conditional distribution of the profitability variable is to be understood then alternative estimation techniques are applicable.

Figure 5.1 plots the coefficients of the five borrowing variables obtained from the quantile regressions at various quantiles of the distribution of profitability. There are two noteworthy findings. First, heterogeneity matters. The impact of debt structure on profitability depends very much on the level of profitability of the firm. Second, the impact of debt structure on a firm's performance is most evident for firms in the bottom 10 per cent of the profitability distribution, that is, for the most poorly performing firms. For these firms, institutional borrowing has a large negative effect on profitability. For the same set of firms, fixed deposits have a strong positive effect on profitability. This provides stronger support for the 'property rights' perspective of the strategic implications of corporate borrowing and against the 'information cost' view.

For firms in the middle quantiles, bottom 25 and 50 per cent respectively, the different types of corporate borrowing do not seem to have appreciable effects on firms' performance, and neither do these effects seem to differ significantly across the five borrowing variables. However, for firms in the upper quantiles (upper 75 and 90 per cent), fixed deposits again have a positive and reasonably large effect on profitability. Surprisingly, for these firms, bank borrowing has a negative effect on profitability, and this could possibly be due to the extraction of surplus from more profitable firms by the banks they borrow from (Diamond, 1991; Rajan, 1992; Weinstein and Yafeh, 1998). Overall, the quantile regression results provide further support for the 'property rights' perspective on corporate borrowing versus the 'information cost' view, and for the importance of fixed deposits as an effective capital structure variable in monitoring firm performance.

CONCLUSIONS

In contrast to the conventional thinking on the importance of bank lending in particular, and monitored debt in general, in determining firms' performance in the Indian context, what matters more is unsecured arm's length lending in influencing firms' profitability, rather than bank borrowing or monitored debt. This can be mainly attributed to the fact that it is both unsecured and privately held, which make the creditors associated with this type of debt the most likely to monitor firms' performance.

Furthermore, the impact of fixed deposits on profitability depends on the level of profitability of the firms, with poorly and well performing firms more likely to be positively impacted by fixed deposit borrowing than firms in the middle of the distribution of profitability. In addition, institutional borrowing has a strong negative effect on firms' profitability for poorly performing firms, and this can be attributed to the state-owned nature of institutional lenders along with the secured nature of institutional lending.

Thus, it is important to take into account institutional differences and a firm's heterogeneity in the analysis of capital structure on firms' performance. The manner in which different corporate debt may affect the performance of firms would depend on the specific institutional characteristics of the economy with, in particular, the legal environment relating to firms' exit and the nature of ownership of corporate debt being important variables that have to be taken into account in analysis of similar phenomena.

From a policy perspective, the findings of this study suggest that if banks and development finance institutions are to play the monitoring role in India that they play in other economies, it may be necessary to reform these institutions by divesting a larger part of the state's ownership of these institutions and allowing the management of these institutions greater independence from the government. Furthermore, it is important to streamline bankruptcy and exit procedures in India so that debt-holders can play a disciplining role on the managers of firms, thus ensuring that the latter are acting in the best interests of the suppliers of finance.

NOTES

1. When we refer to the property rights view, we subsume the agency cost perspective on financial structure in it. Even though these two sets of literature initially developed independently they are concerned with are similar and the approaches highly complementary (see Jensen and Meckling, 1976).
2. Several studies have shown that countries with higher government ownership of banks are associated with lower financial development and lower growth of per capita income and productivity, and that the lending behaviour of state-owned banks is typically politically determined rather than based on economic considerations (La Porta *et al.*, 2002; Sapienza 2004).
3. Scott (1977) provides a theoretical analysis of why secured debt plays a different role in firm's' capital structure than unsecured debt.
4. The Industrial Reconstruction Bank of India has now been renamed the Industrial Investment Bank of India.
5. The Industrial Credit and Investment Corporation of India is now a fully fledged commercial bank.
6. While fixed deposits comprise an average of around 6 per cent of the borrowing of firms in our sample, most fixed deposits issued by these firms are held by other firms (especially the larger corporate firms) rather than by individuals. Thus, the monitoring role that holders of fixed deposits may play in the Indian context is expected to be significantly larger than is suggested by the actual proportion of fixed deposits in the debt structure of firms in India.

REFERENCES

Amsden, A. (1989), *Asia's Next Giant: South Korea and Late Industrialization*, New York: Oxford University Press.
Anant, T. C., S. Gangopadhyay and O. Goswami (1992), 'Industrial sickness in India: initial findings', *Studies in Industrial Development*, Paper No. 2, New Delhi: Ministry of Industry.

Bain, J. S. (1951), 'Relation of profit rate to industry concentration: American manufacturing, 1936–1940', *Quarterly Journal of Economics*, **65**, 293–324.

Bardhan, P. K. (1984), *The Political Economy of Development in India*, Oxford: Basil Blackwell.

Barton, S. and P. Gordon (1988), 'Corporate strategy and capital structure', *Strategic Management Journal*, **9**, 623–32.

Berle, A. A., and Means, G. C. (1932), *The Modern Corporation and Private Property*, New York: Macmillan.

Bertrand, M., P. Mehta and S. Mullainathan (2002), 'Ferreting out tunneling: an application to Indian business groups', *Quarterly Journal of Economics*, **117**, 121–48.

Bettis, R. A. (1983), 'Modern finance theory, corporate strategy and public policy: three conundrums', *Academy of Management Review*, **8**, 406–15.

Bhagwati, J. N. (1993), *India in Transition: Freeing the Economy*, Oxford: Oxford University Press.

Bradley, M., G. Jarrell and E. H. Kim (1984), 'On the existence of an optimal capital structure', *Journal of Finance*, **39**, 857–78.

Boardman, A. E. and A. R. Vining (1989), 'Ownership and performance in competitive environments: a comparison of the performance of private, mixed, and state-owned enterprises', *Journal of Law and Economics*, **32**, 1–33.

Boardman, A. E., D. M. Shapiro and A. R. Vining (1997), 'The role of agency costs in explaining the superior performance of foreign MNE subsidiaries', *International Business Review*, **6**, 295–317.

Burkart, M. M, Panunzi, and A. Shleifer (2003), 'Family firms', *Journal of Finance*, 58, 2167–201.

Capon, N., J. Farley and Hoenig, S. (1990), 'Determinants of financial performance: a meta analysis', *Management Science*, **36**, 1143–59.

Chhibber, P. K. and S. K. Majumdar (1998), 'State as investor and state as owner: consequences for firm performance in India', *Economic Development and Cultural Change*, **46**, 561–80.

Chhibber, P. K. and S. K. Majumdar (1999), 'Foreign ownership and profitability: property rights, control and the performance of firms in Indian industry', *Journal of Law and Economics*, **62**, 209–38.

Chirinko, R. and J. A. Elston (2006), 'Finance, control and profitability: the influence of German banks', *Journal of Economic Behaviour and Organisation*, **59**, 69–88.

Cowling, K. and M. Waterson (1976), 'Price-cost margins and market structure', *Economica*, **43**, 267–74.

Diamond, D. (1991), 'Monitoring and reputation: the choice between bank loans and directly placed debt', *Journal of Political Economy*, **99**, 688–721.

Fama, E. (1985), 'What's different about banks?', *Journal of Monetary Economics*, **15**, 29–39.

Ganesh-Kumar, A., K. Sen and R. R. Vaidya (2003), *International Competitiveness, Investment and Finance: A Case-Study of India*, London: Routledge.

Hoskisson, R. E. and M. A. Hitt (1994), *Downscoping*, New York: Oxford University Press.

James, C. (1987), 'Some evidence on the uniqueness of bank loans', *Journal of Financial Economics*, **19**, 217–35.

Jensen, M. C. and W. Meckling (1976), 'Theory of the firm: managerial behavior, agency costs and capital structure', *Journal of Financial Economics*, **3**, 305–60.

Johnston, J. (1984), *Econometric Methods*, New York: McGraw Hill.

Kay, J. A. and C. P. Mayer (1986), 'On the application of accounting rates of return', *Economic Journal*, **96**, 199–207.

Khanna, T. and K. Palepu (2000), 'Is group affiliation profitable in emerging markets? An analysis of diversified Indian business groups', *Journal of Finance*, **40**, 867–91.

Koenker, R. and G. Bassett (1978), 'Regression quantiles', *Econometrica*, **46**, 33–50.

Koenker, R. and V. D'Orey (1987), 'Computing regression quantiles', *Applied Statistics*, **36**, 383–93.

La Porta, R., F. López de Silanes and A. Shleifer (2002), 'Government ownership of banks', *Journal of Finance*, **57**, 265–301.

Leland, H. E. and D. H. Pyle (1977), 'Informational asymmetries, financial structure and financial intermediation', *Journal of Finance*, **32**, 371–87.

Lummer, S. and J. J. McConnell (1989), 'Further evidence on the bank lending process and the capital-market response to bank loan agreements', *Journal of Financial Economics*, **25**, 99–122.

Majumdar, S. K. (1997), 'The impact of size and age on firm-level performance: some evidence from Indian industry', *Review of Industrial Organization*, **12**, 231–41.

Majumdar, S. K. (1998), 'Slack in the state-owned enterprise: an evaluation of the impact of soft-budget constraints', *International Journal of Industrial Organization*, **16**, 377–93.

Majumdar, S. K. and P. K. Chhibber (1999), 'Capital structure and performance: evidence from a transition economy on an aspect of corporate governance', *Public Choice*, **98**, 287–305.

Mata, J. and J. A. F. Machado (1996), 'Firm start-up size: a conditional quantile approach', *European Economic Review*, **40**, 1305–23.

Mayer, C. (1990), 'Financial systems, corporate finance and economic development', in R. G. Hubbard (ed), *Asymmetric Information, Corporate Finance and Investment*, Chicago, IL: University of Chicago Press.

Mohan, R. and V. Aggarwal (1990), 'Commands and controls: planning for Indian industrial development, 1951–1990', *Journal of Comparative Economics*, **14**, 681–712.

Morck, R., D. Wolfenzon and B. Yeung (2005), 'Corporate governance, economic entrenchment and growth', *Journal of Economic Literature*, **63**, 655–720.

Penrose, E. T. (1959), *The Theory of the Growth of the Firm*, Oxford: Basil Blackwell.

Rajan, R. (1992), 'Insiders and outsiders: the choice between informed and arm's length debt', *Journal of Finance*, **72**, 1367–400.

Sapienza, P. (2004), 'The effects of government ownership on bank lending', *Journal of Financial Economics*, **72**, 357–84.

Scott, J. H. (1977), 'Bankruptcy, secured debt, and optimal capital structure', *Journal of Finance*, **33**, 1–19.

Sen, K. and R. R. Vaidya (1997), *The Process of Financial Liberalization in India*, Delhi: Oxford University Press.

Shepherd, W. G. (1986), 'On the core concepts of industrial organization', in W. G. Shepherd and H. W. De Jong, (eds), *Mainstreams in Industrial Organization*, Dordrecht: Martinus Nijhoff Publishers.

Shleifer, A. and R. Vishny (1994), 'Politicians and firms', *Quarterly Journal of Economics*, **109**, 995–1025.

Shleifer, A. and R. Vishny (1997), 'A survey of corporate governance', *Journal of Finance*, **62**, 737–83.

Singh, A. (1995), *Corporate Financial Patterns in Industrialising Countries: A Comparative International Study*, Washington DC: The World Bank.

Stiglitz, J. and A. Weiss (1983), 'Credit rationing in markets with imperfect information', *American Economic Review*, **71**, 393–410.

Titman, S. and R. Wessels (1988), 'The determinants of capital structure choice', *Journal of Finance*, **43**, 1–19.

Weinstein, D. and Y. Yafeh (1998), 'On the costs of bank-centered financial system – evidence from changing bank relations in Japan', *Journal of Finance*, **53**, 635–72.

Williamson, O. E. (1967), 'Hierarchical control and optimum firm size', *Journal of Political Economy*, **75**, 123–38.

White, M. J. (1989), 'The corporate bankruptcy decision', *Journal of Economic Perspectives*, 129–51.

6. The corporate governance role of capital markets: a Bangladesh perspective

Faizul Haque

INTRODUCTION

The capital market of a country can exert considerable influence on the firm by imposing certain rules and regulations relating to the firm's governance practices. While the legal and regulatory structures are essential, the capital market, with adequate transparency and accountability in place, can ultimately reward or punish firms for their governance practices (Drobetz et al., 2004; Gompers et al., 2003, make a similar observation). The capital market can wield its governance role in mitigating agency problems through disciplining the management and improving the firm's overall governance.

This chapter explores the corporate governance role of the capital market of Bangladesh. It is structured as follows. The next section reviews the literature on the governance role of capital markets, and explains the methodological issues; this is followed by an overview of the securities market of Bangladesh, together with the efficiency of the pricing mechanisms. The fourth section analyses the activism of the regulatory institutions in relation to regulatory provisions and their enforcement. The next section explains the governance role of the financial intermediaries, including institutional investors and banks. A final section concludes the chapter.

LITERATURE REVIEW

In addition to capital allocation (for example mobilizing savings, pooling risks and sharing opportunities), capital markets enhance governance practices through information production and monitoring (Tadesse, 2003). Singh et al. (2002) and Claessens (2003) refer to direct governance measures of the capital markets, which include: tightening listing requirements, controlling insider dealing arrangements, imposing disclosure and accounting rules, ensuring protection of minority shareholders and attracting reputable agents. Conversely, a capital market can exert indirect influence through pricing mechanisms, which include both allocative and disciplinary measures and the takeover mechanisms (Singh, 2003; Samuel, 1996).

Tobin (1984), cited in Singh (2003), distinguishes between the two concepts of share price efficiency of the stock market, namely: information arbitrage efficiency through which all currently available market information is incorporated into the share price; and fundamental valuation efficiency, where share prices accurately reflect the future discounted earnings of the firm. Singh (2003) also mentions that the stock market, with the help of the market for corporate control, can improve the efficiency and performance of a firm by replacing inefficient managers and transferring firm assets to those who can manage it more efficiently. The market for corporate control includes hostile takeovers, management buy-outs, and leveraged buy-outs (Prowse, 1994).

However, several studies (e.g. Claessens, 2003; Morck *et al.*, 2000; Singh, 2003; Demirag and Serter, 2003) observe that the effectiveness of the pricing mechanisms in a developing economy tends to remain rudimentary because of poor corporate governance associated with transparency and disclosures. Singh (2003) and Prowse (1994) criticize the takeover mechanism as being an inherently flawed and expensive method of solving corporate governance problems. Iskander and Chamlou (2000) also state that the signalling measure is likely to be diluted if the capital market is not transparent, investments are costly to exit and institutional investors are poorly governed. Alba *et al.* (1998) argue that the governance role of a developing economy capital market is being constrained by an absolute family dominance, weak incentives to improve disclosure and governance, poor protection of minority shareholders, and weak accounting standards and practices. Demirag and Serter (2003) also mention that the majority of family-based business groups in developing countries appear to own and control banks (through pyramidal or complex shareholding) that act as a substitute for an external capital market. Likewise, Prowse (1994) argues that the managers of firms with less reliance on external finance are unlikely to be disciplined by the capital market. Moreover, Iskander and Chamlou (2000) observe that the capital markets in developing countries provide little incentive for better corporate governance (either in the real sector or in the financial sector), primarily because of the dominance of a few large firms, low trading volumes and liquidity, absence of long-term debt instruments and inactivity of institutional shareholders.

Institutional investors such as insurance companies, pension funds, non-pension bank trusts and mutual funds, being an important part of the capital market, tend to influence the process of corporate governance. For example, Samuel (1996) argues that institutional investors are more efficient than individual investors in collecting, analysing and acting on objective, firm-specific fundamental information, and thus influence a firm's investment and other financial decisions. The Institutional Shareholders' Committee (ISC), the FRC (2003) and Mallin (2004) outline several governance roles of the institutional investors in solving the agency problems, which include (Mallin 2004): (a) engaging in dialogue with the firm based on mutual understanding of objectives; (b) evaluating overall governance disclosures with particular emphasis on board structure and composition; (c) evaluating and monitoring the performance relating to shareholder value and shareholder activism; (d) exercising voting power (either direct or proxy voting) on all major corporate decisions, and (e) intervening whenever necessary, particularly in issues like corporate and operational strategies, investment decisions, acquisition or disposal strategy, internal control mechanism and board and management contracts.

Increased institutionalization seems to improve the efficiency of the governance role of the capital market with which firms are valued and governed. Samuel (1996) argues that the monitoring and disciplinary activities of institutional investors may act as a viable alternative to debt finance as well as the market for corporate control. (However, he does not find any evidence of the impact of institutional ownership on investment performance. Sarker and Sarker (2000), cited in Claessens and Fan (2002), also find no evidence that institutional investors are active in corporate governance.) This is particularly important for developing country firms, because they appear to rely more on debt than equity. However, as Iskander and Chamlou (2000) and Samuel (1996) argue, institutional investors in developing economies generally represent only a small part of a diversified portfolio and also may not be strong enough to impose fairness, efficiency, and transparency. Therefore, the institutional investors are less likely to play a strong governance role in a developing economy.

Stiglitz (1985, cited in Prowse, 1994) and Gul and Tsui (1998) argue that the debt market can mitigate the agency problem by providing debtholders with the incentives and power to monitor and control insiders' expropriation. Shleifer and Vishny (1997) also state that the concentration of debt in the hands of few creditors tends to help the latter exercise significant cash flow as well as control rights, and thus reduce the firm's agency costs, by preventing the managers from investing in unworthy investment projects or extracting private benefits. (The relative power and domination of creditors are much higher for multiple creditors, because each of the individual creditors can take legal action against the firm, and it is reasonably difficult for the firm to renegotiate with several creditors rather than a single one; Shleifer and Vishny, 1997). It is further argued that creditors can liquidate a firm (if it is unable to run efficiently or pay its debts), acquire the assets used as collateral, and participate in the voting process on major corporate decisions (for example reorganization of the firm or removal of the managers). Creditors can also use short-term lending and take the equity ownership of the firm in order to be involved in the investment and other corporate decisions (Shleifer and Vishny, 1997). Nonetheless, irrespective of the nature of creditors' rights, the effectiveness of the country's legal system seems to remain crucial.

METHODOLOGY

This study is based on semi-structured or unstructured interviews (carried out in a field survey from November 2004 to January 2005) with various stakeholders in the corporate sector. The respondents comprise one top executive of the Dhaka Stock Exchange (DSE), three top executives of the Securities and Exchange Commission (SEC), three senior executives of the Bangladesh Bank (BB), three executives of the Investment Corporation of Bangladesh (ICB), one executive of the Institute of the Chartered Accountants of Bangladesh (ICAB), three chartered accountants, three investment bankers, three academic experts and several minority shareholders.

The study also consulted various published (and some unpublished) documents to gain background information and insights into the institutional framework of corporate governance. In this respect, information was collected from the DSE as well as the Chittagong Stock Exchange (CSE), the SEC, the BB, the RJSC and the ICAB. The websites of some of these key stakeholders of corporate governance were also extremely useful in this regard. Archival material from newspapers and periodicals, along with several recent academic or policy studies on corporate governance in Bangladesh, was a valuable source of secondary data.

THE CAPITAL MARKET OF BANGLADESH

This section provides a brief overview of the capital market of Bangladesh, and evaluates the share price efficiency of the capital market.

An Overview of the Capital Market

The capital market of Bangladesh, with its small size, does not seem to have made a significant contribution to the overall economic development of the country, although a recent development can be perceived as encouraging. The ratio of market capitalization of the capital market to GDP increased from 2.42 per cent in 2003 to 6.03 per cent in 2005, according to the DSE's annual report for 2004–5. The securities market is based on two stock exchanges, namely the Dhaka Stock Exchange (DSE) and the Chittagong Stock Exchange (CSE). As at 31 January 2007, there were 317 securities listed with the DSE against a total issued capital of BDT (Bangladeshi Taka) 138610 million, and total market capitalization of BDT 377 759 million (*Dhaka Stock Exchange*, 2007). On the other hand, a total of 213 securities were listed with the CSE against a total issued capital of BDT 63 800 million and total market capitalization of BDT 195 600 million, according to the Bangladesh Bank's annual report of 2005–6.

The prime stock exchange of the country, the DSE, is a self-regulated non-profit organization, which was incorporated as a public limited company in 1954 (since 1964 in its present name). The activities of the DSE are regulated by its Articles of Association, along with the rules, regulations and bye-laws, the Companies Act 1994, the Securities and Exchange Ordinance 1969, and the Securities and Exchange Commission Act 1993. Out of the total 317 securities of the DSE, there were 256 companies (shares), 13 mutual funds and only eight debentures.

The banking sector appears to dominate the capital market, with 53.55 per cent of the total market capitalization, with other major sectors being: fuel and power (9.77 per cent), cement (9.75 per cent), pharmaceuticals (9.67 per cent), textiles (3.65 per cent) and insurance (4.13 per cent) (Dhaka Stock Exchange, 2007). In spite of a growing demand for quality shares in the capital market and several regulatory efforts, most reputable local and foreign firms seem to be reluctant to float their shares, with the exception of a few banks and other financial institutions. In general, firms prefer to keep away from the capital market, partly because of the complex legal formalities of the SEC and stock exchanges, together with the fear of transparency and accountability, high flotation costs and inadequate tax related incentives.

THE EFFICIENCY OF THE PRICING MECHANISMS

During the early 1990s, the capital market of Bangladesh experienced a number of reform initiatives including the establishment of the capital market regulatory body, the Securities and Exchange Commission (SEC) of Bangladesh. Subsequently, there was an upward trend in share price indices, prior to experiencing an unusual boom and collapse in 1996. Since then, the general investor's confidence has been shattered and the share price efficiency of the capital market has come under close scrutiny. While the share market scam partly resulted from the opportunistic behaviour of a group of foreign institutional investors, local entrepreneurs and dishonest executives of the regulatory organs, it occurred primarily because of the inadequacy and inefficiency in the legal and regulatory framework. Over the last couple of years, a number of regulatory and infrastructural reform measures have been implemented, and this has caused an overall steady improvement in the breadth and depth of the capital market. However, a very recent trend of unusual increases in share price indices has made different policy makers, practitioners and researchers debate whether the pricing mechanisms of the capital market are at all efficient.

Share price efficiency (for example information arbitrage efficiency and fundamental valuation efficiency) appears to have been constrained by the critical issues of transparency and accountability at both firm level and operational level of the capital market. The existing regulatory and enforcement mechanisms do not seem to be effective in making sure that the listed firms' financial and non-financial information is available and easily accessible to outsiders in order that everyone can make informed decisions. Moreover, there are numerous examples of fabrication in the disclosure practices of listed financial and non-financial firms, purely to enable the controlling shareholders to protect their economic interests. The unethical business practices of a group of stock market brokers and auditing firms have also played a part.

In general, most of the better governed firms with strong operating performance tend to demonstrate better stock price performance on a continuous basis. However, a rapid or continuous increase in share prices of poorly governed firms with weak financial foundations does not seem to justify the claim that the share prices accurately reflect currently available (or past) market information and future discounted earnings of the firm. (Note that an empirical estimation of the efficiency of pricing mechanisms is beyond the scope of this chapter.) The study reveals that several brokerage houses, in co-operation with ill-motivated sponsors or executives, have violated the SEC rules and regulations through stock price manipulation. This observation corroborates the empirical evidence of Rahman and Hossain (2006) that the stock market of Bangladesh is not weak-form efficient. (Weak-form efficiency refers to the situation when the information relating to the past prices and return is incorporated into the share prices: Fama, 1970).

As previously discussed, the market for corporate control (commonly known as mergers and acquisitions) is a widely recognized tool to resolve corporate governance problems in the developed and many developing economies. Although various researchers and practitioners emphasize mergers and actuations as ways to remove firm inefficiency and to enhance competition, these are not well known practices in the corporate sector of Bangladesh. For example, there are suggestions from many quarters for a straight closure or for the mergers and acquisitions of several private commercial banks in order to overcome their long-lasting inefficiency (Mahmud, 2005). The SEC has recently adopted some regulatory guidelines for the acquisition of substantial shares, mergers and takeover. The SEC rules, among other provisions, require the disclosure of an individual's shareholding of 10 per cent or more in a listed firm. The provisions also require a person to notify other shareholders if the former intends to acquire 10 per cent or more shares of a firm. The price is to be determined by a formula related to the price of the shares over the last six months, or in certain cases, by negotiation. There are also provisions associated with the takeover of financially weak firms (Asian Development Bank, 2003). However, these measures are unlikely to establish the market for corporate control as a corporate governance mechanism, primarily because of the inadequacy of the provisions, together with the small size of the capital market and a significant concentration of ownership by the controlling shareholders in the majority of listed firms.

GOVERNANCE THROUGH REGULATORY PROVISIONS AND ENFORCEMENTS

While the legal system sets a boundary for firms through the judicial system and appropriate laws, the regulatory institutions are responsible for supervisory oversight and disciplinary measures to oblige them to behave in line with relevant rules and regulations. This section explores the regulatory activisms of the SEC, the stock exchanges, and the central bank.

The Securities and Exchange Commission (SEC) of Bangladesh

The SEC, a government-affiliated autonomous regulatory authority of the capital market, was established in 1993 following the enactment of the Securities and Exchange Commission Act 1993. The Act provides the SEC with broader licensing and regulatory powers over the capital market stakeholders and intermediaries such as stock exchanges, brokers and dealers, merchant banks and portfolio managers, whereas the 1969 Securities and Exchange Ordinance (SEO) enabled the SEC to regulate the issuance of securities within the broader framework of the 1994 Companies Act (Sobhan and Werner, 2003). These regulations, along with many other rules, schedules and notifications, tend to establish overall governance structures of the listed firms. The capital market watchdog can be credited with several regulatory initiatives taken in recent times in areas like capacity building, shareholder rights, and transparency and accountability. In a positive move, the SEC issued a notification on Corporate Governance Guidelines for listed companies in Bangladesh, although the success of this initiative is likely to be constrained by the lack of mandatory legal requirements in the Companies Act. Moreover, several provisions (for example, independent directors, audit committees) based on western corporate governance models do not seem to restrain the controlling shareholders from being involved in opportunistic behaviour, as seen in the country's banking sector.

As an independent regulatory body with the responsibility for overseeing the governance practices of listed firms, the SEC does not appear to have adequate enforcement mechanisms, although some progress has been made in areas such as setting rules and regulations. The SEC seems to have failed to develop appropriate surveillance and enforcement systems through which the value of the firm is reflected in the share price without any form of market manipulation. There is also evidence that the institutional investors and other capital market participants exploit the weaker position of the SEC by being involved in opportunistic behaviour. The enforcement organ of the SEC does not have adequate human capital with relevant professional expertise and technological support to detect these irregularities.

While the establishment of the Central Depository System (CDS) is a good initiative of the SEC, the latter appears to have failed to control several related issues, such as the opening of beneficiary owners' (BO) accounts. The recent incidence of the initial public offering (IPO) irregularities of a leading private bank through numerous fake BO accounts has revealed that there can be many loopholes in both the legal system and the existing regulatory bodies' market surveillance mechanisms (for example SEC automation system; see also Mazumder, 2005). This, in turn, has helped a group of businesspeople to gain unethical economic advantages. However, the capital market regulator appears to have become more cautious in recent times, in allowing firms to go public through the IPO. It has taken several actions to streamline the process of opening the BO account and to avoid forgery and other manipulations. The promptness in investigative and punitive actions of the SEC with reference to the said IPO irregularities appears to be a good example of protecting the interests of the outside shareholders. This can, however, be termed as a direct consequence of the close co-ordination between the SEC and the BB, since the latter was more proactive in responding to the violations of the banking rules.

Moreover, the SEC does not seem to be effective in making firms accountable in terms of holding their AGMs regularly, giving fair dividends or resolving shareholder grievances in due time, ensuring minority representation on their boards, and disclosing all relevant financial and non-financial information timely and objectively. The state of shareholder protection and transparency has also been constrained by the absence of an appropriate evaluation system, through which better governed firms are rewarded and errant firms are duly punished. However, the SEC has recently fined the controlling shareholders and management of several firms for not holding their AGMs regularly, although it has failed to prevent other irregularities associated with AGMs. While there are legal provisions for the SEC to sue the errant firms for violating the SEC orders, any use of such legal measures is a lengthy and complex process, and therefore is not a financially feasible solution. Nor do the regulatory bodies have appropriate initiatives to make people aware of the issues of corporate governance.

The capital market regulator does not seem to recognize the significance of credit rating by making it mandatory for listed and prospective listed firms, and thus enhancing transparency. The SEC appears to be reluctant to make the pre-IPO credit rating mandatory, out of concern that this might discourage firms to come to the capital market. Moreover, the SEC does not have adequate enforcement mechanisms to oversee a firm's accounting and auditing practices. There is also a substantial lack of SEC initiatives to oblige external auditors to maintain their professional integrity and to detect various irregularities in financial reporting. Nonetheless, the SEC is striving for the legal authority to hold the dishonest auditing firms accountable and is taking the necessary punitive actions. It is also planning to get the half-yearly accounts of the listed firms audited to improve financial reporting, although it is unlikely to guarantee improved firm transparency. The study reveals that the capital market regulator should set some criteria such as experience and track record, reputation, and staff competence, for the external auditors to be entitled to audit the firms. There are also suggestions for setting standard guidelines for the auditors' remuneration. This is particularly important because the reluctance of a firm to spend more money on external auditors is likely to constrain quality auditing.

The poor state of shareholder protection, transparency and accountability is not a recent trend, but an accumulated outcome of the negligence over many years of the regulatory bodies, the SEC and stock exchanges, to prevent firms from being involved in various forms of irregularity.

The Stock Exchanges

The study reveals that the existing judicial structure, together with the Companies Act and other SEC regulations and poor enforcement, is undermining the stock exchanges' efforts to enforce better governance practices through disciplining opportunistic behaviour in the capital market. The inadequacy of manpower with appropriate expertise is also damaging the regulatory oversight of the stock exchanges. Even though the SEC possesses the authority to empower the exchanges with arbitration jurisdiction, such power is found to be limited to the disputes relating to the securities transaction rather than the expropriation of shareholder rights and the violation of the Companies Act and other regulations. The Asian Development Bank (2003) makes a similar observation.

The Dhaka Stock Exchange (DSE) now appears to ensure, within its capacity, timely financial reporting with minimum disclosure requirements, although these efforts are being constrained by the lack of action on the part of the SEC and the ICAB. The country's premier stock exchange has also been proactive in boosting investors' confidence through close surveillance of share price behaviour, and de-listing (or imposing fines on) several errant firms (for example firms that do not hold AGMs, give dividends or submit regular audited financial accounts). Although there are valid reasons for making the de-listing decisions, often in the interests of the shareholders, the regulatory bodies do not seem to assist outside shareholders with any exit strategy. The shares of the de-listed firms are allowed to be traded through over-the-counter (OTC) arrangements, so de-listing does not resolve the outside investors' problems of getting their investments back. As explained earlier, legal actions (such as seeking liquidation) to compensate investors' losses are not feasible from the perspectives of cost and complexity. The survey reveals that the de-listing decision ought to be preceded by compelling the controlling shareholders to buy back all the shares of the outside investors. Other punitive measures, such as declaring bankruptcy, re-organization of the board and management, or mergers and takeovers, could be part of the solution to these problems.

The Bangladesh Bank

The role of the Bangladesh Bank (BB) in improving the corporate governance of the listed banking institutions is of paramount importance. Several recent amendments to the banking laws and regulations have provided the BB with greater operational and policy autonomy to regulate and supervise the banking sector.

The central bank has taken several policy measures to improve corporate governance standards in the banking sector. It appears to have shown a reasonable degree of success in making a group of bank directors responsible for default loans, taking partial measures through removal (or resignation) of board members, re-scheduling or adjustment of loans, controlling insider lending, and minimizing undue interference of the board members. According to Mahmud (2005), the BB has successfully removed as many as 54 bank directors for defaulting on loans taken from their own banks and eight others for indulging in other improper practices. The central bank is also streamlining the PCBs by setting specific targets to reduce default loan portfolios, introducing an early warning system (EWS) and listing institutions as 'problem banks'. Under the EWS, banks with deteriorating performance in selected indicators are brought under special observation to prevent further deterioration. The BB has also strengthened the monitoring of the 'problem banks' through agreements on clear and quantifiable targets for improvement and monthly returns on performance (Ahmed, 2005).

The activism of the central bank has resulted in overall improvement of corporate governance in banks in relation to firms in other sectors, although its regulatory oversight has not been successful in several areas of governance. In spite of the BB's close vigilance over loan contracts and default loan recovery, various forms of controlling shareholders' expropriations still remain and persistently cause massive default loans in the banking sector. The presence of the default culture seems to have an enormous impact on the development of the corporate governance of the country in general, and the banking sector in particular. The study reveals that many big business groups owned by some powerful families are among the top listed loan defaulters. Several respondents opine that it is hard to get these family conglomerates or other politically powered businesspeople to comply with various rules and regulations so that the interests of the depositors and outside shareholders are protected and the stability of the country's financial system is maintained.

As discussed earlier, several of the BB's regulatory and disciplinary initiatives, intended to limit the opportunistic behaviour of the controlling shareholders and managers, have failed because of the judicial stay order. The interviews also revealed that the BB's efforts to turn its regulatory orders into law, through the proper amendment of the Bank Company Act 1991, have been arrested by various organized moves of the business elites, together with their political allies in Parliament. It is interesting to note that lawmakers from all major political ideologies have made a concerted effort to halt the regulatory initiatives of the Central Bank.

ROLE OF THE FINANCIAL INTERMEDIARIES

As discussed above, the institutional investors and debt holders or creditors can improve the firm's governance practices, and protect the firm's as well as outsiders' interests.

Institutional Investors

The Investment Corporation of Bangladesh (ICB), the only major institutional investor in the country, plays a pivotal role for the small and medium investors through mutual fund operations, investor schemes and portfolio management. The government-controlled ICB was incorporated in 1976 under the Investment Corporation of Bangladesh Ordinance. Since then, the ICB has expanded its operational scope in three broad areas: merchant banking, mutual fund operations, and stock brokerage activities. The ICB has floated ten of the 13 listed mutual funds in the stock exchanges (including one Islamic rules-based and one pension-holders' mutual fund), with the remaining three being issued by the government-owned Bangladesh Shilpa Rin Shangstha (BSRS), a private asset management company, and a micro-finance institution.

The ICB has a record of providing attractive dividends against its mutual funds. Chowdhury and Chowdhury (1998) observe that the ICB is making a significant contribution to the development of the country's capital market by creating both demand for and supply of securities. The ICB investors' account scheme is an attempt to create demand for securities in the capital market through mobilizing the general investors' savings into that market. At the same time, it enhances the supply of attractive securities through the flotation of several mutual funds and unit certificates. As outlined in its annual report for 2003–4, the ICB has recently undergone major reforms in its business policies and operational strategies, including the establishment of three subsidiary companies (ICB Capital Management, ICB Asset Management and ICB Securities Trading) to work in three main operational areas of the capital market. The ICB Securities Trading Company has also launched online trading in major cities to serve general investors across the country. It is important to note that only one private sector mutual fund (issued by the AIMS of Bangladesh Ltd) is listed in the capital market.

The study reveals that institutional investors' activism in mitigating the corporate governance problems of the listed firms is being constrained by the absence of adequate institutional investors, and the limited expertise of the existing mutual funds or investment banks in corporate governance matters. Moreover, the lack of outside investors' awareness of the available investment schemes, and the perceived complexities of these schemes, hinder the development of the institutional investors in the country.

The ICB does not seem to play its due role in protecting the outside shareholders' interests. There are also allegations against the ICB of being involved in deliberate institutional buying or selling, which in turn causes abnormal share price behaviour. A study sponsored by the Asian Development Bank (2003) regards the reluctance of the ICB in complying with SEC mutual fund rules (regulated as per the Securities and Exchange Commission (Mutual Fund) Rules, 2001), together with its preferential treatment as a state-owned organization and other procedural complexities, as a major deterrent which subsequently causes an uneven playing field in institutional investment. In spite of some regulatory initiatives to encourage private participation in institutional investment, there been no positive development in this regard.

Nevertheless, the ICB has recently taken legal measures against several errant firms for their failure to hold AGMs and for non-payment of dividends over many successive years. There have also been legal initiatives against several listed firms to conduct special audits and to re-structure their boards to ensure ICB representation. However, the success of these efforts is hardly noticeable because of the procedural delays in the judicial system.

Banks

The significant role of the debt markets in mitigating firms' governance problems has already been discussed. In the absence of a noticeable corporate debt market and minor presence of the equity market, bank finance (for example term lending) dominates the investment financing of the country. In spite of the initiatives of regulatory bodies, such as those taken by the SEC and BB to ensure trading of government securities and bonds in the stock market, there has been no noticeable development in strengthening the bond market

Since many banks and other financial institutions (for example leasing and insurance firms) have stakes in both financial and non-financial firms in the form of loans and/or equity investments, the former can play a critical role in improving the latter's corporate governance practices. As Caprio and Levine (2002) argue, bank managers can exert significant influence in shaping better corporate governance of the firm through allocating their capital in an efficient way; however, banks and other creditors with concentrated debt may be involved in manipulating the corporations' activities (for example forgoing good investment or taking too little risk) for their personal gain rather than for the benefit of the company in which they invest. Nonetheless, neither banks nor creditors seem to be active in this regard, primarily because of the poor state of corporate governance in their own institutions. While there is some representation of the lending firms on the boards of the borrowing firms, most board representatives tend to be inactive in foreseeing the long-term consequences of their lending or investment decisions.

CONCLUSIONS

This chapter has analysed the corporate governance role of the capital market of Bangladesh. It was revealed that the capital market does not seem to be efficient in its governance functions in relation to information production and monitoring. The lack of activism on the part of the government-controlled (BB and SEC) and non-governmental (ICAB and DSE) regulatory bodies is largely responsible for poor corporate governance role of the capital market. Regulatory activity appears to have been constrained by the absence of co-ordination and the overlap of power and responsibilities of the regulatory agencies, alongside a lack of professionalism, commitment and human capital in the regulatory organs. In spite of some legal protection for outside shareholders by the companies and securities acts, very few investors appear to be aware of the laws and their enforcement. Activity by institutional investors and creditors was largely absent. It was also revealed that the market for corporate control is not present in the corporate sector of Bangladesh.

It is imperative to mention that the performance of regulatory institutions like the BB, SEC and DSE has improved in recent times as a result of broad-based financial sector reforms. Whilst the central bank has made some progress in disciplining the controlling shareholders and managements of banks, undue interference by a group of businesspeople, together with internal management problems and insider lending, appears to be restricting these efforts. It was also revealed that several policy and disciplinary initiatives by the regulatory agencies have failed because of the judicial stay order and enormous political interference. The government seems to be indifferent to taking punitive actions against the controlling owners of the majority of errant financial and non-financial firms, partly because of the latter's political influence.

REFERENCES

Ahmed, F. (2005), 'Financial sector reform, I: banks are today better poised for steady growth than before', *The Daily Financial Express*, 26 March.

Alba, P., S. Claessens and S. Djankov (1998), 'Thailand's corporate financing and governance structures: impact on firm's competitiveness', in *Proceedings of the Conference on Thailand's Dynamic Economic Recovery and Competitiveness*, Bangkok: UNCC.

Asian Development Bank (2003), *Capacity Building of the Securities and Exchange Commission and Selected Capital Market Institutions*, Manila: Asian Development Bank.

Caprio, G. and R. Levine (2002), 'Corporate governance and finance: concepts and international observations', in R. E. Litan, M. Pomerleano and V. Sundararajan (eds), *Building the Pillars of Financial Sector Governance: The Roles of the Private and Public Sectors*, Washington, DC: Brookings Institution Press, pp. 17–50.

Chowdhury, M. U. and T. A. Chowdhury (1998), 'An evaluation of the role of Investment Corporation of Bangladesh (ICB) in the development of Bangladesh capital market', *Dhaka University Journal of Business Studies*, **19** (2), 75–94.

Claessens, S. (2003), 'Corporate governance and development: review of the literatures and outstanding research issues', *Proceedings of the Global Corporate Governance Forum Donors Meeting, 13 March 2003, The Hague*, Washington, DC: The World Bank.

Claessens, S. and J. P. H. Fan (2002), 'Corporate governance in Asia: a survey', *International Review of Finance*, **3**, 71–103.

Demirag, I. and M. Serter (2003), 'Ownership patterns and control in Turkish listed companies', *Corporate Governance: An International Review*, **11** (1), 40–51.

Dhaka Stock Exchange (2007), *The DSE Monthly Review*, January 2007, **22** (1).

Drobetz, W., A. Schillhofer and H. Zimmermann (2004), 'Corporate governance and expected stock returns: evidence from Germany', *European Financial Management*, **10** (2), 267–93.

Fama, E. (1970), 'Efficient capital markets: a review of theory and empirical work', *Journal of Finance*, **25** (2), 383–417.

FRC (2003), 'The Combined Code on Corporate Governance', London: The Financial Reporting Council, Department of Trade and Industry, http://www.frc.org.uk/asb/publications/, 15 December 2004.

Gompers, P. A., J. Ishii and A. Metrick (2003), 'Corporate governance and equity prices', *Quarterly Journal of Economics*, **118** (1), 107–55.

Gul, F. A. and J. Tsui (1998), 'A test of the free cash flow and debt monitoring hypotheses: evidence from audit pricing', *Journal of Accounting and Economics*, **24** (2), 219–37.

Iskander, M. R. and N. Chamlou (2000), *Corporate Governance: a Framework for Implementation*, Washington DC: World Bank.

Mahmud, W. (2005), 'Ethics, economics and the market economy', *Proceedings of the 5th Nurul Matin Memorial Lecture on Ethics in Banking*, Dhaka: Bangladesh Institute of Bank Management.

Mallin, C. A. (2004), *Corporate Governance*, New York: Oxford University Press.

Mazumder, I. (2005), 'Notes on Premier Bank's IPO case', *The Financial Express*, http://www.financialexpress-bd.com, 11 April 2005.

Morck, R., B. Yeung and W. Yu (2000), 'The information content of stock markets: why do emerging markets have synchronous stock price movements?' *Journal of Financial Economics*, **58**, 215–60.

Prowse, S. (1994), 'Corporate governance in an international perspective: a survey of corporate control mechanisms among large firms in the United States, the United Kingdom, Japan and Germany', *BIS Economic Papers,* 41.

Rahman, S. and F. Hossain (2006), 'Weak-form efficiency: testimony of Dhaka Stock Exchange', *Journal of Business Research*, **8**, 1–12.

Samuel, C. (1996), 'Stock market and investment: governance role of the market', *Policy Research Working Paper No. 1578*, Washington DC: World Bank.

Sarker, J. and S. Sarker (2000), 'Large shareholder activism in corporate governance in developing countries: evidence from India', *International Review of Finance*, **1**, 161–94.

Shleifer, A. and R. W. Vishny (1997), 'A survey of corporate governance', *Journal of Finance*, **52** (2), 737–83.

Singh, A. (2003), 'Corporate governance, corporate finance and stock markets in emerging countries', Working Paper No. 258, Cambridge: ESRC Centre for Business Research, University of Cambridge.

Singh, A., A. Singh and B. Weisse (2002), 'Corporate governance, competition, the new international financial architecture and larger corporations in emerging markets', Working Paper No. 250, Cambridge: ESRC Centre for Business Research, University of Cambridge.

Sobhan, F. and W. Werner (eds) (2003), *A Comparative Analysis of Corporate Governance in South Asia: Charting a Roadmap for Bangladesh*, Dhaka: Bangladesh Enterprise Institute.

Stiglitz, J. E. (1985), 'Capital markets and the control of capital', *Journal of Money, Credit and Banking*, **17** (2), 133–52.

Tadesse, S. (2003), 'The allocation and monitoring role of capital markets: theory and international evidence', William Davidson Institute Working Paper No. 624, Ann Arbor MI: University of Michigan Business School.

Tobin, J. (1984), 'On the efficiency of the financial system', *Lloyds Bank Review*, July, 1–15.

7. Corporate governance of banks in developing economies: concepts and issues

Thankom Gopinath Arun and John Turner

INTRODUCTION

Although the subject of corporate governance in developing economies has recently received a lot of attention in the literature (Goswami, 2001; Lin, 2001; Malherbe and Segal, 2001; Oman, 2001), the corporate governance of banks in developing economies has been almost ignored by researchers (Caprio and Levine, 2002). Even in developed economies, the corporate governance of banks has only recently been discussed in the literature (Macey and O'Hara, 2003). In order to address this deficiency, this chapter discusses some of the key concepts and issues for the corporate governance of banks in developing economies.

The corporate governance of banks in developing economies is important for several reasons. First, banks have an overwhelmingly dominant position in developing-economy financial systems, and are extremely important engines of economic growth (King and Levine, 1993a, 1993b; Levine, 1997). Second, as financial markets are usually underdeveloped, banks in developing economies are typically the most important source of finance for the majority of firms. Third, as well as providing a generally accepted means of payment, banks in developing countries are usually the main depository for the economy's savings. Fourth, many developing economies have recently liberalized their banking systems through privatization/disinvestments and reducing the role of economic regulation. Consequently, managers of banks in these economies have obtained greater freedom in how they run their banks.

In the next section, we argue that the unique nature of the banking firm, whether in the developed or developing world, requires that a broad view of corporate governance, which encapsulates both shareholders and depositors, be adopted for banks. In particular, the nature of the banking firm is such that regulation is necessary to protect depositors as well as the overall financial system. Using this insight, in the following section we examine the corporate governance of banks in developing economies in the context of ongoing banking reforms. In the penultimate section, we discuss the changing role of government in developing-economy banking systems and the consequences for corporate governance. The final section provides a summary and policy suggestions.

CORPORATE GOVERNANCE AND THE SPECIAL NATURE OF BANKING

The narrow approach to corporate governance views the subject as the mechanism through which shareholders are assured that managers will act in their interests. Indeed, as far back as Adam Smith, it has been recognized that managers do not always act in the best interests of shareholders (Henderson, 1986). This problem has been especially exacerbated in the Anglo-Saxon economies by the evolution of the modern firm characterized by a large number of atomized shareholders, leading to a separation of ownership and control.[1] The separation of ownership and control has given rise to an agency problem whereby management operate the firm in their own interests, not those of shareholders (Jensen and Meckling, 1976; Fama and Jensen, 1983). This creates opportunities for managerial shirking or empire building and, in the extreme, outright expropriation.[2] However, there is a broader view of corporate governance, which views the subject as the methods by which suppliers of finance control managers in order to ensure that their capital cannot be expropriated and that they earn a return on their investment (Shleifer and Vishny, 1997: 737; Vives, 2000: 1; Oman, 2001: 13).

We will argue below that the special nature of banking means that it is more appropriate to adopt the broader view of corporate governance for banks. Notably, Macey and O'Hara (2003) argue that a broader view of corporate governance should be adopted in the case of banking institutions, arguing that because of the peculiar contractual form of banking, corporate governance mechanisms for banks should encapsulate depositors as well as shareholders. As we shall see below, the special nature of banking requires not only a broader view of corporate governance, but also government intervention in order to restrain the behaviour of bank management.

Depositors do not know the true value of a bank's loan portfolio as such information is incommunicable and very costly to reveal, implying that a bank's loan portfolio is highly fungible (Bhattacharya *et al.*, 1998: 761). As a consequence of this asymmetric information problem, bank managers have an incentive each period to invest in riskier assets than they promised they would *ex ante*. In order to credibly commit that they will not expropriate depositors, banks could make investments in brand-name or reputational capital (Klein, 1974; Gorton, 1994; Demsetz *et al.*, 1996; Bhattacharya *et al.*, 1998), but these schemes give depositors little confidence, especially when contracts have a finite nature and discount rates are sufficiently high (Hickson and Turner, 2004). The opaqueness of banks also makes it very costly for depositors to constrain managerial discretion through debt covenants (Caprio and Levine, 2002: 2). Consequently, rational depositors will require some form of guarantee before they would deposit with a bank. Government-provided guarantees in the form of implicit and explicit deposit insurance might encourage economic agents to deposit their wealth with a bank, as a substantial part of the moral hazard cost is borne by the government.

Nevertheless, even if the government provides deposit insurance, bank managers still have an incentive to opportunistically increase their risk taking, but now it is mainly at the government's expense. This well known moral hazard problem can be ameliorated through the use of economic regulations such as asset restrictions, interest rate ceilings, separation of commercial banking from insurance and investment banking, and reserve requirements. Among the effects of these regulations is that they limit the ability of bank managers to over-issue liabilities or divert assets into high-risk ventures.

Thus far we have argued that the special nature of the banking firm requires public protection of depositors from opportunistic bank management. However, the special nature of the banking firm also affects the relationship between shareholders and managers. For example, the opaqueness of bank assets makes it very costly for diffuse equity holders to write and enforce effective incentive contracts or to use their voting rights as a vehicle for influencing firm decisions (Caprio and Levine, 2002: 2). Furthermore, the existence of deposit insurance may reduce the need for banks to raise capital from large, uninsured investors who have the incentive to exert corporate control (Caprio and Levine, 2002).

A further issue is that the interests of bank shareholders may oppose those of governmental regulators, who have their own agendas, which may not necessarily coincide with maximizing bank value (Boot and Thakor, 1993). Shareholders may want managers to take more risk than is socially optimal, whereas regulators have a preference for managers to take substantially less risk due to their concerns about system-wide financial stability. Shareholders could motivate such risk taking using incentive-compatible compensation schemes. However, from the regulators' point of view, managers' compensation schemes should be structured so as to discourage banks from becoming too risky. For example, regulators could, through directives or moral suasion, restrict the issue of option grants to bank managers. Alternatively, regulators could vary capital requirements depending on the extent to which compensation policies encourage risk taking (Caprio and Levine, 2002: 22).

Some economists argue that competition in the product or service market may act as a substitute for corporate governance mechanisms (Allen and Gale, 2000). The basic argument is that firms with inferior and expropriating management will be forced out of the market by firms possessing non-expropriating managers due to sheer competitive pressure. However the banking industry, possibly due to its information-intensive nature, may be a lot less competitive than other business sectors (Caprio and Levine, 2002). Therefore this lack of competitive pressure as well as the special nature of banking suggests that banks may need stronger corporate governance mechanisms than other firms.

DEREGULATION OF BANKS IN DEVELOPING ECONOMIES

In the section above we argued that the special nature of banking might require government-provided deposit insurance in order to protect depositors. Concomitantly, in order to ameliorate the associated moral hazard problem, we suggested that banks might need to be regulated. However, over the last two decades or so, many governments around the world have moved away from using these economic regulations towards using prudential regulation as part of their reform process in the financial sector. Prudential regulation involves banks having to hold capital proportional to their risk taking, early warning systems, bank resolution schemes and banks being examined on an on-site and off-site basis by banking supervisors. The main objective of prudential regulation is to safeguard the stability of the financial system and to protect deposits. However, the prudential reforms already implemented in developing countries have not been effective in preventing banking crises, and a question remains as to how prudential systems can be strengthened to make them more effective.

The ability of developing economies to strengthen their prudential supervision is questionable for several reasons. First, it is accepted that banks in developing economies should have substantially higher capital requirements than banks in developed economies. However, many banks in developing economies find it very costly to raise even small amounts of capital. Second, there are not enough well trained supervisors in developing economies to examine banks. Third, supervisory bodies in developing economies typically lack political independence, which may undermine their ability to coerce banks to comply with prudential requirements and impose suitable penalties. Fourth, prudential supervision completely relies on accurate and timely accounting information. However, in many developing economies, accounting rules, if they exist at all, are flexible and, typically, there is a paucity of information disclosure requirements. Therefore, if a developing economy liberalizes without sufficiently strengthening its prudential supervisory system, bank managers will find it easier to expropriate depositors and deposit insurance providers.

A prudential approach to regulation will typically result in banks in developing economies having to raise equity in order to comply with capital adequacy norms. Consequently, prior to developing economies deregulating their banking systems, much attention will need to be paid to the speedy implementation of robust corporate governance mechanisms in order to protect shareholders. However, in developing economies, the introduction of sound corporate governance principles into banking has been partially hampered by poor legal protection, weak information disclosure requirements and dominant owners (Arun and Turner, 2003). Furthermore, in many developing countries, the private banking sector is not enthusiastic about introducing corporate governance principles. For example, in India this problem can be summarized in the corporate sector as the privileging of the interests of one group over all other interests in a company (Banaji and Mody, 2001).

THE POLITICAL ECONOMY OF BANK CORPORATE GOVERNANCE IN DEVELOPING COUNTRIES

In many developing economies, the issue of bank corporate governance is complicated by extensive political intervention in the operation of the banking system. The pertinent issues that we briefly want to examine are government ownership of banks, distributional cartels, and restrictions on foreign bank entry.

Government ownership of banks is a common feature in many developing economies (La Porta *et al.*, 2002). The reasons for such ownership may include solving the severe informational problems inherent in developing financial systems, aiding the development process or supporting vested interests and distributional cartels (Arun and Turner, 2002a). With a government-owned bank, the severity of the conflict between depositors and managers very much depends upon the credibility of the government. However, given a credible government and political stability, there will be little conflict as the government ultimately guarantees deposits.

Nevertheless, in economies where there is extensive government owner-ship of banks, the main corporate governance problem is the conflict between the government/taxpayers (as owners) and the managers/bureaucrats who control the bank. The bureaucrats who control government-owned banks may have many different incentives that are not aligned with those of tax-payers. These bureaucrats may maximize a multivariate function which includes, among other things, consumption of prerequisites, leisure time and staff numbers. Also, bureaucrats may seek to advance their political careers by catering to special interest groups, such as trade unions (Shleifer and Vishny, 1997: 768). Furthermore, bureaucrats are by nature risk averse, and will therefore undertake less risk than is optimal from the taxpayers' point of view. In order to partially mitigate such opportunism, bureaucrats may be given little autonomy. In particular, banks may face regulations requiring them to allocate certain proportions of their assets to government securities and various sectors, such as agriculture and SMEs, that are deemed important from a societal viewpoint. However, in the absence of market-provided incentives, the managers of government-owned banks may still be able to engage in opportunism at the taxpayers' expense through shirking or empire building. Perhaps this is why the Basel Committee on Banking Supervision (1999: 4) argues that 'government ownership of a bank has the potential to alter the strategies and objectives of the bank as well as the internal structure of governance. Consequently, the general principles of sound corporate governance are also beneficial to government-owned banks.'

The inefficiencies associated with government-owned banks, especially those emanating from a lack of adequate managerial incentives, have led developing-economy governments (under some pressure from inter-national agencies) to begin divesting their ownership stakes (Arun and Turner, 2002a). The divestment of government-owned banks raises several corporate governance issues. If banks are completely privatized adequate deposit insurance schemes and supervisory arrangements must be estab-lished in order to protect depositors and prevent a financial crash (Arun and Turner, 2002b, 2002c). On the other hand, if divestment is partial, then there may be opportunities for the government as the dominant shareholder to expropriate minority shareholders by using banks to aid fiscal problems or support certain distributional cartels. Therefore, the question in this case is whether or not the government can credibly commit that it will not expropriate private capital owners. For instance, in India the partial divestment of public sector banks has not brought about any significant changes in the quality of corporate governance mechanisms (Arun and Turner, 2002b). Despite a decade of financial reforms in India, the Government has still a major role in appointing members to bank boards. Furthermore, although the reforms have given the public sector banks greater autonomy in deciding the areas of business strategy such as opening branches and introduction of new products,[3] bank boards have little overall autonomy, as they are still to follow the directives issued by the government and central bank (Advisory Group on Corporate Governance, 2001: 10, 30–1, 33). One way it could do this is to reduce its control over managers and give them much more autonomy to act in the interests of all stakeholders, with the caveat that suitable supervisory powers and authority be given to the appropriate regulatory authorities.

A further issue, which complicates the corporate governance of banks in developing economies, is the activities of 'distributional cartels' (Oman, 2001: 20). These cartels consist of corporate insiders who have very close links with or partially constitute the governing elite. The existence of such cartels will undermine the credibility of investor legal protection and may also prevent reform of the banking system.[4] Unsurprisingly, good political governance can be considered as a prerequisite for good corporate governance (Oman 2001: 31).

In many transition economies, it has been observed that competition is more important than change in ownership, and could provide managers with appropriate disciplinary mechanisms (Stiglitz, 1999). Above, it was suggested that competition might act as a substitute for corporate governance. However, banking in developing economies typically has government-imposed barriers to entry, especially on foreign banks. Some notable exceptions are Botswana, Gambia, Lesotho, Rwanda and Zambia (Barth *et al.*, 2001). Nevertheless, in contrast, foreign banks have made few inroads into the developing economies of Asia.

Claessens *et al.* (2000) suggest that the entrance of foreign banks actually increases the efficiency of the developing-economy banking sectors. One possible rationalization of this finding is that foreign banks bring with them new management techniques, corporate governance mechanisms and information technologies which domestic banks have to adopt in order to effectively compete with their foreign rivals (Peek and Rosengren, 2000: 46). A further benefit from permitting foreign bank entry is that it may result in a more stable banking system. Notably, empirical studies suggest that the presence of foreign banks reduces the likelihood of banking crises and may result in banks becoming more prudentially sound (Levine, 1999).

Although foreign banks may have a positive impact on banking system stability and efficiency, developing-economy governments may be reluctant to permit their entry because they lose some ability to influence the economy. Indeed, foreign banks may be less sensitive to indirect government requests and pressures than domestic banks (Stiglitz, 1994: 49). The executives of domestic banks may have connections with the country's governing elite and may be seeking business or political favours in return for acquiescing with government requests. Also, the threat of closure is of greater consequence to a domestic than a foreign bank with an international presence. The ability of foreign banks to ignore government requests may give them a further competitive advantage. However, there is an argument that foreign bank penetration could undermine the ability of governments to use the banking system to achieve social and economic objectives.

CONCLUSIONS AND POLICY IMPLICATIONS

This chapter has argued that the special nature of banking institutions necessitates a broad view of corporate governance where regulation of banking activities is required to protect depositors. In developed economies, protection of depositors in a deregulated environment is typically provided by a system of prudential regulation, but in developing economies such protection is undermined by the lack of well trained supervisors, inadequate disclosure requirements, the cost of raising bank capital and the presence of distributional cartels.

In order to deal with these problems, we suggest that developing economies need to adopt the following measures. First, liberalization policies need to be gradual, and should be dependent upon improvements in prudential regulation. Second, developing economies need to expend resources to enhance the quality of their financial reporting systems, as well as the quantity and quality of bank supervisors. Third, given that bank capital plays such an important role in prudential regulatory systems, it may be necessary to improve investor protection laws, increase financial disclosure and impose fiduciary duties upon bank directors so that banks can raise the equity capital required for regulatory purposes. A further reason as to why this policy needs to be implemented is the growing recognition that the corporate governance of banks has an important role to play in assisting supervisory institutions to perform their tasks, allowing supervisors to have a working relationship with bank management, rather than an adversarial one (Basel Committee on Banking Supervision, 1999).

We have suggested that the corporate governance of banks in developing economies is severely affected by political considerations. First, given the trend towards privatization of government-owned banks in developing economies, there is a need for the managers of such banks to be granted autonomy and be gradually introduced to the corporate governance practices of the private sector prior to divestment. Second, where there has only been partial divestment and governments have not relinquished any control to other shareholders, it may prove very difficult to divest further ownership stakes unless corporate governance is strengthened. Finally, given that limited entry of foreign banks may lead to increased competition, which in turn encourages domestic banks to emulate the corporate governance practices of their foreign competitors, we suggest that developing economies partially open up their banking sector to foreign banks.

NOTES

1. According to Berle and Means (1932), the separation of ownership from control had occurred in the United States by the late 1920s.
2. Various suggestions have been made in the literature as to how this basic principal-agent problem can be ameliorated (Abowd and Kaplan, 1999; Andrade *et al.*, 2001; Hermalin and Weisbach, 2003; Jensen and Meckling, 1976; Jensen and Murphy, 1990; La Porta *et al.*, 1998, 1999, 2000; Shleifer and Vishny, 1986, 1997).
3. G.P. Muniappan in a speech given at the Bank Economist Conference, 2002: *Indian banking: paradigm shift – a regulatory point of view*.
4. Mayer and Sussman (2001: 460) make the pertinent point that regulation and the legal system are endogenous and are an outcome of the political bargaining process.

REFERENCES

Abowd, J. M. and D. S. Kaplan (1999), 'Executive compensation: six questions that need answering', *Journal of Economic Perspectives*, **13**, 145–68.
Advisory Group on Corporate Governance (2001), *Report on Corporate Governance and International Standards*, Delhi: Reserve Bank of India.
Allen, F. and D. Gale (2000), 'Corporate governance and competition', in X. Vives (ed.) *Corporate Governance: Theoretical and Empirical Perspectives*, Cambridge: Cambridge University Press.
Andrade, G., M. Mitchell and E. Stafford (2001), 'New evidence and perspectives on mergers', *Journal of Economic Perspectives*, **15**, 103–20.
Arun, T. G and J. D. Turner (2002a), 'Public sector banks in India: rationale and prerequisites for reform', *Annals of Public and Cooperative Economics*, **73**, 1–19.
Arun, T. G and J. D. Turner (2002b), 'Financial sector reform in developing countries: the Indian experience', *The World Economy*, **25**, 429–45.
Arun, T. G and J. D. Turner (2002c), 'Financial liberalisation in India', *Journal of International Banking Regulation*, **4**, 183–8.
Arun, T. G and J. D. Turner (2003), 'Corporate governance of banking institutions in developing economies: the Indian experience', *South Asia Economic Journal*, **4**, 187–204.
Banaji, J. and G. Mody (2001), 'Corporate governance and the Indian private sector', *QEH Working paper Series* No. 73. Oxford: Queen Elizabeth House.
Barth, J., G. Caprio and R. Levine (2001), 'The regulation and supervision of

banks around the world', *World Bank Working Paper*. Washington, DC: The World Bank.

Basel Committee on Banking Supervision (1999), *Enhancing Corporate Governance for Banking Organisations*, Geneva: Bank for International Settlements.

Berle, A. and G. Means (1932), *The Modern Corporation and Private Property*, New York: Macmillan.

Bhattacharya, S., A. W. A. Boot and A. V. Thakor (1998), 'The economics of bank regulation', *Journal of Money, Credit and Banking*, **30**, 745–70.

Boot, A. W. A and A. V. Thakor (1993), 'Self-interested bank regulation', *American Economic Review*, 83, 206–12.

Caprio, G. and R. Levine (2002), 'Corporate governance of banks: concepts and international observations', unpublished paper presented at the Global Corporate Governance Forum Research Network Meeting, 5 April.

Claessens, S., A. Demirguc-Kunt and H. Huizanga (2000), 'The role of foreign banks in domestic banking systems', in S. Claessens and M. Jansen, (eds) *The Internationalization of Financial Services: Issues and Lessons for Developing Countries*, Boston, MA: Kluwer Academic Press.

Demsetz, R. S., M. R. Saidenberg and P. E. Strahan (1996), 'Banks with something to lose: the disciplinary role of franchise value', *Federal Reserve Bank of Minneapolis Quarterly Review*, Winter, 3–13.

Fama, E. and M. Jensen (1983), 'Separation of ownership and control', *Journal of Law and Economics*, **26**, 301–25.

Gorton, G. (1994), 'Bank regulation when banks and banking are not the same', *Oxford Review of Economic Policy*, **10**, 106–19.

Goswami, O. (2001), 'The tide rises, gradually: corporate governance in India', *OECD Development Centre Discussion Paper*, Paris: OECD.

Henderson, J. P. (1986), 'Agency of alienation? Smith, Mill and Marx on the joint-stock company', *History of Political Economy*, **18**, 111–31.

Hermalin, B. E. and M. S. Weisbach (2003), 'Boards of directors as an endogenously determined institution: a survey of the economic literature', *FRBNY Economic Policy Review*, April, 7–26.

Hickson, C. R. and J. D. Turner (2004), 'Free banking and the stability of early joint-stock banking', *Cambridge Journal of Economics*, **28**, 903–19.

Jensen, M. C. and W. Meckling (1976), 'Theory of the firm: managerial behaviour, agency costs and capital structure', *Journal of Financial Economics*, **3**, 305–60.

Jensen, M. C. and K. Murphy (1990), 'Performance pay and top-management incentives', *Journal of Political Economy*, **102**, 510–46.

King, R. G. and R. Levine (1993a), 'Finance and growth: Schumpeter might be right', *Quarterly Journal of Economics*, **108**, 717–37.

King, R. G and R. Levine (1993b), 'Finance, entrepreneurship and growth: theory and evidence', *Journal of Monetary Economics*, **32**, 513–42.

Klein, B. (1974) 'The competitive supply of money', *Journal of Money, Credit and Banking*, **6**, 421–53.

La Porta, R., F. López de Silanes and A. Shleifer (1999), 'Corporate ownership around the world', *Journal of Finance*, **54**, 471–517.

La Porta, R., F. López de Silanes, and A. Shleifer (2002), 'Government ownership of banks', *Journal of Finance*, 57, 265–301.

La Porta, R., F. López de Silanes, A. Shleifer and R. W. Vishny (1998), 'Law and finance', *Journal of Political Economy*, **106**, 1113–55.

La Porta, R., F. López de Silanes, A. Shleifer and R.W. Vishny (2000), 'Investor protection and corporate governance', *Journal of Financial Economics*, **58**, 3–27.

Levine, R. (1997), 'Financial development and economic growth: views and agenda', *Journal of Economic Literature*, **35**, 688–726.

Levine, R. (1999), 'Foreign bank entry and capital control liberalization: effects on growth and stability', University of Minnesota, mimeo.

Lin, C. (2001), 'Private vices in public places: challenges in corporate governance development in China', *OECD Development Centre Discussion Paper*, Paris: OECD.

Macey, J. R. and M. O'Hara (2003), 'The corporate governance of banks', *Federal Reserve Bank of New York Economic Policy Review*, April, 91–107.

Malherbe, S. and N. Segal (2001), 'Corporate governance in South Africa', *OECD Development Centre Discussion Paper*, Paris: OECD.

Mayer, C. and O. Sussman (2001), 'The assessment: finance, law and growth', *Oxford Review of Economic Policy*, **17**, 457–66.

Oman, C. P. (2001), 'Corporate governance and national development', *OECD Development Centre Technical Papers*, No. 180, Paris: OECD.

Peek, J. and E. Rosengren (2000), 'Implications of the globalization of the banking sector: the Latin American experience', *New England Economic Review*, September/October, 45–62.

Shleifer, A. and R. W. Vishny (1986), 'Large shareholders and corporate control', *Journal of Political Economy*, **94**, 461–88.

Shleifer, A. and R. W. Vishny (1997), 'A survey of corporate governance', *Journal of Finance*, **52**, 737–83.

Stiglitz, J. E. (1994), 'The role of the state in financial markets', *Proceedings of the World Bank Annual Conference on Development Economics 1993*. Washington, DC: The World Bank, 19–52

Stiglitz, J. E (1999), 'Reforming the global financial structure: lessons from recent crises', *Journal of Finance*, **54**, 1508–22.

Vives, X. (2000), 'Corporate governance: does it matter', in X. Vives (ed.) *Corporate Governance: Theoretical and Empirical Perspectives*, Cambridge: Cambridge University Press.

8. Improving corporate governance of banks: issues and experience from Bangladesh

M. Masrur Reaz

INTRODUCTION

Banks execute a crucial function of financial intermediation between savers and investors. Hence, it is essential for economies to develop efficient and stable banking sectors, and this need is particularly acute in developing countries. Having recognized the need, many developing countries have initiated financial reform measures in order to improve the efficiency of banking firms. Seminal studies by McKinnon (1973) and Shaw (1973) presented the theoretical arguments for the widespread adoption of financial reform measures, both authors strongly arguing that such reforms support the development of deeper financial systems which can, in turn, support economic growth. However, despite the implementation of rigorous financial sector reform measures, many argue that the results have been disappointing (Jalilian and Kirkpatrick, 2001). In many cases, a failure to recognize the imperfect characteristics of financial markets, and premature deregulation, has led to adverse consequences for the stability of the financial system itself (Brownbridge and Kirkpatrick, 2000). Hence, it is important to develop appropriate institutional mechanisms in advance of, or alongside, financial reform measures, which will ensure the smooth operation of liberalized financial systems. Since financial intermediaries gain total control of funds owned by depositors, mechanisms to mitigate moral hazard on the part of the intermediaries require particular attention. Corporate governance is considered to be one such institutional means that aims to align decision making in financial institutions with that of the best interest of their stakeholders.

This chapter aims to highlight, using the case of the Bangladesh banking sector, issues that require attention from policy makers in improving corporate governance of banks in developing nations. The study first lays out a framework which explains the role of corporate governance from the very reason why financial institution exists, that is, by highlighting the link between financial development and governance. The chapter then provides several banking firm-specific arguments that provide the reason for paying attention to corporate governance of banks. Having provided the conceptual evidence, the chapter then outlines the problems and inefficiencies in the Bangladesh banking sector, followed by a sketch of the banking sector governance including a comparative analysis on governance quality and performance of various banks, and thereby underlining the need for sound governance for an efficient and stable banking industry.

FINANCIAL DEVELOPMENT AND CORPORATE GOVERNANCE: A CONCEPTUAL FRAMEWORK

The value of a developed financial system in a developing country originates from its contribution to growth through efficient resource allocation (World Bank, 1989).[1] Different cross-country studies support the idea that countries with efficient and strong financial markets also experience higher rates of economic growth.[2] Developing nations' financial systems rely heavily on banking firms as they are usually the largest and most common intermediary in their financial systems. Banks largely dominate the financial systems of developing countries and remain extremely important engines of economic growth (King and Levine, 1993a, 1993b; Levine, 1997). In the absence of strong, efficient financial markets, banks almost solely supply the credits required to run the economic activities (Arun and Turner, 2004). The banks also facilitate the payment and settlement systems as well as functioning as the main depository in developing economies.

While the role of banks in financial development is of enormous importance, the role of corporate governance has been considered as vital to reach the goals of developing a strong and sustainable financial and banking sector. To mitigate various risks and ensure fair return in their financial systems, countries must develop structural and institutional mechanisms. As demonstrated in Figure 8.1, corporate governance is one such mechanism which reduces risks such as adverse selection or expropriation of funds by the financial intermediaries. Winkler (1998) insists that the quality of corporate governance of financial institutions in fact determines the success of financial development.

There remains, however, considerable concern among experts with regard to the quality of corporate governance in developing states.

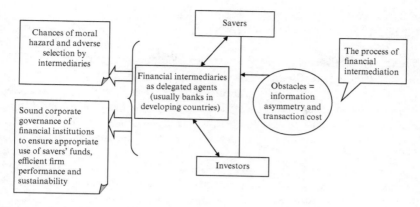

Source: Author's own compilation

Figure 8.1 Corporate governance, banking institutions and financial development in developing countries

Corporate governance in developing economies has only recently attracted attention (Oman, 2001; Lin, 2001), as the East Asian crises, along with debacles in Russia and Brazil, exposed the problems of poor corporate governance in developing as well as emerging markets (Allen, 2005; Oman *et al.*, 2003).

Attention to the developing world's corporate governance becomes more necessary when it is realized that the success of ongoing economic reforms largely depends on the quality of corporate governance (Nenova, 2004). Oman (2001) has stressed the importance of implementing sound corporate governance for the sake of development, suggesting its presence in order to increase the flow, and decrease the cost, of financial capital and to stimulate productivity growth.

In a seminal World Bank study that outlines the corporate governance agenda for developing nations, Nenova (2004) argues that developing countries face challenges in various areas in terms of sound corporate governance. The author argues that the main governance problem in low-income countries is value transfer from non-controlling shareholders or stakeholders to dominant large shareholders. Such abuse becomes easier with concentrated ownership (firms often in the hands of a few families), ineffective disclosure practices, weak legal framework and enforcement, and problems in the audit environment.

Building on the argument put forward in the literature, the following section elaborates why corporate governance of banking firms requires priority attention, particularly in developing economies.

BANKING FIRMS: A CRITICAL CASE FOR CORPORATE GOVERNANCE

There are several unique characteristics of banking firms which call for special attention to their corporate governance. Opacity of bank portfolios, the broader extent of claimants, heavy reliance on debt, high social costs, and enhanced moral hazard, all support the case for urgent attention being directed towards banking sector governance.[3]

The case is more pressing in developing countries where special interest groups are active, government ownership of banks is dominant, an optimal level of competitive market pressure is often missing, prudential regulation and supervision is largely absent or ineffective, and legal backup is weak.[4] These conditions make it simple for banking agents and distributional cartels to misappropriate bank funds and thus raise the risk of bank failures. In fact, a number of bank failures and financial crises have shaken economies around the world over the last two decades (Caprio and Klingebiel, 1996; Caprio, 1997), and such financial crises in different countries have demonstrated how the lack of sound governance practices in financial institutions can lead towards the collapse of financial sectors, causing serious and long-term damage to the entire economy (Singh and Weisse, 2002; Mitton, 2002; Winkler, 1998).

The greater contribution of the banking system towards development itself is the very first reason why banking sector governance should be addressed properly in developing economies (Arun and Turner, 2002a, 2002b). Banks largely dominate the financial systems of developing countries and remain extremely important engines of economic growth (King and Levine, 1993a, 1993b; Levine, 1997). In the absence of strong, efficient financial markets, banks almost solely supply the credits required to run economic activities (Arun and Turner, 2004). Given the unique features of banking firms, the imperfect characteristics of developing countries' banking systems, and evidence of bank failures due to low quality of banking governance, this chapter aims to explore the contention that corporate governance of banks must be addressed in order to improve banking performance.

BANKING SECTOR AND ITS GOVERNANCE IN BANGLADESH

As in many other developing countries, banks constitute the lion's share of Bangladesh's financial sector. According to the Bangladesh Bank (2001), more than 90 per cent of the financial system's contribution toward GDP is generated by banks. The financial system of Bangladesh is predominantly composed of an organized or institutionalized banking system and an unorganized credit market (Hossain and Rashid, 1996). The banking system includes the central bank and 49 scheduled banks, of which nine are public sector. Of these nine public sector banks, four are commercial banks and the other five are specialized banks. Of the 49 scheduled banks, 30 are local private commercial banks and ten are foreign commercial banks (Bangladesh Bank, 2006).

After independence in 1971, the then government nationalized the entire banking system and used the banks to achieve its social and political objectives. Until the mid-1980s, the Bangladesh banking sector was characterized by a financially repressed regime. The sector witnessed low interest rates, the distortion of resource allocation, a low rate of savings leading to financial distress, and it was being used to service the needs of the public sector and a few business houses (Hassan, 1994). The internal control system of the commercial banks was weak, the published accounts never reflected the actual financial health, the quality of the assets of the banks was never evaluated on strict accounting principles, profitability and liquidity aspects of portfolio management were unfamiliar concepts among management personnel, and the elements of capital adequacy for banking operations were never given due importance (Raquib, 1999).

The cumulative effect of mismanagement in the banking system led to a huge accumulation of non-performing loans for the financial sector which, at points, had risen to more than 40 per cent of the total advances of the banking sector (Financial Sector Reform Project, 1996). The financial sector was in a state of complete disarray, and in an attempt to bring about structural, institutional and policy changes in the fragile financial sector, the National Commission on Money, Banking and Credit was formed in 1984.[5] Based on the Commission's report, the government initiated reform measures under the Financial Sector Reform Project (1990–6). Later, the report of the Banking Reform Commission (1998–2001) produced guidelines for continuing reform measures. The reforms affected areas such as ownership, interest rates, prudential aspects, restructuring of public sector banks, and directed lending policies. A snapshot of such reforms is provided in Table 8.1.

The financial sector in Bangladesh has come a long way since its inception. From complete nationalization and economic regulation, the sector has moved on to a largely liberalized phase. Having recognized the importance of an efficient financial system in supporting economic growth, successive governments have carried out financial reform programmes expected to enhance the performance of the financial sector, particularly the banking sector, through fostering a competitive banking environment.

Table 8.1 Reforms in Bangladesh banking

Areas of reform		Pre-reform scenario	Changes through reform
Ownership		Nationalized banking sector with all banks under government ownership and control	Two government banks privatized. Formation of private banks allowed by both local and foreign investors
Interest rate		Economic regulations by government set fixed interest rate levels	Partially deregulated in 1989 where banks could set the rate within a stipulated band fixed by the Central Bank. The band ceiling and floors were allowed several times. Banks were allowed to charge differentiated interest rates to individual borrowers and priority sectors in 1992. The rate structure was simplified by reducing lending categories from 29 to 12. Later in 1992, lending rate band and deposit rate ceiling were abolished leaving it to market
Prudential aspects	Credit information database	None until 1992	Credit information bureau set up at BB in 1992 containing information regarding individual and institutional borrowers of bank credit
	Loan classification guideline	No mandatory guidelines until 1989	Standardized guidelines introduced in 1989. A series of subsequent measures were taken to make the guidelines more stringent. They also involved upgrading of accounting standards, disclosure and audit standards
	Minimum capital adequacy	None until 1991	The BCA 1991 required 6 per cent of total time and demand liabilities. FSRP imposed minimum risk-weighted capital requirement of 8 per cent

On-site and off-site supervision	Very weak and unorganized audit by the BB. Off-site monitoring non-existent till mid-1990s	FSRP provided stringent guidelines for on-site inspection by BB audit teams. Camel rating and some other off-site risk analysis mechanisms initiated. Dedicated off-site supervision and problem bank monitoring departments established
Linking classified loan level with large loan approval	Banks could sanction any amount of large loans regardless of their classified loan level which actually	From 2002, different slabs have been introduced limiting the level of large loan approval depending on the banks' respective classified loan amount
Relevant legal reform	Outdated banking ordinance of 1962 governed banking until 1991. No bankruptcy act and court until 1997. No courts to deal exclusively with financial sector related cases until mid 1990s	Banking Company Act was introduced in 1991. Financial Institutions Act enacted in 1993 to deal with NBFIs. Bankruptcy Act and bankruptcy courts introduced in 1997. Financial loan courts established with bank loan defaulters
Restructuring of public sector banks	Closure/merger of loss-making branches of NCBs & SCBs	Many areas of the country had redundant presence of government banks such as five different public banks' branches within one kilometre radius	In 2002, MoF decided to close or merge the NCB and SCB branches which were making losses for five consecutive years and chance of moving to profit bleak

Table 8.1 (continued)

Areas of reform	Pre-reform scenario	Changes through reform
Delegation of power and responsibility between board and management	No clear guidelines until 1996. Officially majority of authorities lied to the board. Management carried out board and MoF directives	First set of specific guidelines provided in 1996. The revised guidelines imposed in 2002. Board has the responsibility of formulating and approving business goals, targets, strategies, income-expenditure policies, loan policies and monitoring the progress. The CEO was given the power to approve loans up to a certain limit without board's approval. CEO's responsibility to ensure compliance with relevant legal and regulatory framework and achieving business goals
Directed lending	Credit policy totally dominated by government until 1982.	Gradually relaxed since then. Largely free of directed credit which come as part of economic regulations. However, directed credit still prevalent in NCBs and PCBs to render benefit to politicians, bank owners and their beneficiaries

Source: Author's own compilation based on literature

These financial reforms have indeed generated more than sufficient competition in the banking sector, yet the performance of banks is far from satisfactory, with the majority of local banks struggling to achieve basic efficiencies and operating with an alarmingly low level of financial solvency.

Since those reforms, the banking sector has substantially expanded, but its efficiency still remains low, and losses amount to about 1.18 per cent of the GDP (Sayeed, 2002). Two decades after the commencement of the reforms, the performance of banks and the banking sector continues to be gloomy (Bangladesh Enterprise Institute, 2003 (BEI); Banking Reform Commission, 1999) and the current scenario can be termed a fully fledged banking crisis.[6] The question, therefore, remains as to whether the failure of reforms to rescue the ailing banking sector and firms can be attributed to the state of corporate governance in the banks. Many have indeed termed the quality of banks' corporate governance as substandard. According to Reaz and Arun (2006), the lack of sound governance in banking firms was one of the primary causes behind the lacklustre performance of the sector. The following part of this section provides a snapshot of the banking sector governance as it prevails in Bangladesh.

CORPORATE GOVERNANCE IN THE BANGLADESH BANKING SECTOR

Corporate governance in the Bangladesh banking sector has always been poor, and the presence of special interest groups, abusive owners/directors, heavy government ownership, executive corruption, collusion among bankers, politicians and business groups, and weak legal and regulatory frameworks has exacerbated the governance problems in Bangladesh banking (Banking Reform Commission, 1999). The Banking Reform Commission (BRC) Report (1999) described banking sector governance as a 'shambles', hinting that many of the serious banking problems such as large non-performing and/or bad loans, insolvency of many banks, and low profitability of domestic banks, were linked to the low quality of corporate governance prevailing in the banks.

A recent study by the BEI (2003), designed to develop codes of best practice in relation to corporate governance for Bangladesh generally, sheds some light on the state of banking sector governance. This study was highly critical of the quality of bank governance, suggesting that the public banks were forced by the government to lend to priority sectors and special interest groups, regardless of risks. Political patronization was pin-pointed as one of the main causes of abuse in PCBs as political figures, their family members, and business or social associates held the majority shares as well as board positions. Both the BRC and BEI studies suggest that governance quality was better in foreign banking firms operating in Bangladesh. In addition, both reports indicated that the weak role of relevant regulatory agencies had contributed significantly towards the current problems in banking sector governance.

Independent auditors have a definite role in maintaining good governance (World Bank, 1998), but unfortunately the auditors have not played their due role in this respect in Bangladesh (Centre for Policy Dialogue, 2001).[7] The inherent problems in the audit environment coupled with ineffective disclosure and lack of accountability have largely made audit a crippled pillar of banking governance (Banking Reform Commission, 1999). The BEI (Bangladesh Enterprise Institute, 2003) report also indicated that the disclosure level in banking was inadequate, the quality low and the system flawed. Accounting and audit standards are important components of corporate governance (OECD, 1999), but according to the BEI (Bangladesh Enterprise Institute, 2003), in Bangladesh these yardsticks lag far behind the minimum international standard.

Financial control systems in most financial institutions are also weak and flawed (World Bank, 1998). In the current environment, characterized by inappropriate approval and authorization policies and inadequate financial procedures and control, there is a grave risk that financial statements are mis-reporting loan recoveries, assets, liabilities, revenues and expenses, and are adversely affecting the operations of business (Raquib, 1999). On this theme, Raquib (1999) has argued that such misclassifications have serious implications for various operations such as deposit taking, lending, cash handling, customer relations and regulatory reporting, as well as impacting upon the reliability of financial and management information.

In the absence of any prior empirical study or database on corporate governance in the banking sector of Bangladesh, an earlier paper by Reaz and Arun (2006) empirically outlined the structure and quality of banking governance. While exploring banking governance in Bangladesh, the study found that large shareholdings, total board control, lack of accountability, and the weak role of regulatory bodies have led many local banks' owners and their beneficiaries to engage in self-benefiting activities at the expense of depositors' funds. Efficient accountability, employment contracts, and incentive systems were found to be unfamiliar concepts in public sector banks, while they played a crucial role in deterring bank executives from misappropriation of bank funds in local private and foreign banks. The audit mechanisms of local banks, which are largely ineffective due to political interference, biased intervention by owners, flawed accounting standards, and unethical practices by many auditors, assist in encouraging misappropriation by owners and executives. Disclosure remains at a low point in terms of its extent and quality, thus enabling many irregularities to go unnoticed by depositors or other important stakeholders.

In the next section the study moves on to investigate the findings of earlier case studies which explored the governance mechanisms in different types of banks.

A COMPARATIVE ANALYSIS ON GOVERNANCE AND PERFORMANCE OF BANGLADESHI BANKS

Earlier research in banking governance, both empirical and conceptual, claims that banks originating from the practice in developed economies exhibit a better standard of governance, and that corporate governance measures vary greatly among public, private and foreign banks in Bangladesh.[8] This section will attempt to address the claim that banks with foreign ownership practise a better standard of governance than do their locally owned counterparts in developing nations, and hence post a better financial performance.

A case study comprising three banks (one each from the public, private and foreign sectors) was conducted to further address the research question laid out above. The study, using data from the author's field research in 2004, compares three banks from the perspective of four corporate governance pillars: ownership and control, boards, management contracts and transparency through audit and disclosure. Data were extracted through in-depth interviews with the officials of the respective banks, and secondary literature such as annual reports and websites.

These banks together make up the majority of banking firms in Bangladesh. Both the foreign and public sector banks are among the largest and oldest in their respective categories. The private bank has been in operation for about 14 years. The methodology, however, carries the inherent weakness of case studies, that is the limited potential for generalization of the findings. The public sector bank is referred to as Bank X, the private bank as Bank Y, and the foreign bank as Bank Z hereinafter.

OWNERSHIP STRUCTURE AND CONTROL

The entire share of Bank X is owned by the Bangladesh government, and at no time has X ever floated any share in the capital market. To be more specific, the Ministry of Finance (MoF) on behalf of the government carries out the ownership responsibilities. Bank Y is a local bank under total ownership of local private entrepreneurs. Sponsor shareholders, 49 in number, own 50 per cent of the bank while the rest is owned by 2733 general shareholders. The ownership structure of Bank Z is very simple, the entire bank being owned by its parent company which is registered in the UK as a commercial bank.

Neither Bank X nor Bank Z has significant family shareholdings, while some seven families own a significant number of shares in Bank Y. Institutions own 3.91 per cent of Bank Y while government and a foreign financial institution own 100 per cent shares of Banks X and Z respectively.

In terms of control, Bank X remains under total control of the owner. MoF, on behalf of the government, decides on and interferes with everything about the bank ranging from board formation to executive appointments, and from loan decisions to the transfer, promotion and hiring of staff. Politicians belonging to ruling parties play a very influential role. Coherence through personal, business and social relationships, and ownership of 50 per cent of the shares, means that sponsor shareholders dominate the board seats, and hold total control of Bank Y; they interfere with all the bank's operation including heavy borrowings for themselves. Corporate policies regarding delegation of power mean that Bank Z is under the total control of the board, which comprises executives.

BOARD DYNAMICS

The boards of all three banks are supervisory in nature. The private bank has the largest board with 26 members, while the foreign and public banks have 12 and seven members respectively. The board members of Bank Z are all executives. With one exception, the CEO, all board members of both Banks X and Y are non-executive independent or owner directors.

Except for the CEO, all board members of Bank X are selected by MoF, from both the public and private sectors. All private sector appointees are required to be aligned with the political ideology of the ruling party. There is no provision for election to the board, and appointments are largely non-transparent. In Bank Y, sponsor directors are selected by sponsor shareholders, general shareholders are elected by all shareholders, and the CEO is an ex officio member of the board. Here, the sponsors' selection is always based on a unanimous understanding among themselves, and sponsors also influence elections in the general category to get their preferred individuals elected. All board members of Bank Z are ex officio, and executives holding certain positions automatically become board members. While all board members of Bank Z have extensive banking experience, directors of X and Y, except for their CEOs, have no banking experience.

Until recently the board held all authority in Bank Y. The Central Bank has now empowered private bank CEO positions with more authority in terms of dealing with management, loans and other decisions. However, in practice, the board still influences all decision making as the CEO gives in to the board's demands. The majority of authorities in Bank Z are delegated to respective divisions. The board only monitors the division activities and takes corrective measures in case of problems and irregularities. Unlike local banks, the board does not approve loan applications, and neither can board members borrow from the bank for commercial purpose. In Bank X, the board is in charge of preparing policy guidelines for operation and monitoring management. In practice, almost all policy guidelines come from the MoF who often interferes with management operations in order to benefit special quarters.

Monitoring by the board in Bank Z is extremely strict; corrective and punitive measures would always and strictly follow inefficiencies and corruption by bankers. In Bank Y, board monitoring is strict; the board usually follows up with corrective/punitive actions in the case of slackness or corruption by executives. However, exceptions take place when corruption by executives involves sponsor owners' interests. In the case of Bank X, board monitoring is very lax as the board is dominated by independent directors with no interests at stake. The board also lacks proactive initiatives for proper monitoring.

Bank X's board remains accountable to the MoF. However, in practice MoF never holds boards accountable for a bank's performance. In the case of Bank Y, the board is accountable to no-one within the firm. Externally, accountability remains with the Central Bank which, since the late 1990s, has required some accountability by the private banks' boards. The board of Bank Z is fully accountable to the global and regional headquarters of the parent company, and there are past instances of action against board members.

MANAGEMENT BEHAVIOUR, CONTRACTS, AND COMPENSATION

To start with the CEO's authority and accountability, the CEO of Bank X has limited authority in terms of loan approval and executive promotion and transfers. The board in some cases and MoF in most cases dictate to the CEO in terms of decision making. Accountability, in practice, remains with the ministry. Keeping official accountability with the boards, the central bank has delegated significant authority to private bank CEOs in terms of loan processing, management hiring, transfer, promotion, audit decisions, and so on. In practice, however, the CEO's authority in Bank Y is curtailed as the board interferes with the majority of decisions. In Bank Z, the CEO is responsible for the overall performance of the bank in Bangladesh, and hence holds supreme authority to take any decisions. However, the CEO is accountable to both the regional CEO and a group executive director at the global headquarters.

The performance of the CEO is not linked to continuation or job promotion in Bank X. Inefficiencies and failures are rarely followed up by punitive measures in this institution. In contrast, advancement and continuation for Bank Z executives are strictly linked to performance, without exception. Similarly, performance is linked to advancement and continuation in the job in Bank Y, the only exception being for those favoured by sponsor shareholders. Unless sponsor owners are involved, inefficiencies and failures are followed up by punitive measures. While pay and performance are very strongly linked in Banks Z and Y, there is no such incentive for the executives of Bank X, and as a result, executives in Bank X are corrupt in the absence of accountability, efficient contracts and compensation. While the incentive and accountability system ensures that Bank Z managers are absolutely free of corruption, executives of Bank Y are largely free of corruption due to strict monitoring, accountability and efficient contracts and compensation.

AUDIT AND DISCLOSURE

Audit in Bank X is largely ineffective, because of political and union interference. Due to such pressures, initiating corrective actions following audit findings is difficult and rare. In the case of Bank Y, audit can be considered effective. However, exceptions take place where irregularities involve sponsor shareholders. Bank Z has extremely effective audit mechanisms and audit objections are always given serious attention.

When it comes to disclosure of operating and financial performance, Bank Z makes full disclosure; the opposite is true for Bank X. Bank Y discloses such data, although there has been evidence they have been 'doctored' at times. Both Banks Y and Z disclose their performance through annual reports, while publication of an annual report is rare in the case of Bank X. Neither of the local banks X and Y, makes any disclosures to their core stakeholder group, that is depositors. Bank Z, however, does disclose financial performance to depositors. Bank Z also makes full disclosure of methods to determine salary and benefits of top executives, while this is absent in Banks X and Y. Similarly, Bank Z makes a full disclosure of connected lending and third party transactions. Bank Y now makes public connected lending, due to Central Bank regulations, but does not disclose third party transactions. Neither connected lending nor third party transactions are made public by Bank X.

Field research indicated that both stock and stakeholders' rights are greatly violated by both owners and executives through self-benefiting swindling in Bank X. In Bank Y, both depositors' and small general share-holders' rights are massively violated by sponsor shareholders; however, misappropriation by executives is not common. Both owner institution and executives in Bank Z make best effort to uphold stock and stakehold-ers' rights and benefits.

In summary, the case analysis clearly ranks the governance structure/ quality of the foreign bank operating in Bangladesh as very sound. The summary also suggests a slightly better governance scenario prevails in the local private bank as opposed to the public bank. The case findings strongly support the conclusions of the earlier survey (Reaz and Arun, 2006) regarding the superiority of governance practice in foreign banks in Bangladesh.

The cases strongly indicate a concentration of ownership in the hands of founders, abuse by founders and special interest groups, problems regard-ing board authority, accountability, contrasting executive behaviour at local and foreign banks, collusion between auditors and bank owners, and insufficient and flawed disclosure practices in the banking sector in Bangladesh. A separation of ownership and control, efficient executive contracts, efficient and qualified boards with accountability, and adher-ence to local and international transparency practices make the govern-ance of foreign banks in Bangladesh of sound nature. While this does not necessarily suggest transferring ownership of the sector to foreigners to improve the governance scenario, policy makers in banking must take lessons from the foreign-owned banks and initiate changes along the same lines, to instal pillars and practices of good governance in the local banking institutions. A priority need is to strengthen the board's capac-ity along with their accountability, and improve executive contracts and empowerment in the short term. In the medium to long term, separation of ownership and control, and improved transparency must be aimed at in order to bring good governance. Much of this would require the gov-ernment to initiate reform processes along with improving its supervisory capacity.

CONCLUSION

The political changes of the late twentieth century have led to huge deregulation and privatization around the world, particularly in the developing economies. The industrial economies have also seen their corporations grow bigger and more global in the wake of an expanding business world, which has become more complex than ever before. These changing developments have brought forward the issue of sound corporate governance in the context of corporate sustainability and efficiency. Amongst various firms, banking institutions are demanding priority attention to their governance quality due to the unique firm-specific features of banking institutions as well as the dominant position of banks in developing economies' financial systems.

Over the last two decades, Bangladesh has undertaken various financial reforms in an attempt to develop an efficient and stable banking sector. Nevertheless, the sector has failed to yield satisfactory performance in the stipulated time. Many argue that lack of attention and improvement to the corporate governance of banks in Bangladesh may have greatly impeded the ability of competitive markets to improve the overall efficiency and health of the banking sector generally, and individual banking institutions in particular. The literature often points a finger at crony capitalism, special interest groups, ineffective boards, lack of appropriate executive incentives, flawed transparency mechanisms and weak regulatory backup as major problems of banking governance in Bangladesh.

Significant differences in governance practices between foreign and locally owned banks in Bangladesh have emerged through the comparative analysis in the last section of this chapter. The analysis has provided evidence that concentration of ownership, if not separated from control, allows manipulation of depositors' fortunes by controlling owners. The findings highlight the need for qualified and accountable boards to oversee banking firms. This is particularly true in systems where boards have been bestowed with ultimate authority in decision making and/or overseeing individual firms. The findings go on to suggest that experienced and expert employees, if empowered under a strict executive contract and accountability system, are more likely to steer towards better interest for all stakeholders. It is obvious from the findings that transparency through strict audit and effective disclosure works as a deterrent to misuse of depositors' funds by those in control. Transparent systems help to develop effective accountability at both management and board level.

The findings above impart some vital lessons for policy makers in Bangladesh and similar developing economies. In the absence of an efficient stock market, dispersed ownership will perhaps not bring much benefit in the short term. Policies should encourage concentrated shareholding with decision-making authority placed in the hands of professional experts, and efficiently designed contract, monitoring, accountability and transparency mechanisms developed by the owners. The findings underscore the need to construct efficient contracts to limit the behaviour of those in control of firms. The presence of large, reputable institutional shareholders in well governed foreign banks suggests consideration of the possibilities of involving more institutional owners; with their greater level of motivation, expertise and voting power, respected institutional owners could play a vital role in improving the corporate governance of firms.

The issue of foreign ownership in the banking sector is supported in the context of this study as the entry of foreign banks would not only enhance competitive pressure, but would also introduce the relatively better functioning and more prudent governance mechanisms of western economies into developing economies. Therefore, policies regarding financial sector and corporate governance reform must ensure the participation of foreign banks, as well as investors in the banking sectors.

ACKNOWLEDGEMENT

The views expressed in this article are the author's own and do not necessarily represent the views of DFID Bangladesh.

NOTES

1. This point is emphasized by the World Bank (1989: 26): 'The biggest difference between rich and poor countries is the efficiency with which they have used their resources. The financial system's contribution to growth lies precisely in its ability to increase the efficiency.'
2. See King and Levine (1993a, 1993b), Levine and Zervos (1998), Rajan and Zingales (1999), Cetorelli and Gambera (2001).
3. See Nam (2004), Jensen and Meckling (1976), Fama and Jensen (1983), Shleifer and Vishny (1997), Vives (2000), Oman (2001), Macey and O'Hara (2001), Arun and Turner (2002b, 2004).
4. See Basel Committee on Banking Supervision (1999), Arun and Turner (2004), Fan (2004).
5. Ownership reforms were, however, initiated in 1982–3 through privatization of some banks and formation of new private sector banks.
6. According to Demirguc-Kunt and Detragiache (1997), a fully fledged systemic banking crisis exists if the ratio of non-performing assets to total assets in the banking system exceeds 10 per cent.
7. According to CPD (2001), the problem is not unskilled auditors, but rather the overall culture and environment in which the auditors operate, which limit their work to legal responsibilities, making them disclose the bare minimum to the public, along with very low audit fees.
8. See Arun and Turner (2004), Reaz and Arun (2006).

REFERENCES

Allen, F. (2005), 'Corporate governance in emerging economies', *Oxford Review of Economic Policy*, **21** (2), 164–77.

Arun, T. G. and J. Turner (2002a), 'Public sector banks in India: rationale and prerequisites for reform', *Annals of Public and Cooperative Economics*, **73** (1), 89–109.

Arun, T. G. and J. Turner(2002b), 'Financial sector reforms and corporate governance of banks in developing economies: the Indian experience', *South Asian Economic Journal*, **4**(2), 187–204.

Arun, T. G. and J. Turner (2004), 'Corporate governance of banks in developing economies: concepts and issues', *Corporate Governance: An International Review*, **12** (3), 371–7.

Basel Committee on Banking Supervision (1999), *Enhancing Corporate Governance for Banking Organizations*, Basel: Bank for International Settlements.

Bangladesh Bank (2001), *Economic Trends*, Dhaka: Bangladesh Bank.

Bangladesh Bank (2006), *Annual Report*, Dhaka: Bangladesh Bank.

Bangladesh Enterprise Institute (2003), *A Comparative Analysis of Corporate Governance in South Asia: Charting a Roadmap for Bangladesh*, Dhaka: BEI.

Banking Reform Commission (1999), *The Report of the Banking Reform Commission*, Dhaka: BRC.

Brownbridge, M. and C. Kirkpatrick (2000), 'Financial regulation in developing countries', *Journal of Development Studies* **17** (1), 1–24.

Caprio, G. (1997) 'Safe and sound banking in developing countries – we're not in Kansas anymore', *The World Bank, Working Paper No. 1739*, Washington DC.

Caprio, G. and Klingebiel, D. (1996) 'Bank insolvency: bad luck, bad policy or bad banking?' Paper prepared for the World Bank's Annual Bank Conference on Development Economics, Washington DC.

Cetorelli, N. and M. Gambera (2001), 'Banking market structure, financial dependence and growth: international evidence from industry data', *Journal of Finance*, **56**, 617–48.

Centre for Policy Dialogue (2001), *Financial Sector Reforms: A Report by CPD Financial Sector Task Force*, Dhaka: CPD.

Demirguc-Kunt, A. and E. Detragiache (1997), 'Determinants of banking crises: evidence from developing and developed countries', *IMF Working Paper* No. 97/106, Washington DC: IMF.

Fama, E. and M. Jensen (eds) (1998), *Separation of Ownership and Control in Foundations of Organizational Strategy*, Cambridge MA: Harvard University Press.

Fan, J. (2004), 'What we know about corporate governance of banks', Paper presented at Asian Development Bank Institute's Seminar on Corporate Governance of Bank in Asia, 10–11 June, Tokyo.

Feinberg, P. (1998), 'Study: good governance aids profits', *Pensions and Investments (Chicago)*, September, **28**, 2–63.

Financial Sector Reform Project (1996), *An Evaluation of the Impact of Reform on the Financial Sector, Studies in Bangladesh Banking*, Dhaka: FSRP, Ministry of Finance.

Greuning, H. and S. Bratanovic (eds) (2003), *Analyzing and Managing Banking Risk: A Framework for Assessing Corporate Governance and Financial Risk*, Washington DC: World Bank.

Hassan, K. (1994), 'The financial sector reform in Bangladesh', in K. Hassan (ed.), *Banking and Finance in Bangladesh*, Dhaka: Academic Publishers.

Hossain, A. and S. Rashid (1996), '*In Quest of Development: The Political Economy of South Asia*', New Delhi: Vedam Publications.

Jalilian, H. and C. Kirkpatrick (2001) 'Financial Development and Poverty Reduction in Developing Countries, *Working Paper No. 30, Finance and Development Research Program, IDPM,* Manchester: University of Manchester.

Jensen, M. and W. Meckling (1976), 'Theory of the firm: managerial behavior, agency costs and ownership structure', *Journal of Financial Economics*, **3** (4), 305–60.

Johnson, L. D. and J. Neave (1994), 'Governance and competitive advantage', *Managerial Finance*, **20**, 54–69.

King, R. and R. Levine (1993a) 'Finance and growth: Schumpeter might be right', *Quarterly Journal of Economics*, **108**, 717–37.

King, R. and R. Levine (1993b), 'Finance, entrepreneurship and growth', *Journal of Monetary Economics*, **32**, 1–30.

Levine, R. (1997), 'Financial development and economic growth: views and agendas', *Journal of Economic Literature*, 35 (June), 237–57.

Levine, R. and S. Zervos (1998), 'Stock markets and economic growth', *American Economic Review*, **88**, 537–58.

Lin, C. (2001), *Private Vices in Public Places: Challenges in Corporate Governance Development in China*, Paris: OECD Development Centre, www.oecd.org/devl (accessed on 27 February 2005).

Macey, J. and M. O'Hara (2003), 'The corporate governance of banks', *Economic Policy Review*, 9(1).

McKinnon, R. (ed) (1973), *Money and Capital in Development*, Washington DC: Brookings Institute.

Mitton, (2002) 'A cross-firm analysis of impact of corporate governance on the East Asian financial crisis', *Journal of Financial Economics*, **64**(2), 215–41.

Nam, S. (2004), 'Corporate governance of banks: review of issues', Working Paper, Asian Development Bank Institute.

Nenova, T. (2004), 'A corporate governance agenda for developing ccountries', World Bank Discussion Paper, Washington DC: World Bank.

OECD (1999), *Principles of Corporate Governance*, Paris: OECD.

Oman, C. (2001), 'Corporate governance and national development', Technical Paper, No. 180, Paris: OECD Development Centre.

Oman, C., S. Fries, and W. Buiter (2003), 'Corporate governance in developing, transition, and emerging-market economies', Policy Brief No. 23, Paris: OECD Development Centre.

Rajan, R. G. and L. Zingales (1999), 'The politics of financial development', Working Paper, Chicago, IL: University of Chicago.

Raquib, A. (1999), 'Financial sector reform in Bangladesh: an evaluation', *Bank Porikroma*. Dhaka: Bangladesh Institute of Bank Management.

Reaz, M. and T. Arun (2005), 'Corporate governance and competition: conceptual thoughts', *Corporate Ownership and Control*, Fall, 45–51.

Reaz, M. and T. Arun (2006), 'Corporate governance in developing economies: perspective from the banking sector in Bangladesh', *Journal of Banking Regulation*, 7 (1, 2), 94–106.

Sayeed, Y. (2002), 'Bangladesh: strategic issues and potential response initiatives in the finance sector: banking reform and development', Paper Presented at Seminar Organized by Asian Development Bank and AIMS of Bangladesh, Dhaka, 22 July.

Shaw, E. (ed.) (1973), *Financial Deepening in Economic Development*. New York: Oxford University Press.

Shleifer A. and R. Vishny (1997), 'A survey of corporate governance', *Journal of Finance*, **52**, 737–83.

Singh, A., and Weisse, B. (2002) 'Corporate governance, competition, the new international financial architecture and large corporation in emerging markets', Working paper No. 250, ESRC Center for Business Research, University of Cambridge, December.

Vives, X. (2000), 'Corporate Governance: Does it Matter', in Vives, X. (ed.) *Corporate Governance: Theoretical and Empirical Perspectives*. Cambridge: Cambridge University Press.

Winkler, A. (1998), 'Financial development, economic growth and corporate governance', Paper No. 12, Finance and Accounting Working Paper Series, Frankfurt: Goethe University.

World Bank (1989), *World Development Report*. Washington DC: World Bank.

World Bank (1998), *Bangladesh: Strategy for Establishing a Sound and Competitive Banking Sector,* vol. 1–2, Washington DC: Finance and Private Sector Unit, South Asia Region, World Bank.

9. Corporate governance regulation and board decision making during takeovers

Blanaid Clarke

INTRODUCTION

This chapter examines the legal and regulatory framework which applies to the provision of advice by directors of a target company to shareholders during a takeover bid. Adopting a regulatory perspective, it considers whether this framework functions effectively. Regulation stems from initiatives both at EU level and at national level. Reconciling and bedding down these different initiatives has not always proven easy. Three points may be made in this regard. First, each market is different in terms of ownership patterns, structure and stage of development of the securities market, availability of finance, importance and role of the banking sector, socio-economic influences and political cultures. In addition, the regulation of takeovers falls within the remit of different types of bodies in different Member States each with their own particular structures, agendas, experiences and powers. Consequently, the task of agreeing harmonizing regulation, which can operate efficiently within each of these different marketplaces, has proven difficult. The European Commission's response to this challenge has been to adopt what might be viewed as a light regulatory touch. Second, takeover law (either nationally or at an EU level) is not in itself a coherent body of law in the way that one might describe constitutional or tort law. It has many different areas feeding into it such as company law, securities law, contract law and, of particular relevance to this chapter, corporate governance. Each area has its own specific norms, objectives, policies and regulatory mechanisms and these too vary from Member State to Member State. Third, as this chapter will show, a mixture of binding 'hard law' and non-binding 'soft law' regulates the takeover process and in particular the giving of advice to shareholders. This chapter suggests that regulators have not always been consistent in their approach to corporate governance and takeover regulation and, in the context of advice to offeree shareholders, regulatory gaps have resulted.

THE TAKEOVERS DIRECTIVE

As early as the 1970s, a consensus appeared to emerge that since takeovers had an overall positive economic effect, harmonized European legislation was required to facilitate takeovers and to provide a level playing field for takeover bids. Despite the introduction in 1985 of a White Paper on Completing the Internal Market, which announced an intention to propose a directive on the approximation of Member States' regulations governing takeovers, almost 20 years passed before a directive was actually adopted. During this time the Commission put forward one proposal after another, all of which failed to yield a consensus. The process was beset with disagreement about the nature of the directive (detailed rules versus framework), the viability of self-regulatory supervisory authorities, the necessity of mandatory general bids, the treatment of employees during a bid and, importantly, the possibility of defensive actions. In June 2001, the Conciliation Committee actually reached a common agreed position but the text was rejected by the European Parliament on a tied vote. At that time, the Parliament identified for specific criticism the principle that shareholder approval was required before directors could institute defensive measures in the face of a bid. The Rapporteur, Klaus-Heiner Lehne, recommended that such a requirement could only be justified if a level playing field existed for European companies facing a takeover bid and that since this was not then the case the agreement should be rejected. Following this setback, the Commission established a High Level Group of Company Law Experts under the chairmanship of Jap Winter to present recommendations for resolving the matters raised by Parliament (the Winter Report). A further proposal was introduced in 2002 taking broad account of these recommendations; following significant amendment, much of it last minute, Directive 2004/25/EC on Takeover Bids (the Directive) was finally adopted in April 2004.

In the light of available economic evidence, the Winter Report opined that the availability of a mechanism which facilitates takeover bids is basically beneficial (Winter *et al.*, 2002a: 9). The Winter Report identified three specific reasons why this might be the case. First, takeovers are a means for the offeror to create wealth by exploiting synergies between their existing business and the offeree. Second, takeover bids also offer shareholders the opportunity to sell their shares to offerors who are willing to offer a price above the prevailing market price. Finally, the market for corporate control suggests that actual and potential takeover bids are an important means to discipline the management of listed companies (Manne, 1965; Jensen and Meckling, 1976; Fama, 1980). This theory is based on the idea that inefficient management leads to share price decreases and shareholders seeking to exit these companies. Opportunities thus arise for other persons to acquire the companies cheaply, to install new management and to achieve greater returns for the new shareholders. The theory suggests that not only do takeovers lead to the removal of under-performing directors but also that the threat of such takeovers encourages directors to perform to the best of their abilities in order to avoid losing their jobs following such takeovers. All that regulators must do in such a scenario is to ensure that the takeover market operates freely and without hindrance from the directors themselves.[1] The Winter Report was emphatic in its assertion that 'such discipline of management and reallocation of resources is in the long term in the best interests of all stakeholders and society at large' and that these views 'form the basis for the Directive' (Winter *et al.*, 2002a: 19).

In the Irish market, the evidence supports the first two contentions but is weaker on the third. A study was undertaken of all 35 companies subjected to a takeover offer since the inception of the Irish Takeover Panel in 1997. The study was based on the same industries, 36 per cent involved bids by management buy-out (MBO) vehicles and a further 15 per cent involved bids by newly established companies run by individuals often with experience in these areas. Synergistic gains were stated to be the reason behind the acquisitions from companies in the same industry. In particular, the opportunity to expand in the Irish markets was emphasized. Interestingly, all the cross-border bids in the sample (28 per cent) fell into this category. In terms of premiums, the average recorded for the bids was 33 per cent.[2] This is clearly attractive for the offeree's shareholders. It also explains perhaps why all but one of the companies in the sample experienced a change in control following the bid. Finally, the evidence sheds some light on the health of the market for corporate control in Ireland. On a general level, only 5 per cent of relevant companies were subjected to a bid in any one year.[3] In considering which specific bids might be the result of inefficient management, the MBO situations would not appear relevant.[4] These bids were stated to be driven overwhelmingly by perceptions of 'negative small cap sentiments' in the Irish market. Of the acquisitions from offerors in the same industry which disclosed these details,[5] only one involved all the offeree's directors resigning and the remaining bids retained the CEO and/or at least half the board. Of the six bids from new offeror companies in the sample, one retained the CEO and finance director, four did not disclose whether any of the directors were resigning and only one declared that all directors were resigning. None of these companies cited poor management as the rationale for the acquisition. However, before using this as evidence to question the existence of the market for corporate control, one must remember that the effect of the market for corporate control lies as much in the threat it poses to directors as the production of changes in control. It is arguable thus that where the threat operated effectively, there would not be high incidence of takeovers. All that one might conclude from the survey is that there does not seem to be substantial evidence of the stick aspect of the market for corporate control being used.

Because of the structural and regulatory differences referred to in the introduction above, it was acknowledged that takeover bids could not be undertaken with the same expectation of success in different Member States (Winter *et al.*, 2002a: 19). Thus shareholders in Member Sates did not have equivalent opportunities to tender their shares. This is referred to as the 'lack of a level playing field'. The Winter Committee was set the task of reviewing whether and to what extent a level playing field for takeover bids could and should be created with respect to the mechanisms and structures allowed and created under company law in Member States, which might frustrate or inhibit takeover bids. The Committee acknowledged at the outset that any approach on this basis would leave the various general and structural differences existing in Member States untouched. However, it expressed the opinion that its recommendations with respect to company law mechanisms and structures would, in addition to market driven changes, mark an important step forward in developing a general level playing field for takeover bids in the EU (Winter *et al.*, 2002a: 20). The Report firmly acknowledged that there was a need for a level playing field for shareholders in the EU and that a directive on takeover bids was an important part of it. In this context, the Winter Report noted that:

> managers are faced with a significant conflict of interests if a takeover bid is made. Often their own performance and plans are brought into question and their own jobs are in jeopardy. Their interest is in saving their jobs and reputation instead of maximising the value of the company for shareholders. (Winter *et al.*, 2002a: 21)

As a consequence of its deliberations, the Winter Report suggested that a guiding principle of any European company law regulation aimed at creating a level playing field should be the right of shareholders to make the ultimate decision in respect of whether to tender their shares and at what price. It concluded that the risk was too great that directors would negate the positive economic benefits of takeovers by engaging in actions which would frustrate hostile takeovers (Winter *et al.*, 2002a: 2, n.2.). This is the view which appeared to find favour in the Directive. Recital 16 states that 'in order to prevent operations which could frustrate a bid, the powers of the board of an offeree company to engage in operations of an exceptional nature should be limited, without unduly hindering the offeree company in carrying on its normal business activities'.

This theme is continued in Article 3(1)(c) which provides *inter alia* that 'the board of an offeree company . . . must not deny the holders of securities the opportunity to decide on the merits of the bid'. Article 9(2), giving effect to this principle, requires the specific prior authorization of shareholders for 'any action . . . which may result in the frustration of the bid' and specifically 'before issuing any shares'. Importantly, the identification of an alternative bidder is expressly excluded from the prohibition on the basis that in an auction shareholders are afforded an opportunity to sell their shares. The Winter Report also stated that European company law regulation aimed at creating a level playing field should be guided by a second principle, proportionality between risk bearing and control (Winter *et al.*, 2002a: 20). Article 11 introduces the break-through rule which was designed to increase the number of takeovers in the EU by eliminating these corporate governance arrangements which might otherwise impede takeovers (Winter *et al.*, 2002a: 29). Despite the subsequent optionalization in Article 12(1) of the prohibition on frustrating action in Article 9 and the break-through rule in Article 11, it may be argued that the Directive clearly sets the benchmark of Articles 9 and 11 being applied by Member States and indeed that market pressure will provide incentives to adopt this benchmark (Winter, 2004: 18).

ROBUST DEFENCE

However, a further significant opportunity exists for directors to thwart a bid. Directors may frustrate a bid by mounting a robust defence. The Winter Report emphasized that the offeree board's 'insight into, and responsibility for, the strategy and day-to-day affairs of the company enable and require it to advise the shareholders on the takeover bid' (Winter *et al.*, 2002a: 20). Empirical studies have consistently found that the recommendations of target company directors in takeovers are the most important variable in determining takeover outcome (Walking, 1985; Eddey and Casey, 1989; Cotter and Zenner, 1994; Holl and Kyriazis, 1996; Cotter *et al.*, 1997; O'Sullivan and Wong, 1999). This increases the urgency of ensuring that effective corporate governance mechanisms exist to regulate the process of making these recommendations in order to ensure that directors are acting in the best interests of the company and its shareholders. One would thus expect this subject to be included in the Directive. It would be consistent for example with its aim, set out in Recital 3, of creating a level playing field and preventing patterns of corporate restructuring within the EU from being distorted by arbitrary differences in governance and management cultures.

There is a clear requirement in the Directive for the target company board to provide advice to shareholders. When an offer is made, Article 9(5) requires the board to draw up and make public a document setting out its opinion of the bid and the reasons on which it is based. The directors are also required to include their views on the effects of the implementation of the bid on certain matters such as the company's interests, the company's strategic plans, employment and business locations. However, absolutely no reference is made to the composition of the board giving such advice. There is no requirement, for example, for directors with a particular conflict of interest to stand down. Article 3(2)(c) sets out as a General Principle merely the requirement that the board of the target company 'act in the interest of the company as a whole'. While this duty clearly applies to the giving of advice to shareholders, it appears to amount to a restating of the traditional common law fiduciary duty.[6]

The Higgs Report acknowledged the 'natural potential for conflict between the interests of executive management and shareholders' in the making of a range of routine decisions such as remuneration or audit (Higgs, 2003: para.9(2)). In such circumstances, the Report noted that the legal duty on directors to act in the best interests of the company in itself is 'insufficient to give full assurance that these potential conflicts will not impair objective board decision-making' (Higgs, 2003: para. 9(3)). Yet, in the more extreme circumstance of a takeover bid, only this duty is prescribed by the Directive. It is submitted thus that by failing to regulate this crucial area of corporate governance, the Directive is failing in its objective to protect fully the interests of shareholders. One possible reason for its omission is that it was deemed more appropriately left to individual Member States to provide for it in their domestic regulations pursuant to Article 3(2). Article 3(2) expressly authorizes Member States to lay down additional conditions and provisions more onerous than those of the Directive with a view to ensuring compliance with the General Principles. Within these limits, each Member State may introduce or retain its own particular rules. Thus, the provisions of the Directive must be seen merely as minimum requirements for EU takeover regulation. However, such a delegation of responsibility would appear surprising given the significance of directors' recommendations to the ultimate outcome of the takeover and the importance placed by the EU on a level playing field. The penultimate section of this chapter examines the relevant takeover regulations in Ireland and the UK in order to determine whether this has happened in practice. A second possibility is that this area of takeover regulation was omitted from the Directive because it was viewed as essentially a matter of corporate governance which was adequately covered in general EU corporate governance regulation. This will be considered in the next section.

CORPORATE GOVERNANCE REGULATION

The European Commission emphasized that a dynamic and flexible company law and corporate governance framework in the EU is essential for a modern, dynamic, interconnected industrialized society (Commission of the European Communities, 2003: Introduction). However, both a Commission-sponsored review of the main corporate governance codes relevant to the EU (2002) and the High Level Group of Company Law Experts in its final report (Winter *et al.*, 2002b) advised against establishing an EU corporate governance code. This final Winter Report noted that while fixed rules in primary legislation may offer 'the benefits of certainty, democratic legitimacy and strong possibilities of enforcement' this comes at 'the cost of little or no flexibility, and disability to keep pace with changing circumstances.' It recommended making use of alternative forms of regulation and identified corporate governance as the first area where this would be required. In the Action Plan on Modernising Company Law and Enhancing Corporate Governance in the European Union of 2003, the Commission emphasized the need for any regulatory response at European Union level to be firm in the principles but flexible in application. It admitted that a self-regulatory market approach, based solely on non-binding recommendations, would not always be sufficient to guarantee the adoption of sound corporate governance practices. It stated that markets would only be able to play their disciplining role in an efficient way in the presence of a certain number of made-to-measure rules. The Commission thus decided against developing an EU corporate governance code on the basis that differences in underlying company law and securities regulations in Member States would mean either that such a code would involve a significant number of different options or it would have to confine itself to abstract principles. It decided thus to adopt a common approach at EU level with respect to these few essential rules and principles and to consider, where possible, the use of alternatives to legislation. In doing so, the Commission expressed a preference for disclosure requirements, viewing them as less intrusive in corporate life and yet a highly effective market-led way of rapidly achieving results (Commission of the European Communities, 2003: para.12).

The presence of independent directors on the board, capable of challenging the decisions of the management, was identified in the Action Plan as a means of protecting the interests of shareholders and, where appropriate, other stakeholders. The Commission had expressly accepted that 'in key areas where executive directors clearly have conflicts of interests . . . decisions in listed companies should be made exclusively by non-executive or supervisory directors who are in the majority independent'. It also indicated its intention to establish at EU level certain minimum standards of what cannot be considered to be independent (Commission of the European Communities, 2003: para. 3.1.3). However, the EU Consultation Paper on the Role of Non-Executive or Supervisory Directors of Listed Companies and on the Committees of the (Supervisory) Board (EU, 2004) explained that precise definitions of 'independence' vary in different codes and there is an absence of 'a universal understanding of what independence precisely entails' (EU, 2004: para. 2.2.3). In February 2005, a non-binding Recommendation was duly published on the Role of Non-Executive or Supervisory Directors of Listed Companies and on the Committees of the (Supervisory) Board ('The Recommendation') (EU, 2005). Recital 4 notes that 'In view of the complexity of many of the issues at stake, the adoption of detailed binding rules is not necessarily the most desirable and efficient way of achieving the objectives pursued'.

Article 13 of the Recommendation deals with the issue of 'independence'. Article 13.1 provides that 'a director should be considered to be independent only if he is free of any business, family or other relationship, with the company, its controlling shareholder or the management of either, that creates a conflict of interest such as to impair his judgment'. Article 13.2 also provides that a number of criteria for assessment of the independence of directors should be adopted at national level, taking into account the guidance set out in Annex II, which identifies a number of situations reflecting the relationships or circumstances usually recognized as likely to generate material conflict of interest. The Annex prefaces these circumstances with a comment that 'it is widely understood that assessment of the independence of any particular director should be based on substance rather than form'. Article 13.2 thus provides that the board may consider that, although a particular director meets all the criteria laid down at national level for assessment of the independence of directors, he cannot be considered independent owing to the specific circumstances of the person or the company, and the converse also applies.

The EU Recommendation is consistent with the Combined Code (Financial Reporting Council, 2006) which was adopted by both the London and the Irish Stock Exchanges on a 'comply and explain' basis in their Listing Rules. Article 3 states that the board should include a balance of executive and non-executive directors and in particular independent non-executive directors. It also provides that the decision as to whether a director is independent 'in character and judgment' rests with the board which must decide whether there are 'relationships or circumstances which are likely to affect, or could appear to affect, the director's judgment'. Article 3.1 provides that such relationships or circumstances include:

- the existence of 'a material business relationship between the director and the company either directly, or as a partner, shareholder, director or senior employee of a body that has such a relationship with the company';
- the receipt by the director of 'additional remuneration from the company apart from a director's fee';
- the existence of 'close family ties with any of the company's advisers, directors or senior employees'; and
- The representation by the director of a significant shareholder.

The inclusion of circumstances which 'could appear to affect' a director's independence is reduced somewhat by the statement in Article 3.1 of the Combined Code that where such relationships or circumstances exist which may appear relevant to its determination, that is which might appear to affect a director's judgement, the board may still decide that a director is independent but should state its reasons for doing so.

A number of comments can be made about the application of the Combined Code rules in the context of a takeover. First, the rules may be avoided by merely explaining non-compliance. Second, it is easier to claim compliance because of the absence of a precise definition of the term 'independent' or 'conflict of interest'. Like other forms of soft law, this leads to criticism that it lacks the clarity and precision needed to provide predictability and a reliable framework for action (Trubek *et al.*, 2005). Third, the Combined Code is further weakened by the statement that it is up to the board itself to determine what constitutes 'independence'. The outcome of all of this is that in most cases where directors have been categorized as 'independent' despite not meeting the Combined Code guidelines, the explanation given is that the board was satisfied that they should be deemed so. This is sufficient to ensure compliance with the Combined Code. Finally, the provision in the Combined Code does not apply to specific decision-making scenarios. It only applies to the general board position. What it refers to is independence from the company, not, for example, independence from a bidder. Although Article 13.3.2 of the Recommendation provides for periodic reconfirmation of independence, it does not provide for reconfirmation on an issue by issue basis. For this reason, the guidelines pertaining to independence in the Combined Code and Recommendation might be seen as merely illustrative. All of this might be said to support a criticism which is often made of soft law, that it undermines EU legitimacy because it creates expectations but does not or cannot bring about change (Trubek *et al.*, 2005).

TAKEOVER RULES

The Irish Takeover Panel was authorized by the Irish Takeover Panel Act 1997 to ensure that takeovers and other relevant transactions of relevant companies[7] were conducted in accordance with the principles set out in the 1997 Act (Irish Takeover Panel, 1997). Recently, the European Communities (Takeover Bids (Directive 2004/25/EC)) Regulations 2006 appointed the Irish Panel as the competent supervisory authority for takeover bids under the Takeovers Directive. Like the London Takeovers Panel, the Irish Panel regulates on the basis of specific rules and General Principles. Since its inception, these rules and principles, which mirror in content those of the City Code, have had statutory effect. As in the City Code, notes are provided alongside the Rules for practitioners, but these do not have statutory effect.

Rule 3.1 and Rule 25 of both the City Code and the Irish Rules require the target company's board to provide advice to shareholders and to set out the details which must be included in the offer document. However, both go further than the Directive in attempting to deal with the conflict of interest which arises in the context of a takeover. Rule 3.1 of the Irish Rules states clearly that any director with a conflict of interest should be excluded from the formulation and communication of advice to shareholders. Rule 25.1(d) reiterates this and states that the nature of the conflict should be explained clearly to the shareholders in any document issued by the offeree. The City Code is less prescriptive, merely stating in the Note to Rule 25.1 that directors with a conflict 'should not normally be joined'. Even in such closely aligned Rules as those of the UK and Ireland and in countries with similar corporate cultures, it is clear that a disparity in the treatment of directors is possible. It can be argued thus that the objectives of the Directive are not being achieved in this regard.

Prior to the implementation of the Directive, the General Principles set out in both the City Code and the Irish Rules required competent independent advice to be provided to the shareholders of the target company. For example, General Principle 8 in the Irish Act originally stated that the directors of the target company owe a duty to the target company and its shareholders 'to act in disregard to personal interest' when giving advice and furnishing information in relation to the offer.[8] General Principle 9 of the City Code required the directors 'in advising their shareholders' to 'act only in their capacity as directors and not to have regard to their personal or family shareholdings or to their personal relationships with the companies'. However, the General Principles in the Irish Rules[9] like those in the City Code were subsequently replaced with the General Principles set out in the Directive.[10] They are less helpful as a consequence. General Principle 2 now requires that the offeree's shareholders 'must have sufficient time and information to enable them to reach a properly informed decision on the offer' and General Principle 3 requires *inter alia* that the board of an offeree must act in the interests of the company as a whole. While it is of course a strong argument to suggest that 'sufficient' information includes independent advice, the removal of an express obligation on directors in this regard is significant.

In terms of what constitutes a conflict, the non-statutory Notes to Rule 3.1 of the Irish Rules give three examples of circumstances in which a conflict will exist:

- if there are significant cross shareholdings between an offeror and the offeree;
- if a director is common to both companies; or
- if a person is a substantial shareholder in both companies.

Significantly, the Notes to Rule 3.1 state that 'the Panel will normally consider in the absence of evidence to the contrary that it is appropriate for executive directors of the offeree to participate in giving advice to shareholders'. This deals with the contention that during a takeover, all directors are conflicted because they risk losing their jobs. However, it provides that such directors must satisfy themselves that they do not have a conflict of interest, and that if any director considers that he has, he should withdraw from the independent board. Both the City Code and the Irish Rules deal specifically with a takeover offer which constitutes a management buy-out or MBO. The Notes on Rule 25.1 of the Irish Rules provide that a director will be regarded as having a conflict of interest if it is intended that he or she will have 'a continuing role', whether in an executive or non-executive capacity, in either the offeror or offeree if the offer is successful. The notes on Rule 25.1 of the City Code state that such a person will 'normally be regarded' as conflicted. In this context, one issue which could be usefully imported from the corporate governance codes is the point made by Higgs that this new definition addresses not just relationships or circumstances that would affect the director's objectivity but also those that could appear to do so (Higgs, 2003: para. 9.11).

A final point to note is that there are a number of clear differences in the

Table 9.1   Comparison of takeover rules with the combined code

	Takeover Rules	Combined Code
Hostile takeover	Can advise	No conflict
Member of MBO team	Cannot advise	Conflict
Ongoing role	Generally can advise	Conflict
Association with shareholder in the Bidder	Generally cannot advise	Conflict
Association with shareholder in the Target Company	Generally can advise	Conflict

categorization of directors as independent as between these Rules and the various corporate governance codes. Some of these differences are set out in Table 9.1.

In actual fact, the existence of these differences may be positively unhelpful in the determination of independence in the context of a takeover. The research undertaken to date explains the difficulty of applying consistent rules to this area. A study of the 39 offer documents reveals that while 31 per cent of directors declined to participate in the advisory team, 69 per cent felt able to give advice to shareholders. In 28 per cent of the bids made, it was declared that at least some of the advisers would become part of the new board or become consultants to the newly acquired company.[11] In a further 31 per cent of the bids, all advisers were expressly stated to have no further role. However, in the remaining 41 per cent of cases, there was no disclosure at all as to the future role, if any, of the directors. In these cases, the shareholders did not have the benefit of this information in evaluating the advice. Clearly, hard rules would be difficult to formulate in relation to independent directors as in practice 'one size does not fit all' and there are a myriad different definitions of independence all with different criteria (Higgs, 2003: para. 9.8). This is one of the consequences of operating within a hybrid system where hard and soft law operates in the same policy domain. The facets of soft law which appear to make it the appropriate form of regulation can also lead to significant difficulties in terms of application and enforcement.

CONCLUSION

There has been an acknowledgement at EU level of both the need to ensure a level playing field and the threat of conflicted directors to the achievement of this objective. Despite this, existing EU takeover regulation concentrates almost exclusively on the prohibition of frustrating actions by directors and ignores the impact of directors' advice on the outcome of a takeover. Although domestic takeover regulation provides for the giving of independent advice, it does so in such a way as to allow the directors themselves significant discretion as to their role. Finally, while the composition and objectivity of the committees of directors giving advice can equally be categorized as a corporate governance issue, this has largely been overlooked in EU and national corporate governance regulation; it appears to have fallen between two regulatory stools. As a consequence, there exists independently and without reference to each other, systems of corporate governance and takeover regulation in this area which, when taken separately, are not fully effective and which, when combined, create new problems: a negative synergy.

Clearly, hard rules would be difficult to formulate in this regard as in practice one can see that 'one size does not fit all'. As Higgs noted, there exists a myriad different definitions of independence all with different criteria (Higgs, 2003: para. 9.8). Although the Irish Rules do not attempt to set out all the circumstances in which a conflict arises, they do set out a number of circumstances in which they will exist. This is helpful because at the very least it shifts the onus of proof on to the directors in such cases to prove that no conflict arises. It is submitted that a solution, if one can be found, might exist in the identification of a compromise between hard and soft law. A description of the nature of independence could be set out clearly in the Rules, or indeed in the Directive which gives the relevant supervisory authorities greater control over the board in this regard. Unlike the Recommendation, the regulator and not the board would become the final arbiter of independence. A somewhat similar treatment is given in the Directive and the Takeover Rules to the definition of 'concert party'.

However, on the European stage at least, there appears to be little appetite for further regulation. Instead, there are constant complaints of 'regulatory fatigue' in the EU. That said, while the focus in the Commission is still on strengthening shareholders' rights and fighting management entrenchment (Borges, 2006), one might do well to remember that one of the ultimate means of empowering shareholders is by providing them with sufficient information. In the context of takeover offers, advice received from an independent board is crucial to the achievement of the positive economic benefits associated with takeovers and the failure to regulate this area reduces the opportunities for such benefits.

ACKNOWLEDGEMENTS

Any opinions stated and interpretations suggested constitute personal opinions and interpretations and are not intended to represent the views or practices of any other person or body.

NOTES

1. Though beyond the scope of this chapter, it is submitted that the market for corporate control as a form of external market force suffers from its reliance on a number of disputable assumptions, limited application and ambiguous empirical support. See further Clarke (2006).
2. This does not include offers where there was no actual value for the share listing, for example because of the lack of a market, suspension or otherwise.
3. The average number of relevant companies during the period 1997 to 2005 was 74. The term 'relevant company' is determined in accordance with section 2 of the Irish Takeover Panel Act 1997.
4. Even if the poor share price was caused by inept management, it would seem to pervert the market for corporate control theory, if the management themselves were able to benefit from the fruits of their ineptitude.
5. Six out of the 19 bids did not disclose any details of resignations. A further one indicated the finance director and an undisclosed number of other directors were remaining.
6. An argument might perhaps be made that unlike the traditional common law duties, this duty is owed to shareholders and other stakeholders.
7. Relevant companies are defined in section 2 of the Act (as amended by section 75 of the Investment Funds, Companies and Miscellaneous Provisions Act 2005 and section 26 of the Investment Funds, Companies and Miscellaneous Provisions Act 2006) and include Irish registered companies listed on the Irish Stock Exchange, the London Stock Exchange, the New York Stock Exchange and Nasdaq.
8. It might be argued, however, that this seems to contradict the Rule prohibiting the director from involving himself or herself in the decision.
9. With the exception of General Principle 12 dealing with the SARS which has remained.
10. This was done by section 30 of the Investment Funds, Companies and Miscellaneous Provisions Act 2006 in Ireland and the Takeovers Directive (Interim Implementation) Regulations 2006 in the UK (and subsequently the Companies Act 2006).
11. In four of these cases, the majority of the advisers remained, in one an equal number remained, in five a minority remained (although often in an important role like CEO or financial director) and in one an unidentified minority remained.

REFERENCES

Borges, A. (2006), 'Speech to the Hearing on Future Priorities for the Action Plan on Company Law and Corporate Governance, Brussels, 3 May 2006', http://64.233.183.104/search?q=cache:N0GXC5OzU-kJ:ec.europa.eu/internal_market/company/consultation/index_en.htm + Borges, + a + member + of + the + European + Corporate + Governance + Forum, + to + the + Hearing + on +

Future + Priorities + for + the + Action + Plan&hl = en&ct = clnk&cd = 1&gl = ie, 12 December 2007.

Clarke, B. (2006), 'European Takeover Regulation and Directive 2004/25/EC', *The Company and Securities Law Journal*, **24**, 93–106.

Commission of the European Communities (2003), *Modernising Company Law and Enhancing Corporate Governance in the European Union: A Plan to Move Forward,* COM/2003/0284 final.

Cotter, J., A. Shivdasani and M. Zenner (1997), 'Do independent directors enhance target shareholder wealth during tender offers?' *Journal of Financial Economics,* **39**, 3–43.

Cotter, J. and Zenner, M. (1994) 'How managerial wealth affects the tender offer process', *Journal of Financial Economics,* **35**, 63–97.

Eddey, P. and R. Casey (1989) 'Directors' recommendations in response to takeover bids: do they act in their own interests?', *Australian Journal of Management* **14**, 1–28.

EU (2002), 'Comparative Study of the Corporate Governance Codes relevant to the European Union and its Member States (January 2002)'. http://ec.europa.eu/internal_market/company/otherdocs/index_en.htm, 12 December 2007.

EU (2004), *Commission Consultation Paper on the role of non-executive or supervisory directors of listed companies and on the committees of the (supervisory) board* (May 2004).

EU (2005), *Commission Recommendation on the role of non-executive or supervisory directors of listed companies and on the committees of the (supervisory) board (2005/162/EC).*

Fama, E. (1980) 'Agency problems and the theory of the firm', *Journal of Political Economics,* **88**, 288–307.

Financial Reporting Council (2006), *The Combined Code on Corporate Governance,* London: FRC.

Higgs, D. (2003), *Review of the Role and Effectiveness of Non-Executive Directors,* London: Department of Trade and Industry.

Holl, P. and D. Kyriazis (1996), 'The determinants of outcome in UK takeover bids', *International Journal of Economics and Business,* **3**, 165–84.

Irish Takeover Panel (1997), *Irish Takeover Panel Act 1997 Takeover Rules 2007.*

Jensen, M. and W. Meckling (1976), 'Theory of the firm: managerial behaviour, agency costs and ownership structure', *Journal of Financial Economics,* **3**, 305–60.

Manne, H. (1965) 'Mergers and the market for corporate control', *Journal of Political Economics,* **73**, 110–20.

O'Sullivan, N. and P. Wong (1999), 'Board composition, ownership structure and hostile takeovers: some UK evidence', *Accounting and Business Research,* **29**, 139–55.

Panel on Takeovers and Mergers, (2007) *The City Code on Takeovers and Mergers,* London: Panel on Takeovers and Mergers.

Trubek, D., P. Cottrell and M. Nance (2005), ''Soft law' 'hard law' and European integration: toward a theory of hybridity', *Legal Studies Research Papers Series* Paper No. 1002.

Walking, R. (1985) 'Predicting tender offer success: a logistic analysis', *Journal of Financial and Quantitative Analysis,* **20**, 461–78.

Winter, J. (2004) 'EU Company Law at the Cross-Roads' in G. Ferrarini, K. Hopt, J. Winter and E. Wymeersch (eds), *Reforming Company and Takeover Law in Europe,* London: Oxford University Press.

Winter, J., J. S. Christensen, J. M. Garrido Garcia, K. J. Hopt, J. Rickford, G. Rossi and J. Simon (2002a) 'Report of the High Level Group of Company Law Experts on issues related to takeover bids', http://ec.europa.eu/internal_market/en/company/company/official/index.htm, 12 December 2007.

Winter, J., J. M. Garrido Garcia, K. J. Hopt, J. Rickford, G. Rossi, J. S. Christensen and J. Simon (2002b) 'Final Report of the High Level Group of Company Law Experts on a modern regulatory framework for company law in Europe', http://ec.europa.eu/internal_market/company/modern/index_en.htm#background, 12 December 2007.

10. Shareholder protection: a leximetric approach

Priya P. Lele and Mathias M. Siems

INTRODUCTION

The discussion of shareholder protection has various dimensions: it is topical in the context of the new EU Directive on Shareholder Rights (EU, 2007; for a critical comment see Siems, 2005b). It is significant for the consideration of good corporate governance (Bebchuk, 2005a, 2005b; see also Bebchuk and Fried, 2004), and time and again comes to the forefront in the growing literature on 'law and finance'. Following the pioneering work of a group of financial economists, there is an increasing trend to quantify the law in relation to shareholder protection. However, in our view, this has not been done in a satisfactory manner. Thus, the next section identifies some of the problems with the existing indices, and the following section discusses the building of a more meaningful shareholder protection index; in particular, it addresses the question of selection of variables and method of coding. The penultimate section presents some of the results that are indicative of interesting possibilities that a leximetric approach (the term was first used by Cooter and Ginsburg, 2003) opens up into the study of comparative shareholder protection law and the final section offers conclusions on the chapter.

Our results contribute to the contemporary discussion on comparative company law and corporate governance. Adopting a leximetric approach, we have made some interesting findings on questions such as which of the studied countries scores the maximum on our shareholder protection index, how much legal systems have changed over the years, whether differences follow the distinction into civil-law and common-law countries, and whether the laws on shareholder protection are converging or diverging.

As a point of clarification, it should be noted that this chapter is about 'leximetrics' and not 'econometrics'. 'Leximetrics' can be understood as every quantitative measurement of law. Moreover, the coding of shareholder rights can be the first part of an econometric study which seeks to find a statistical relationship between legal and economic data;[1] this is, however, the topic of a different paper (Armour *et al.*, 2008).

THE PROBLEMS WITH EXISTING INDICES

The most popular shareholder protection index so far is the one constructed by La Porta *et al.* (1998) in their article on 'Law and Finance'. Their index uses eight variables as proxies for shareholder protection in 49 countries. These variables code the law for 'one share one vote', 'proxy by mail allowed', 'shares not blocked before the meeting', 'cumulative voting', 'oppressed minorities mechanism', 'preemptive rights to new issues', 'share capital required to call an extraordinary shareholder meeting' and 'mandatory dividend'. Since the publication of 'Law and Finance', many studies have used these variables on shareholder protection (Dyck and Zingales, 2004; Licht *et al.*, 2005; Pagano and Volpin, 2005; see also Spamann, 2006). However, as admitted in a recent article (Djankov *et al.*, 2008), the initial index has also been subjected to many criticisms. For instance, Spamann (2006), Cools (2005) and Braendle (2006) have criticized the *ad hoc* selection of variables and found various coding errors. Pistor (2000) has gone a step further and extended the number of variables in order to capture particular problems for the transition economies of Eastern Europe and the former Soviet Union (see also Pistor *et al.*, 2000).

To elaborate, the first problem is the very limited number of variables, which hardly provides a meaningful picture of the legal protection of shareholders. To be sure, one cannot take all aspects of shareholder protection into account. The company law of most countries consists of several hundred sections or articles, so that the coding of all the details would lead to an unworkable index of several hundred (or more likely thousand) variables. Thus, it is necessary to construct a limited number of variables, but the selection of these variables must be intelligible and wide enough to function as a proxy for shareholder protection in general. This is not the case with La Porta *et al.*'s eight variables, which do not fully capture the most significant aspects of the law.[2] For instance, although the variables for 'one share one vote', 'proxy by mail allowed', 'shares not blocked before the meeting', and 'share capital required to call an extraordinary shareholder meeting', deal with different aspects of shareholders' voting power, they miss the more crucial question of the extent of this power, that is the issues over which the shareholders in a general meeting can exercise decision-making power. For our index see Table 10.1, variable I 1. Similarly, while the variable 'cumulative voting' may be important to the extent that it seeks to measure the power of shareholders in the

Table 10.1   Shareholder protection index (variables)

Variables	Description[1]
I. Protection against board and management	
1. Powers of the general meeting[2]	The following variables equal 0 if there is no power of the general meeting and 1 if there is a power of the general meeting. (1) Amendments of articles of association (2) Mergers and divisions (3) Capital measures[3] (4) *De facto* changes: the decisive thresholds are the sale of substantial assets of the company (e.g., if the sale of more than 50 per cent requires approval of the general meeting it equals 1; if more than 80 per cent, it equals 0.5; and otherwise 0). (5) Dividend distributions: equals 1 if the general meeting can effectively influence the amount of dividend (for example if it decides about the annual accounts and the annual dividend, and if the board has no significant possibility of 'manipulating' the accounts); equals 0.5 if there is some participation of the general meeting; equals 0 if it is only the board that decides about the dividend. (6) Election of board of directors (7) Directors' self-dealing of substantial transactions
2. Agenda-setting power[4]	(1) General topics: equals 1 if shareholders who hold 1 per cent or less of the capital can put an item on the agenda; equals 0.5 if there is a hurdle of more than 1 per cent but less than 10 per cent; equals 0 otherwise. (2) Election of directors: *ditto* (3) Costs: equals 1 if shareholders do not have to pay for their proposals; equals 0 otherwise.
3. Extraordinary shareholder meeting[5]	(1) Right: equals 1 if the minimum percentage of share capital to demand an extraordinary meeting is less than or equal to 5 per cent; equals 0.5 if it is more than 5 per cent but less than or equal to 10 per cent; equals 0 otherwise. (2) Enforcement: equals 1 if shareholders can call the meeting themselves or have a right that the court will enforce it; equals 0 if the court has discretion.
4. Anticipation of shareholder decision	(1) Restrictions on proxy voting: equals 0 if there are restrictions on who can be appointed or which rights the proxy has so that it is likely that proxy voting does usually not take place; equals 0.5 if there are some restrictions which reduce the relevance of proxy voting; equals 1 if there are no restrictions. (2) Anticipation facilitated: equals 1 if postal voting or proxy solicitation with two-way voting proxy form has to be provided by the company; equals 0.5 if two-way proxy form has to be provided but not proxy solicitation; equals 0 otherwise.

Table 10.1   (continued)

Variables	Description[1]
	(3) Costs of proxy contest: equals 1 if the costs of proxy solicitations are paid by the company or if proxies have the right to have their proposals included in the company's proxy form; equals 0 otherwise.
5. Information in the run-up of the general meeting	(1) Amendments of the articles of association: Equals 1 if the exact wording has to be sent in advance ('push-system'); equals 0.5 if the share-holders have to request it ('pull-system'); equals 0 otherwise.
	(2) Mergers: equals 1 if a special report has to be sent in advance ('push-system'); equals 0.5 if the shareholders have to request it ('pull-system'); equals 0 otherwise.
6. Shares not blocked before general meeting	Equals 0 if shareholders have to deposit their shares prior to the general meeting and if this has the consequence that shareholders are prevented from selling their shares for a number of days; equals 1 otherwise.
7. Individual information rights	(1) Right to demand information (1): equals 1 if an individual shareholder or shareholders with 5 per cent or less capital can demand information which will be answered at the general meeting; equals 0.5 if shareholders with 10 per cent or less capital have this right; equals 0 otherwise.
	(2) Right to demand information (2): equals 1 if an individual shareholder or shareholders with 5 per cent or less capital can demand information independent of the general meeting; equals 0.5 if shareholders with 10 per cent or less capital have this right; equals 0 otherwise.
8. Communication with other shareholders	(1) Right to access the register of shareholders and (if necessary) beneficial owners: equals 1 if the right of inspection can be used by a single shareholder; equals 0 if there is no such right.
	(2) Equals 1 if communication is not affected by proxy rules; equals 0 otherwise.
9. Board composition	(1) Division between management and control: equals 1 if there is a two-tier system or at least half of the board members are non-executive; equals 0.5 if at least 25 per cent of the board members are non-executive; equals 0 otherwise.
	(2) Independent board members:[6] equals 1 if at least half of the board members must be independent; equals 0.5 if at least 25 per cent of them must be independent or if the independence requirement is very low; otherwise equals 0.
	(3) Committees: equals 1 if companies have to install an audit and a remuneration committee with a majority of independent members; intermediate scores are possible if the requirement is partial, (for instance requires setting up of one of the committees or the independent members of the committees constitute less than a majority); equals 0 if committees are not necessary or if they are not required to have independent members.

Table 10.1   (continued)

Variables	Description[1]
10. No excessive remuneration for non-executive and executive directors	(1) General meeting power:[7] equals 1 if the general meeting has to approve all compensation schemes; equals 0.5 if this is limited (for example, applies to stock option plans only, or if some directors are excluded); equals 0 otherwise. (2) Annual disclosure: equals 1 if there is full and specific disclosure about the individual remuneration of each director; equals 0.75 if there is information about the individual remuneration of some directors; equals 0.5 if there is disclosure about the top 2 directors (executives); equals 0.25 if there is only disclosure about the overall remuneration; equals 0 otherwise. (3) Substantive requirements placing limit for remuneration in order to protect shareholders: equals 1 if there is a direct regulation; equals 0 otherwise.
11. Performance based remuneration	Equals 1 if performance based remuneration of directors and managers is fostered (for example facilitation of stock options to reward performance); equals 0 otherwise.
12. Duration of director's appointment	(1) Normal duration: equals 1 if this is one year or less; 0 if this is five years or more; equals 0.5 if this is more than 1 but less than 5 years. (2) Dismissal feasible: equals 1 if there are no special requirements; equals 0 if an important or good reason is required; intermediate scores are possible if there are no special requirements but there may be financial burden for the company (for example in the form of compensation under a statute or contract or damages for breach of contract or salary under a fixed term contract).
13. Directors' duties[8]	(1) Directors' liability – duty of care: equals 0 if there are narrow criteria which virtually exclude liability; equals 0.5 if there are some restrictions (for example, business judgement rule; gross negligence); equals 1 if there are no or little restrictions regarding business judgment and standard of care. (2) Directors' liability – duty of loyalty: equals 1 if there is a duty not to put personal interests ahead of the company; equals 0 otherwise. (3) Private enforcement: equals 0 if this is typically excluded (for example, because of strict subsidiary requirement, hurdle which is at least 10 per cent; cost rules); equals 0.5 if there are some restrictions, for example certain percentage of share capital (unless the hurdle is at least 10 per cent); cost rules; demand requirement; equals 1 otherwise.
14. Shareholder supremacy	(1) General principle: equals 1 if the board always has to give priority to shareholders' interests; equals 0 if the board have to give priority to the interests of other stakeholders; equals 0.5 in other cases.

Table 10.1   (continued)

Variables	Description[1]
	(2) Takeover law: equals 1 if there is the principle of strict neutrality in case of takeovers; equals 0.5 if the principle of neutrality is subject to exceptions; equals 0 otherwise.[9]
15. Preemptive right[10]	Equals 1 when the law grants shareholders the first opportunity to buy new issues of shares, and this right can be waived only by the general meeting;[11] equals 0 otherwise.
16. Director's disqualification	Equals 1 if negligent conduct can lead to disqualification; 0.5 if directors are disqualified only in specific instances of negligence (for example, failure of financial reporting); equals 0 if negligent conduct itself is not sufficient for disqualification
17. Corporate governance code	Equals 1 if companies have to disclose and explain whether they comply with a corporate governance code; equals 0.5 if this is only recommended; equals 0 otherwise.
18. Public enforcement of company law	The following variables equal 0 if there is no power of public authority and 1 if public authority has power. (1) Authorization for director's self dealing of substantial transactions (2) Authorization for appointment of managers (3) Power to intervene in cases of prejudice to public interest or interest of the company for instance due to 'mismanagement of company' or in cases of oppression of shareholders

II. Protection against other shareholders

1. Quorum[12]	Equals 1 if there is a 50 per cent quorum for the extraordinary shareholder meeting (when it is called for the first time); equals 0.5 if the quorum is ⅓; equals 0.25 if the quorum is ¼; equals 0 otherwise.
2. Supermajority requirements	Equals 1 if there are supermajority requirements (for example, ⅔ or ¾) for amendments of the articles of association, mergers, and voluntary liquidations; equals 0 if they do not exist at all.
3. One share – one vote[13]	(1) Default rule: equals 1 if this principle exists as a default rule; equals 0 otherwise. (2) Prohibition of multiple voting rights (super voting rights): equals 1 if there is a prohibition; equals ⅔ if only companies which already have multiple voting rights can keep them; equals ⅓ if state approval is necessary; equals 0 otherwise. (3) Prohibition of capped voting rights (voting right ceilings): equals 1 if there is a prohibition; equals ⅔ if only companies which already have voting caps can keep them; equals ⅓ if state approval is necessary; equals 0 otherwise.
4. Cumulative voting	Equals 1 if shareholders can cast all their votes for one candidate standing for election to the board of directors or if there exists a mechanism of proportional representation in the board by which minority interests may name a proportional number of directors to the board (default or mandatory law); equals 0 otherwise.

Table 10.1   (continued)

Variables	Description[1]
5. Voting by interested shareholders prohibited	Equals 1 if a shareholder cannot vote if this vote favours him or her personally (that is, only 'disinterested shareholders' can vote); equals 0 otherwise.
6. No squeeze out (freeze out)	Equals 0 if a shareholder holding 90 per cent or more can 'squeeze out' the minority; equals 1 otherwise.
7. Right to exit	(1) Appraisal rights: equals 1 if they exist for mergers, amendments of the articles and sales of major company assets; equals 0 if they do not exist at all. (2) Mandatory bid: equals 1 if there is a mandatory bid for the entirety of shares in case of purchase of 30 per cent or ⅓ of the shares; equals 0 if there is no mandatory bid at all. (3) Mandatory public offer: equals 1 if there is a mandatory public offer for purchase of 10 per cent or less of the shares; equals 0.5 if the acquirer has to make a mandatory public offer for acquiring more than 10 per cent but less than 30 per cent of the shares; equals 0 otherwise.
8. Disclosure of major share ownership	Equals 1 if shareholders who acquire at least 3 per cent of the companies capital have to disclose it; equals 0.75 if this concerns 5 per cent of the capital; equals 0.5 if this concerns 10 per cent; equals 0.25 if this concerns 25 per cent; equals 0 otherwise
9. Oppressed minority	(1) Substantive law: equals 0 if majority decisions of the general meeting have to be accepted by the outvoted minority; equals 1 if some kind of substantive control is possible (for example in cases of amendments to the articles of association, ratification of management misconduct, exclusion of the pre-emption right, related parties transactions, freeze outs); equals 0.5 if this control covers only flagrant abuses of majority power. (2) Shareholder action: equals 1 if every shareholder can file a claim against a resolution by the general meeting because he or she regards it as void or voidable; equals 0.5 if there are hurdles such as a threshold of at least 10 per cent voting rights or cost rules; equals 0 if this kind of shareholder action does not exist.
10. Shareholder protection is mandatory[14]	(1) Exclusion of director's duty of care (see variable I 13.1) in articles: equals 0 if possible and equals 1 otherwise. (2) Rules on duration of director's appointment (see variable I 12.1 and 2): equals 1 if mandatory and 0 otherwise. (3) Board composition (supervisory boards, non-executive directors) (see variable I 9.1 and 2): equals 1 if mandatory and 0 otherwise. (4) Other topics: equals 1 if there is the general rule that company law is mandatory; equals 0 if company law is in general just a model 'off-the-shelf'; equals 0.5 if there is no general rule.

Table 10.1   (continued)

Notes:
1. Even where the description of the variables does not mention so specifically, we have given intermediate scores wherever necessary. See p. 158 on non-binary coding.
2. For the power of the general meeting for remuneration see variable I 10.1.
3. The possibility of authorized capital does not lead to a reduction from 1 to 0.5 because the default rule does not change.
4, 5. Variables I. 2 and 3 could also be used as mechanisms for protecting minority from majority shareholders. However, in this study we have considered them as part of protection against directors because the directors are responsible for and decide the agenda and the calling of the shareholders meetings and therefore the legal rules of these variables primarily protect shareholders against directors.
6. Having independent board members may also be a method to protect minority shareholders against majority shareholders. This depends, however, on the definition of 'independence', which is not coded in this variable.
7. For the involvement of boards and committees generally see variable I 9.
8. For approval of directors' conduct by the general meeting, the supervisory board, or independent board members see variables I 1, 9; for exclusion of liability in the articles see variable II 10.1.
9. For preventive measures see, for example, variable II 3.
10. Usually, the directors decide about the issuance of new shares. Preemptive right is perceived as an important protection against directors as it prevents them from disregarding the interests of shareholders in general. Of course, in some cases this may also be a method to protect minority against majority shareholders.
11. For the requirements for a waiver (for example supermajority, good reason) see variables II 2, 9.
12. The purpose of requiring a substantial percentage of shareholders to constitute a valid quorum could be to prevent decisions of the general meeting which are not supported by a significant majority, much like the supermajority requirements. But see also note 20 to the main text.
13. Preference shares without voting rights are not addressed because they are feasible in all countries.
14. Variables II 10.1-3 do not code the content of the law (this is already done in variables I 9.1-2 to 12, 13.1) but only its nature, i.e. whether 'mandatory' or 'default'. I 2, 9.

appointment of directors, it misses the more critical question of removal of directors and the extent to which entrenchment is possible, as also certain other aspects of the terms of directors, for example, their tenure, remuneration and so on (see Table 10.1, variables I 10, 12). Further, despite using the term 'anti-director index' (La Porta *et al.*, 1998: 1123), the variables do not address the aspects of law relating to issues such as composition of the board, extent of directors' self dealing or their disqualification (Table 10.1, variables I 1.6, 13.2, 9, 10, 16).

Additionally, La Porta *et al.*'s choice of variables can be criticized as suffering from a US bias (for a similar point see Berglöf and von Thadden, 1999, and for further references see Cools, 2005: 700–1). For instance, in the US the use of cumulative voting has been thoroughly debated (see, for example, Gordon, 1989), as a result of which some US states have 'opt out' and some have 'opt in' provisions in their corporate laws.[3] From an American perspective cumulative voting is therefore an important topic and its regulation can be seen as a good proxy for shareholder protection in general. However, this is not the case in other countries. For example, although in France and Germany cumulative voting can be provided for in the articles (see Cools, 2005: 718, for France; and Hüffer, 2004: 33, for Germany), its use does not play any role and some of the most elaborate and voluminous books on company law ignore it altogether.[4]

On the other hand, the US bias can be seen from the absence of certain variables in the index. The exclusion of the law on removal of directors, against the background of the fact that the law on entrenchment of directors in the US is the subject of strong criticism (Bebchuk and Cohen, 2005; Table 10.1, variable II 10.2), points towards a possible US bias. The focus on protection of shareholders from directors and the comparative disregard of the expropriation of minority shareholders by majority blockholders is another example. This fact has also been illustrated in a study in which a German scholar (Berndt, 2002: 17–18) constructed an 'alternative minority protection index', on the basis of what he believed to be more important rules for (minority) shareholder protection. He omitted 'shares not blocked' and the 'oppressed minorities mechanism' and instead included two new variables: 'minority protection regarding authorized capital' and 'minority protection regarding share repurchases'. It is little surprise that, on the resultant index, Germany performed better than the US.

Whilst their choice of variables indicates a possible US bias, their coding has been subjected to pointed criticism of their common-law bias. For instance, the difference between default and mandatory rules has not been sufficiently taken into account, so that the random reliance on mandatory law and default rules for the coding of variables across countries has therefore been identified as part of the common-law bias.[5]

Finally, there is trouble with the definitions of some of the variables. Many of the La Porta *et al.* variables are too broad or too vague. For instance, the variable 'proxy voting' is unsatisfactory because most countries have some kind of proxy voting; see the following section for how we have disintegrated these variables and recast them into more meaningful ones. Even fuzzier is the variable 'oppressed minority' (Spamann, 2006: 37); given its extremely broad description[6] it covers various substantive and procedural aspects of shareholder protection, which should have been scrutinized separately. For our index see Table 10.1, variables I 13.1–3, 18, II 7.1, 9.1–2.

BUILDING A MEANINGFUL SHAREHOLDER PROTECTION SCHEME

This lack of reflection on the difficult topic of choosing the variables and of coding legal rules in detail is conspicuous in the earlier studies, resulting in ambiguity and criticism. For instance, the lack of appropriate explanation and treatment of mandatory and default rules has given rise to criticism of bias, as described in the previous section. We have therefore decided to pass over the existing studies and make a fresh start for quantification of shareholder protection. Our new shareholder protection index traces how shareholder protection in five countries has developed over a period exceeding three decades.[7] In this section we discuss how we made the choice of variables and decided how 'the law' should be coded.

The Variables

Our new shareholder protection index traces how shareholder protection in the UK, US, Germany, France and India has developed over the last 35 years. We have endeavoured to include variables which best reflect shareholder protection in these countries. To be sure, it is unrealistic to attempt to include all the possible considerations in the index. The effective protection of shareholders is linked with contract law, civil procedure, questions of legal effectiveness, as well as social, economic, and cultural differences. These aspects will be taken into account when our shareholder index is used for our future econometric study. Conversely, the present chapter deliberately focuses on a diligent coding of only those legal rules which concern shareholder protection because a mixed coding of shareholder rights and rule of law in one set of variables would lead to confusion rather than illumination.

The variables used as proxies for shareholder protection in the index are divided into those which protect shareholders against directors and managers, and those which protect (minority) shareholders against other shareholders. Many of the variables contain sub-variables; for instance, the overall variable 'power of the general meeting' consists of seven sub-variables which address different issues over which the general meeting may or may not have decision-making power, namely, amendments of articles of association, mergers and divisions, capital measures, *de facto* changes, dividend distributions, election of board of directors, and directors' self-dealing of substantial transactions. In total, our shareholder protection index has 60 (sub-)variables whose development has been coded for the five countries. The list of these variables and a description of their coding is given in Table 10.1.

Some variables used in the existing literature have been disintegrated, modified and recast into more precise variables with detailed sub-variables. For instance, as observed earlier, the use of the variables 'proxy voting' and 'oppressed minority' in the previous studies is too vague. With respect to 'proxy voting' it is important to distinguish between a variety of aspects, such as who can be appointed, whether companies have to facilitate proxy voting, who bears the costs of a proxy contest, and whether the proxy rules affect communication between shareholders (Table 10.1, variables I 4.1–3, 8.2). We have therefore recast it into two separate variables, 'anticipation of shareholder decision' and 'communication with other shareholders', which are further divided into meaningful sub-variables (Table 10.1, variables I 4.1–3, 8.2). With respect to 'oppressed minority', we have first of all distinguished between substantive law for protection against mismanagement of the directors and managers, and fraud on minority by or transferring of assets and profits out of firms by majority (or controlling) shareholders for their benefit (Table 10.1, variables I 6.1 and II 9.1). Moreover, there are various ways in which enforcement may operate; for instance, private law remedies, intervention by public authorities, and disqualification are equally conceivable. We have therefore built separate sub-variables to reflect enforcement (Table 10.1, variables I 6.3, 16, 18.1, II 9.2).

In our choice of variables, we have taken account of the fact that different legal instruments can be used to achieve a similar function. For example, there are various ways in which a decision of the general meeting may be prevented from harming minority shareholders: rules of company law may be mandatory so that the majority shareholders cannot abuse their power in the general meeting in this respect (the opportunistic amendment hypothesis: see Gordon, 1989: 1549, 1573). Company law may require approval of a public authority so that the powers of the majority shareholders are restricted.[8] Quorum and supermajority requirements may ensure that a significant majority has approved the decision in question; fiduciary principles may control the voting of the majority shareholder; or appraisal rights may provide the minority shareholder with a way to exit the company for full compensation. For details see Table 10.1, variables II 1, 2, 7.1, 9.1. If one of these elements is disregarded, a study which uses quantified legal variables for econometric purposes may be flawed because it does not measure shareholder protection properly. Similarly, for a leximetric study of this nature, important functional equivalents must not be ignored in providing a coherent and meaningful characterization of the law.

Finally, it is crucial to consider basic insights of comparative law. A comparative lawyer must not impose his or her own conceptions on a foreign legal system. The concept is summed up well in one of the leading comparative law textbooks:

> Europeans and Americans must be constantly aware, when studying non-Western legal systems and cultures, that they must not approach or appraise these systems from their Western viewpoints or judge them by European or American standards. For example some Western lawyers concluded in the 1970s that China has no legal system because she has no attorneys in the American or European sense, no independent judiciary, no Codes, and, since the Cultural Revolution, no system of legal education. Yet, this is surely to judge a non-Western system by Western standards, rather like the Western visitor who assumed that there was no 'proper' music played in China because he did not see any Western instruments in the Chinese concert hall he visited. (De Cruz, 1999: 223)

In order to minimize any 'home bias', in the construction of our variables we have therefore looked at the OECD's 'Principles on corporate governance' (OECD, 2004), the comparative literature on company law (for example Cools, 2005; Zetzsche, 2004; Siems, 2008a), as well as the laws of the countries themselves. We have also considered that there can be significant differences between developed and developing countries in terms of the crucial concerns for protection of shareholders.[9] We have therefore endeavoured in our choice of variables to reflect some of the distinctive features of Indian company law for the protection of shareholders (Table 10.1, variables I 18, II 7 (3).

The Coding

Attributing and comparing legal differences by numbers is contrary to the traditional way of doing comparative law. The use of a quantitative methodology to account for variations across legal systems is inevitably reductive and, as such, may be subjected to some searching criticisms (Siems, 2005a: 521). However, we believe that with a cautious approach, it has the potential to open new vistas of research in the area of comparative law and as such should not be shunned. In fact, the penultimate section of this chapter provides an illustration of interesting possibilities that diligent quantification of legal rules offers for comparing variations across time series and across legal systems.

The coding of legal rules is difficult, because law is not a 'thing' which can be quantified as easily as money, cars, or persons. In this exercise, it is often easier to define a variable, we realized, than to actually ascertain the law and code it by assigning it a number. It is sometimes a matter of legal judgment (as in variables I. 13, II. 17 in Table 10.1). The way we have sought to tackle this issue is to ensure that lawyers trained in the

Table 10.2   Shareholder protection index (extract: France)

	70	71	72	73	74	75	76	77	78	79	80	81
I[1]	1[2]	1	1	1	1	1	1	1	1	1	1	1
	1[3]	1	1	1	1	1	1	1	1	1	1	1
	1[4]	1	1	1	1	1	1	1	1	1	1	1
	0[5]	0	0	0	0	0	0	0	0	0	0	0
	½[6]	½	½	½	½	½	½	½	½	½	½	½
	1[7]	1	1	1	1	1	1	1	1	1	1	1
	1[8]	1	1	1	1	1	1	1	1	1	1	1

jurisdictions did the actual coding; alternatively, we have sought such experts to validate our coding. But as is common knowledge, lawyers even from the same jurisdiction may disagree on the position of law. We believe that transparency is a solution to this problem. Space prevents us from including all but a few variables as illustration (see Table 10.2); our entire coding and explanatory notes are, however, available online (Lele and Siems, 2007).

In this interesting and often treacherous journey through the legal systems of five countries, we encountered some difficult patches; for instance, where our path reached a fork or was unclear we had to choose which direction to follow. However, throughout this exercise we have been guided by the underlying principles of 'functionality' and 'transparency'.

Areas of law

Our coding concerns shareholder protection only, as opposed to investor protection in general. We started by looking at company law. However, in some cases it was necessary to take securities law into account, because certain aspects of the protection of shareholders from directors and majority shareholders may be addressed in securities law. An example is the US securities law on the appointment of proxy, which is to a large extent regulated in federal securities law (SEC Regulation 14a; SEC Rules 14a-1 to 14b-2). Functionally it makes no difference which area of law addresses a particular topic. We should mention here that in coding we considered law as it applies to listed companies, which also explains why we find provisions relevant for some of the variables in securities law. This is because the economic data that will be combined and tested in the further econometric study for which these indices form the basis is available with respect to listed companies (see now Armour *et al.*, 2008).

However, because of our focus on rules which address the protection of 'shareholders as such' and not investors in general, most areas of securities law have not been taken into account. For instance, the rules on insider trading, on public disclosure and transparency of financial information, as well as accounting requirements, are not coded in detail (but see Table 10.1, variables I 7, 10.2 and II 8). The prohibition of insider trading aims at protection of investors and capital markets in general but not specifically at the protection of 'shareholders as such'.[10] The disclosure of financial information and accounting requirements are general topics which also target the protection of bondholders, other lenders, financial markets, and perhaps even society as a whole. We therefore believe these legal topics should be addressed in separate indices (similar La Porta *et al.*, 2006 and Djankov *et al.*, 2008).

Mandatory as well as default rules
One of the difficult questions that we had to decide was to what extent we should code default rules as well as mandatory law. In Part I of our variables (see Table 10.1) no distinction has been made between default and mandatory law. Since these variables address the protection of shareholders against directors and managers, the thinking is that the shareholders can together prevent deviation from a default rule which aims at their protection. Conversely, with respect to the protection of shareholders against major shareholders (Part II of our variables), there are some variables which only code mandatory law (specifically, variables II 3.2–3, 10; the law on variables II 6, 7.2–3, 8 is also mandatory in all countries). The reason for this is the principle of functionality, as mandatory rules can be an instrument to protect minority shareholders against tunnelling by the majority. Furthermore, three (sub-)variables address the question of whether minority shareholders can prevent the majority of shareholders from opting out of the protection of shareholders against directors and managers (variables II 10.1–10.3). This is important if the board can control the shareholder meeting or if the majority shareholders and board act together, because in these cases the protection against the board and other shareholders is rendered interchangeable.

As far as default rules are concerned, the corporate governance codes and, in the case of the UK and India Table A of British and Indian company law, have also been taken into account, for instance in variables I 4.6, 9.2–3; see also variable I 17. Since all companies in these countries need articles of association, the Table A regulations operate as an 'off-the-shelf' model. Likewise, for listed companies, corporate governance codes can be at least as important as default rules. This is because non-compliance of corporate governance codes may severely hinder corporate finance and thus the very purpose of being listed may be impaired. Thus, at least in developed countries, compliance with corporate governance codes is the rule. For the UK see Arcot and Bruno (2006); for Germany, Werder *et al.* (2005); for France, Hebert (2004).

We also coded the British City Code on Takeovers and Mergers. Although it is not statutory law and legal sanctions are often not available, compliance is the rule (Armour and Skeel, 2007). Our index takes the City Code into account to provide a meaningful picture of how shareholders are protected in the case of takeovers in the UK.

Non-uniform law and listing rules

For federal states, coding may lead to a problem if the law on shareholder protection is not regulated in a uniform way. From among our five countries, this was a concern with respect to the US alone; company law is uniform in Germany, India and the UK. More than half a million business entities have their legal home in Delaware, including more than 50 per cent of all US publicly-traded companies and 58 per cent of the Fortune 500 (see Delaware, 2006). We therefore decided to look at the Delaware General Corporation Law (DGCL).

A related problem exists where there is more than one stock exchange in one country. Here we have chosen the dominant stock exchange, for instance we considered the NYSE rules in coding for the US.

Furthermore, listing rules are sometimes based on statutory law and sometimes on self-regulation of the stock exchange. For example, in the UK the listing rules were only the LSE's own private requirements until 1985, when they were given a statutory basis (see Powell, 1988: paras. 2–3, 5–11). In 2000 the Financial Services and Markets Act shifted the competence for the listing rules from the LSE to the UK Listing Authority, a component of the Financial Services Authority. Similarly, in India the Listing Agreement Form has had statutory force only since 1995 (see the amended s. 21 of the Securities Contract (Regulation) Act 1956). However, from a functional perspective these differences do not matter, as even in the past listed companies could not escape the listing requirements, and so these self-regulatory rules have also been taken into account in our coding.

Statutory and case law

A particular legal rule can be based on statutory law or case law. With respect to case law, a doctrinal approach may be put forward that in common-law countries case law is regarded as a source of law, whereas in civil law countries court decisions are merely seen as a clarification of the existing law (see, for example, Glenn, 2004: 177, 237). However, our index does not make this distinction. Despite the different starting point, in both common-law and civil-law countries court decisions can have an effect which is as important as a statutory provision (see, for example, Markesinis, 1997, 2001). Thus, following a functional approach we have taken into account statutory law as well as court decisions and the legal changes brought about by them.

Statutory law has been coded in the year in which it came into force, and case law in the year in which it was delivered and reported. There are questions about statutes passed but not yet in force, or decisions either unpublished or expected, but these are aspects of the law that cannot be considered for coding. For further discussion, see Bhagat and Romano (2007).

Unweighted variables

Another issue that we considered in coding the variables for this study was that of weighting of variables.[11] It is conceivable that not all of our variables will have the same significance in all the countries. Naturally, geopolitical considerations, economic concerns, or cultural differences may mean that some of the measures coded here have more importance in some countries than others. However, having considered the option of weighting the variables, which presents the subjective decision of how much weight to give to each variable in each country, we decided in favour of unweighted measures. It is arguable therefore that our index does not fully capture the comparative shareholder protection. In our defence we yet again rely on our functional approach, which has meant that we have taken into account the existence of functional equivalents across jurisdictions. This explains the large number of variables. To be sure, we do not claim that the variables coded are the only or the maximum or even the optimum rules for protection of shareholders: what we have attempted here is to choose and code variables that are capable of acting as proxies for the protection of shareholders in these countries.

Non-binary coding

Finally, it had to be decided whether to use binary coding only (0, 1) or non-binary numbers too (½, ⅓, ¼, ⅔, ⅝, and so on). Against the use of binary coding in some of the previous studies it was argued that binary evaluation of legal systems according to '0 or 1' is a very simplified method to judge the extent of shareholder protection (Braendle, 2006: 264, 276 on La Porta *et al.*, 1998; Baums and Scott, 2003). However, one can equally criticize the use of non-binary coding: whereas the use of '0' and '1' can easily be translated as 'yes' and 'no', the non-binary use of numbers for law can appear to be arbitrary (Siems, 2005c: 305).

Here, we decided to use binary as well as non-binary numbers because it is not always possible to translate legal rules into 'yes'-'no' questions. For instance, the statutory law may be ambiguous, or judges may disagree. If no clearly predominant opinion exists, it is more accurate to code a variable as '½' or some other intermediary score than to randomly decide that either the '1' or the '0' score is more persuasive. Furthermore, non-binary coding has the advantage that more information can be included in a single variable. For example, according to our index, the variable which measures the information which shareholders get in case of amendments of the articles of association 'equals 1 if the exact wording has to be sent in advance (push-system), equals 0.5 if the shareholders have to request it (pull-system), and equals 0 otherwise' (Table 10.1, variable I 5.1). Here it might be objected that there is no reason why a 'pull-system' is exactly half as good as a 'push-system'. This is indeed a fair point, and non-binary coding is undeniably to some extent a matter of judgment. However, law is complex and we believe that a faithful coding should also reflect this very feature of law. Non-binary coding can therefore lead to more meaningful results than the mere use of '0' and '1'.

LEXIMETRICS: THE RESULTS

Using our shareholder protection index, various interesting questions can be addressed: For instance, it can be asked which country scores the maximum on our shareholder protection index; how much these legal systems have changed over the years; whether differences follow the distinction into civil-law and common-law countries; and whether the laws of the five countries are converging or diverging. In this section we consider some of these questions using graphical representations of values of the five indices that we constructed for our panel countries.

General Shareholder Protection Aggregate

At the outset, we simply aggregated all 60 variables from our shareholder protection index for each of the countries and represented it graphically. The resultant graph is shown in Figure 10.1.

The five curves in Figure 10.1 demonstrate some common features. First, all of them exhibit a general upward movement, which means that the aggregate value of the indices increased with time. Thus, legal shareholder protection has been improving over the last three decades. In particular there has been an enhancement in shareholder protection in the last five years, which given the recent attention to good corporate governance is hardly surprising. Second, at times the curves climbed down a few

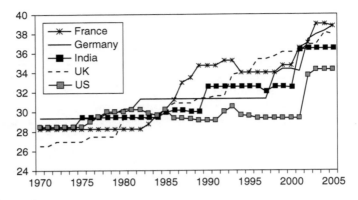

Figure 10.1   General aggregate (60 variables)

points. This phenomenon, which took place particularly in the 1980s and
1990s, can be explained by the desire to make the law more flexible as it
is believed to be more business friendly. For instance, in some countries
the issuing of stock options without approval of the general meeting, the
exclusion of pre-emptive rights, or the squeeze out of minority shareholders was introduced or became easier.[12] Third, most curves have plateaux
and steps: law does not usually change gradually. On the one hand, there
may be years when a particular part of the law, such as the protection
of shareholders, does not change at all. On the other, a law reform or a
bundle of court decisions may lead to amendments to various aspects of
shareholder protection resulting in a sharp rise in the value of an index in
a short time.

In addition to the common features above, the curve for each country
has specific features of its own. In particular, regarding the UK law one
can see a fairly constant improvement of shareholder protection. The
steps in 1980, 1985 and in the 1990s were caused mainly by the company
law reforms and the codes of best practice (Cadbury Committee, 1992;
Greenbury Committee, 1995; Hampel Committee, 1998). There are also
relatively smaller steps which were, for example, the result of the strengthening case law on directors' duties.[13] The US curve looks quite different.
As we have coded Delaware corporate law, which is famous for its 'light
approach' in regulating the internal affairs of companies, it is no surprise
that for most of the time-series the US values are lower than the ones of
the other countries. Critics call this a 'race to the bottom' (Cary, 1974);
others emphasize its efficiency (Romano, 1993: 14). There are certainly
frequent changes in the Delaware General Corporation Law, which is normally amended every year, as well as important decisions by the Delaware

courts.[14] However, these events have not led to major reorientations of Delaware's law on shareholder protection. The steep rise in 2002 reflects the changes brought about by the Sarbanes Oxley Act 2002 which led to a strengthening of shareholder protection.[15]

In contrast, French shareholder protection law shows a remarkable improvement in the late 1980s and early 1990s,[16] and in these years it was, perhaps surprisingly, clearly more shareholder friendly than the law of the other countries. The curve dropped a few points during the mid-90s, because of the belief that French company law should become more flexible.[17] As with the other curves, the French curve has again followed an upward movement since 1999.[18] In this respect, only the German situation is similar to the French; apart from changes in the late 1990s and early 2000,[19] the German law on shareholder protection has been relatively stable. An explanation could be that some of the European company law directives of the 1970s and early 1980s were based on German company law.[20] Furthermore, in the 1980s and early 1990s other legal topics such as the reform proposals on the German contract law and insolvency law, and problems related to German unification, were at the fore.

Lastly, the Indian curve also shows phases of relative stability during most of the mid-1990s, as also in the 1970s and early 1980s, and a giant leap in 2001. Apart from developments in the takeover law,[21] the shareholder protection law during the 1990s remained largely unchanged.[22] There could be at least two possible explanations for this: first, the Indian economy was opening up, so other areas of law were deemed more crucial for the process of liberalization and therefore deserved more attention from the legislators: for instance, the liberalization of the internal regulatory framework, reduction in tariffs, adoption of appropriate exchange rates, and permitting foreign investment to play a significant role in the economy. Second, with the onset of liberalization the stock market capitalization rose, shareholding became relatively more dispersed (and included foreign investors); the issues concerning corporate governance came to the fore only after this initial period of stock market growth. The series of corporate scandals (see Goswami, 2003: 105 for a discussion on these early scandals) that followed the initial period of liberalization emphasized the need for better corporate governance, culminating in the adoption of improved corporate governance provisions, reflected in the gain of significant points around 2001.[23] What emerges therefore, from the Indian experience, is a pattern where the law follows rather than leads investor expectations as well as economic development.[24]

In analysing these differences and developments one cannot help wondering whether French law really offers 'better' shareholder protection than US law, and if so, whether investors should redirect their capital.

The clear answer is that this implication cannot be made. First of all, it has to be remembered that we coded the law on shareholder protection alone, and have not considered other aspects such as financial disclosure, the rule of law or socio-economic attitudes, which may also be related to shareholder protection. Second, the extent and manner in which shareholders should be protected can vary with time, dependent on a number of factors, such as the extent of blockholder control or dispersed share ownership structures, and the level of development of legal and economic institutions. Thus, not the absolute score but the legal adaptability of a particular legal system may be more important (Siems, 2006). In this respect it is often said that Delaware has a particular advantage because of its judiciary (Romano, 1993: 37). However, legal adaptability is not restricted to case law alone because, for example, the frequent changes in French company law in the 1980s were mainly caused by reforms of the codified law (see note 16). Third, more shareholder protection need not necessarily be better. Company law has to balance different interests so that an 'optimum' rather than a 'maximum' of shareholder protection has to be found. (For related lines of reasoning see Anabtawi, 2006; Bainbridge, 2006; Stout, 2002.) For example, while the value of the shareholder protection index for the US has increased considerably in recent years as a result of the Sarbanes Oxley Act, the changes brought about by the Act and its implications have received criticism and some scepticism as to whether it would actually mean an improvement in corporate governance (see, for example, Romano, 2005).

A related point, and fourth, is that some of the variables in our index have been included and coded because they are relevant for shareholder protection but they may actually be unsatisfactory because they excessively restrict companies.[25] For example, mandatory company law protects minority shareholders, because it prevents the majority from changing the articles in order to exploit the minority.[26] However, its inflexibility may in the end be a problem not only for the majority of shareholders but may also harm the company in general and thus the shareholders as a whole. Reference can also be made to the 'nexus-of-contracts' conception of the company; see, for example, Easterbrook and Fischel (1991). Another example is the control of appointment of managers by government or public authority (Table 10.1, variable I 18.2). In a country like India where many companies have traditionally been family dominated enterprises, the majority shareholders would typically fill managerial places with their own kinship. Therefore, control over appointment of managers by the government in the interest of the shareholders can seem to be protective of the shareholders. Yet, this control mechanism can lead to delays and foster rent-seeking behaviour that could hinder business and be harmful

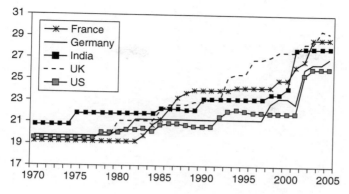

Figure 10.2   Protection against boards (42 variables)

to shareholders as a whole. For instance, in India the requirement of prior authorization of the government for appointment of managerial personnel has been relaxed since 1988, with the introduction of Schedule XIII (as amended from time to time), admittedly to make the law more flexible and to give companies more freedom in this respect.

Aggregates of Specific Groups of Variables

In order to obtain a more meaningful picture than that provided by the general aggregate above it can be useful to deconstruct our index of 60 variables and look at aggregates of specific groups of variables. One way of doing this is to look at the variables which protect shareholders against board and managers on the one hand, and those that protect minority shareholders against majority shareholders on the other (Table 10.1, variables I and II). The result can be seen in Figures 10.2 and 10.3.

First, it is clear that protection of shareholders against directors and managers has increased considerably in all the countries, whereas protection against other shareholders has not changed significantly. The exception is the US curve, which loses a few points in the 1980s and 1990s in particular because of introduction of flexibility in issuance of shares with varying voting rights and in exclusion of liability for breach of duty of care (variables II 3.2–3, 10.1). One way to explain this could be that the growing importance of capital markets leads to more dispersed shareholder ownership (for details see Siems, 2008a: 277–88); this increased shareholder base may exert pressure to improve the protection of shareholders against directors and managers. Second, distinguishing between different countries, protection against other shareholders is more important in blockholder countries, because here there is a danger that major

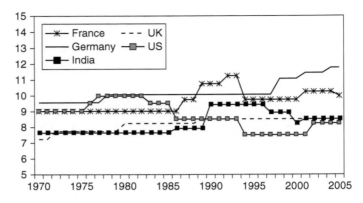

Figure 10.3   Protection against other shareholders (18 variables)

shareholders exploit the minority. Given the fact that blockholders often dominate public companies in India, France and Germany, this could be the reason why these countries perform better, according to Figure 10.3, than the UK and the US, where dispersed shareholder ownership is more common. On differences in shareholder structure see, for example, Barca and Becht (2001) and Van den Berghe (2002: 34). Third, however, Figure 10.2 does not show similar differences between blockholder and dispersed ownership countries. This is noteworthy because it refutes the argument that there is an indispensable link between dispersed shareholder owner-ship and strong shareholder protection (La Porta *et al.*, 1998). This does not, of course, mean that shareholder protection is unimportant in this respect; a certain level of shareholder protection can still be a necessary (but not sufficient) precondition for the separation of ownership and control through dispersed holdings (Roe, 2002: 233).

Convergence and Divergence of the Law

At first glance, Figure 10.1 may give the impression that in 2001 the laws of the UK, India, France and Germany were identical because all four coun-tries have approximately the same score of 38 out of 60 variables. This would, however, not be a fair assessment. As Figure 10.1 simply shows the aggregate of all the variables, it is perfectly possible and indeed is the case, that different variables have led to similar scores for the UK, India, France and Germany. Therefore to highlight the differences between the countries with a view to identifying trends of convergence or divergence we have calculated the differences between each variable in the law of a particular legal system and the same variable in the law of the other

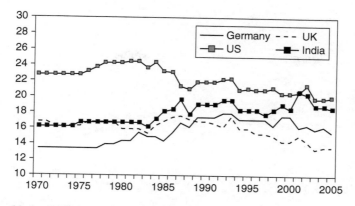

Figure 10.4 Difference from French law (max. 60)

countries. Subsequently, the absolute values of these differences have been added together and represented graphically in Figures 10.4 and 10.5. For example, Figure 10.4 displays four curves that represent the difference between French law and each of the other panel countries. The lower a country's score, the more similar is its law to French law. Thus, a country would, for instance, produce a score of 0 if it were completely identical to French law, and 60 if it were completely different.

With respect to the differences from French law in Figure 10.4 the most interesting curves are those that represent Germany and the UK. One may expect that German and French law would be least different because both countries belong to the civil-law family and in both countries blockholders have typically dominated public companies. This can indeed be confirmed until the late 1980s. Since then, however, UK law is the least different from French law, because French and UK law have converged[27] and French and German law have diverged.[28] Path dependencies based on legal families have not prevented this development. Furthermore, it is interesting to note that all along the indices for the two European countries (UK and Germany) have had values considerably more similar to French law values than have the two non-European countries (US and India). Here again, communication between the European countries, or even a common European legal culture, appears to be stronger than the categorization into different legal families.

With respect to the difference from UK law in Figure 10.5, Indian law is least different, then French, then German and once again US law is the most different. Indian law is predictably similar to UK law because of its common-law legal origin. However, it has developed certain features of its own to suit its socio-economic conditions, such as the law in relation to

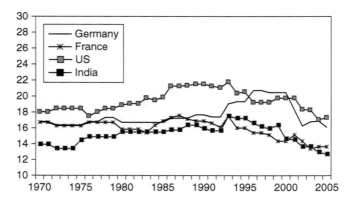

Figure 10.5   Difference from UK law (max. 60)

public enforcement of company law (Table 10.1, variable I 18), and these variables seem to ensure a constant difference between the two countries for the entire duration of the time-series. Changes in UK law[29] took the two countries further away from each other during the 1990s, although the introduction of Indian corporate governance provisions based largely on the UK codes has reduced the difference in the last few years.[30] A comparable recent development can be seen for the other countries. It is remarkable, however, that for almost the entire period French law has been similar to UK law and that US law has been very different.[31] Our results therefore contradict any claims to the effect that there are deep differences between shareholder protection in the civil-law and the common-law origin countries. For such claims see La Porta *et al.* (1998) and Djankov *et al.* (2008).

The differences from German, Indian and US law have not been included for lack of space. However, the next two figures display differences between all the countries and therefore compensate for the absence. Figure 10.6 shows the mean of all the differences of all five countries from every other country. For example, the US curve indicates how different US law is from the law of the UK, Germany, France and India. Once again, a score of 0 would mean that it was completely identical, and 60 that it was completely different. Finally, Figure 10.7 displays the mean of the five curves of Figure 10.6.

The fact that in Figure 10.6 the US curve has the highest scores means that US law has always been more different than the law of the other four countries, while the US curve occasionally climbing down a few points, especially since 2000, may indicate some Americanization of the law of the other countries. Indeed, our data suggests that, in some respect, the

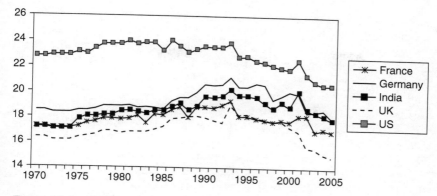

Figure 10.6   Difference from other countries (max. 60)

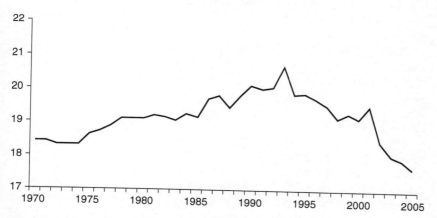

Figure 10.7   Mean of all differences (max. 60)

law of the other countries has become more similar to US law.[32] Equally, with respect to some variables US law has become more similar to the law of the other countries.[33] But, given the continuing differences between US law and the law of the other countries, Figure 10.6 shows that there is no general Americanization of the law on shareholder protection. It is also interesting that UK law has always been more 'mainstream', that is the UK law has been the least different from the law of all the other countries. The explanation may be that the UK is a member of both the common-law and the European families, and thus influences and/or absorbs different legal traditions. Finally, it is remarkable that the curves of the five countries hardly ever overlap. The differences in the level of internationality are therefore fairly stable. Perhaps the degree to which a country takes foreign ideas into account is a deep factor in legal culture which does not change considerably over time.

Non-quantitative research disagrees about the question of whether there is convergence in company law (see Gordon and Roe, 2004; McDonnell, 2002: 341; Branson, 2001; Gilson, 2001; Hansmann and Kraakman, 2001; and Siems, 2008a). Our quantitative result is that the dropping curves in Figure 10.6 indicate that the laws of the five countries are converging over recent years. This overall tendency becomes even clearer in Figure 10.7. Two points in time are particularly important: 1993/4 and 2001/2. During 1993/4, France made its law more flexible, and thus the values of variables I 12.2, II 1, 6 dropped, whereas in the UK the Cadbury Code of Best Practice was applied, and the values of variables I 9.1–3, 12.2, 17 rose. This led to a divergence, but in the succeeding years the other countries followed the UK model and enacted similar corporate governance codes. The convergence has increased significantly since 2001/2. Following the burst of the dot-com bubble and the string of corporate scandals at the beginning of the century in many parts of the world, all five countries changed the law in a similar pattern. Consequently, Figure 10.7 indicates that globalization in shareholder protection is indeed taking place.

CONCLUSION

In this chapter we have built a new and meaningful shareholder protection index for five countries and have coded the development of the law over three and a half decades. Attributing and comparing legal differences by numbers is contrary to the traditional study of comparative law, and the use of a quantitative methodology to account for variations across legal systems has been subjected to some searching criticisms (Siems, 2005a). However, we believe that with a cautious approach, it has the potential to open new vistas of research in the area of comparative law and as such should not be shunned. In fact, this chapter provides an illustration of the interesting possibilities that diligent quantification of legal rules provides for comparing variations across time-series and across legal systems.

Our leximetric study has found, first, that in all of the countries studied (UK, US, Germany, France, India), shareholder protection has been improving over the last 35 years. Second, our data shows that the law on shareholder protection in the US is weaker than the law of the other four countries. Third, we have found that one of the reasons for this is that the protection of minority against majority shareholders is considerably stronger in the 'blockholder countries' of France, Germany and India. Fourth, our examination of the legal differences between the five countries does not confirm the distinction between common-law and civil-law countries. Our results therefore suggest that, on diligent coding of shareholder protection law based on a meaningful shareholder protection index and in particular taking into account functional equivalents of legal instruments for protection, the claims that there are deep differences between shareholder protection in civil-law and common-law countries seem to wither away. Finally, we have found that convergence in shareholder protection has been taking place since 1993 and has increased considerably since 2001.

It should be noted that we have not examined whether a better 'score' in our shareholder protection index does matter for good corporate governance and ultimately for the economic development of a country. It could be the case that more shareholder protection hinders companies and thus has a contrary effect. We will, however, be examining this question in the future, when our indices will constitute a basis for an econometric study combining financial data to find statistical relationships between legal and economic criteria (see now Armour *et al.*, 2008).

NOTES

1. This chapter is adapted from the first of a series of papers that we are producing as part of the project on 'Law, Finance and Development' at the Centre for Business Research, University of Cambridge. The project aims to consider the mechanisms by which legal institutions shape national financial systems, so as to identify the implications of legal reform for economic development. It is an interdisciplinary project which combines qualitative and quantitative research methodology to yield a uniquely complete set of empirical results.
2. See also Coffee (2001); in note 6 he states, 'by no means is it here implied that these rights are unimportant, but only that they supply partial and sometimes easily outflanked safeguards, which have little to do with the protection of control and the entitlement to a control premium'. Similar observations have been made with respect to the indices for creditor protection and labour law: see Armour *et al.* (2002) and Ahlering and Deakin (2007).
3. For example, the California General Corporation Law, § 301.5(a) on the one hand and the Delaware General Corporation Law, § 214 on the other.
4. See, for example, Schmidt (1997), a book of almost 2000 pages, which discusses the appointment of directors at 838–41 but does not mention cumulative voting even once.
5. For example Braendle (2006: 275) has observed that 'The formulation of the framework of the different criteria often seems strange. In some parts it is sufficient to score if company laws provide for an option for a right, in other parts rights have to be mandatory to acquire a point. It is obvious that this framework benefits Common Law.'
6. La Porta *et al.* (1998: 1122) state that this variable 'equals one if the company law or commercial code grants minority shareholders either a judicial venue to challenge the decisions of management or of the assembly or the right to step out of the company by requiring the company to purchase their shares when they object to certain fundamental changes, such as mergers, asset dispositions, and changes in the articles of

incorporation. The variable equals zero otherwise. Minority shareholders are defined as those shareholders who own 10 per cent of share capital or less.'

7. In the expansion of our research we shall include some transition economies, as well as more developed and developing economies; when we include these countries, we may modify or add to our existing list of variables to better reflect the laws on shareholder protection in these countries; see now Siems (2008b); Armour *et al.* (2008).

8. In India, for example, any amendment to the articles of association which has the effect of converting a public company into a private company does not have any effect unless approved by the Central Government (CA 1956, s. 31 (1), proviso).

9. See, for example, Berkman *et al.* (2005: 47), who have observed that, 'although it is critical to improve on the transparencies of business practices, especially in developing countries, it seems that it is inappropriate to merely follow the corporate governance measures prepared by other developed countries. The mere imposition of minimum proportion of independent directors on every listed company does not seem to be a panacea to the problems of corporate governance.' Similar opinions are expressed by Varma (1997), Chakrabarti (2005) and Khanna (2000).

10. Indirectly, however, shareholders may be protected; on the divisive nature of the prohibition of insider trading see Manne (1966), Romano (1993: 103), and Calaba (2001: 457, 474).

11. Previous studies have received criticism on this count: see Braendle (2006: 276) on the shareholder protection index; Siems (2005) on the securities law index; and Ahlering and Deakin (2007) on the labour law index. Ahlering and Deakin suggest that 'One possible answer to this objection is that weightings for cross-national indices are extremely difficult to determine, and that an unweighted index might be less biased than one based on subjective attempts at weighting'.

12. Exchange Act Release No. 34-36356, 60 Fed. Reg. 53 832 (1995); Gesetz für kleine Aktiengesell-schaften und zur Deregulierung des Aktienrechts, 2. 8. 1994, BGBl. I 1961; Loi no 1993-1444 du 31 décembre 1993.

13. *Norman v Theodore Goddard* [1991] BCLC 1027; *Re D'Jan of London* [1994] 1 BCLC 561; *Bishopsgate Investment Management Ltd. v Maxwell (No. 2)* [1994] 1 All ER 261; *Re Barings plc (No.5)* [1999] 1 BCLC 433, esp. 486–9; *Re Landhurst Leasing plc* [1999] 1 BCLC 286.

14. For example on takeover law *Unocal Corp. v Mesa Petroleum*, Co., 493 A.2d 946 (Del. Supr. 1985); *Moran v Household Int'l, Inc.*, 500 A.2d 1346, 1350 (Del. 1985); *Revlon, Inc. v MacAndrews & Forbes Holdings, Inc.*, 506 A.2d 173 (Del. Supr 1986); *Paramount Communications, Inc. v Time, Inc.*, 1989 WL 79880 (Del Ch. 1989); *Paramount Communications, Inc. v QVC Network, Inc.*, 637 A.2d 34 (Del. Ch. 1994); *Unitrin, Inc., v American General Corp.*, 651 A.2d 1361 (Del. 1995).

15. Sarbanes-Oxley Act (Public Company Accounting Reform and Investor Protection Act) (USA) of 30.07.2002, Pub. L. No. 107-204, 116 Stat. 745; for example with respect to committees, independence requirements, corporate governance guidelines, and disqualification.

16. For example by Loi no 83-3 du 3 janvier 1983; Loi no 84-148 du 1er mars 1984; Loi no 85-98 du janvier 1985; Décret no 86-584 du 14 mars 1986; Loi no. 87-416 du 17 juin 1987; Loi no 88-17 du 5 janvier 1988; Loi 89-531 du 2 août 1989; Arrête du 15 mai 1992.

17. Loi no 94-126 du 11 février; Loi 94-679 du 8 août 1994; Loi no 1993-1444 du 31 décembre 1993.

18. Caused by Code de Commerce 2000; Loi no 2001-420 du 15 mai 2001; Décret no 2002-803 du 3 mai 2002; Loi no 2003-706 du 1er août 2003; Loi no. 2005-842 du 24 juilliet 2005; also Principes de gouvernement d'entreprise résultant de la consolidation des rapports conjoints de l'AFEP et du MEDEF, 2003.

19. Gesetz zur Namensaktie and zur Erleichterung der Stimmrechtsausübung (NaStraG), 18.1.2001, BGBl. I 123; Unternehmensübernahme-Regelungsgesetz, 20.12.2001, BGBl. I 3822; Viertes Finanzmarktförderungsgesetz, 21.6.2002, BGBl. I 2010;

Transparenz-und Publizitätsgesetz (TransPuG), 19.7.2002, BGBl. I 2681; Gesetz zur Unternehmensintegrität und Modernisierung des Anfechtungs-rechts (UMAG), 22.9.2005, BGBl. I 2802; Gesetz über die Offenlegung der Vorstandsvergütungen (VorstOG), 3.8.2005, BGBl. I 2267.

20. For example, the Second Council Directive 77/91/EEC; Third Council Directive 78/855/EEC; Sixth Council Directive 82/891/EEC.

21. With the introduction of Clause 40A and 40B of Listing Agreement in 1990 and then the introduction of SEBI (Substantial Acquisition of Shares and Takeovers) Regulations of 1994 and 1997.

22. This was in fact the period of most dramatic change in India, with the onset of liberalization. However, the concentration on shareholder protection is probably too narrow to adequately capture the changes taking place in corporate finance in developing countries; see Singh *et al.* (2002).

23. As a result of the introduction of Clause 49 to the Listing Agreement and also amendments to the Companies Act 1956 itself. Although Clause 49 was introduced by the Securities and Exchange Board of India (SEBI) in 2000, the changes brought about have been coded from 2001, because compliance with the clause was required in a phased manner depending on the size of the listed companies, beginning from March 2001.

24. For instance see Singh *et al.* (2002: 20). A similar view has been put forward in relation to the development of securities markets in the US and UK; see Coffee (2001: 77). See also Cheffins (2001); and for a different view La Porta *et al.* (2006).

25. Apart from the examples mentioned in the text, one may, for example, criticise the inflexibility of quorum and supermajority requirements (Table 10.1, variables II 1 and 2) and the deterrent effect of the mandatory bid (variable II 3.2) on takeovers. On this topic see, for example, Enriques (2004).

26. See Table 10.1, variable II 10; the aggregate scores for this variable in our data for 2005 are Germany: 4 points; France: 3 points; India: 2.5 points; UK: 2 points; US: 1.5 points.

27. For example, comparing our data on shareholder protection in 1980 and 2005, there are now fewer differences between the two countries with respect to proxy voting (variable I 4), shares not blocked (variable I 6), board division (variable I 9.1), duty of care (variable I 13), and disclosure of major shareholder ownership (variable II 8).

28. For example, comparing our data on shareholder protection in 1980 and 2005, there are now more differences between the two countries with respect to the power of the general meeting for *de facto* changes (variable I 1.4), proxy voting (variable I 4), individual information rights (variable I 5), the right to access the register of shareholders (variable I 8.1), the 'one share one vote' principle (variable II 3), and appraisal rights (variable II 7).

29. See the Cadbury (1992), Greenbury (1995) and Hampel (1998) Committees on best practice, and the cases listed in Note 13.

30. Clause 49 of the Listing Agreement, introduced in 2000 by the SEBI, see its circular dated 21-2-2000 and implemented from 2001 onwards.

31. Differences between US and UK law concern, for example, the power of the general meeting (variable I 1), the right to call an extraordinary shareholder meeting (variable I 3), proxy voting (variable I 4), duration of director's appointment (variable I 13), board neutrality in case of takeovers (variable I 14.2), supermajority requirements (variable II 2), the mandatory bid (variable II 7.2), pre-emptive rights (variable II 15), and entrenched boards (variable II 10.2).

32. This concerns, in particular, the variables on proxy voting (variable I 4), committees (variable I 9.2), performance based remuneration (variable I 11), private enforcement (variable I 13.3), one share one vote (variable II 3), and disclosure of major shareholder ownership (variable II 8).

33. In particular, the variables on board division (variable I 9.1), general meeting power for remuneration (variable I 10.1), public enforcement (variable I 18.3), and shareholder protection mandatory (variable II 10).

REFERENCES

Note: all websites were accessed on 11 August 2006.

Ahlering, B. and S. F. Deakin (2007), 'Labour regulation, corporate governance and legal origin: a case of institutional complementarity?', *Law & Society Review*, **41**, 865–98.

Anabtawi, I. (2006), 'Some skepticism about increasing shareholder power', *UCLA Law Review*, **53**, 561–600.

Arcot S. R. and V. G. Bruno (2006), 'In letter not in spirit: an analysis of corporate governance in the UK', http://fmg.lse.ac.uk/~arcot/CGPaper1.pdf.

Armour, J. and D. A. Skeel (2007), 'Who writes the rules for hostile takeovers, and why? The peculiar divergence of US and UK takeover regulation', *Georgetown Law Journal*, **95**, 1727–94.

Armour, J., B. R. Cheffins and D. A. Skeel (2002), 'Corporate ownership structure and the evolution of bankruptcy law: lessons from the United Kingdom', *Vanderbilt Law Review*, **55**, 1699–785.

Armour, J., S. Deakin, M. Siems, P. Sarkar and A. Singh (2008), 'Shareholder protection and stock market development: an empirical test of the legal origins hypothesis', http://ssrn.com/abstract=1094355.

Bainbridge, S.M. (2006), 'The case for limited shareholder voting rights', *UCLA Law Review*, **53**, 601–36.

Barca, F. and M. Becht (eds) (2001), *The Control of Corporate Europe*, London: Oxford University Press.

Baums, T. and K. Scott (2003), 'Taking shareholder protection seriously? Corporate governance in the United States and Germany', http://ssrn.com/abstract=473185.

Bebchuk, L. A. (2005a), 'The case for increasing shareholder power', *Harvard Law Review*, **118**, 833–914.

Bebchuk, L. A. (2005b), 'The case for shareholder access: a response to the business round table', *Case Western Reserve Law Review*, **55**, 557–68.

Bebchuk, L. A. and A. Cohen (2005), 'The costs of entrenched boards', *Journal of Financial Economics*, **78**, 409–33.

Bebchuk, L. A. and J. M. Fried (2004), *Pay Without Performance: the Unfulfilled Promise of Executive Compensation*, Cambridge MA: Harvard University Press.

Berglöf, E. and E. L. von Thadden (1999), 'The changing corporate governance paradigm: implications for transition and developing countries', http://ssrn.com/abstract=183708.

Berkman, H., R. A. Cole, A. Lee, and M. Veeraraghavan (2005), 'The effect of board composition and ownership structure on firm performance: evidence from India', http://www.hhs.se/NR/rdonlyres/74CEDE8D-A06F-4D90-85EA-6645610A8B32/0/Veeraraghav-an_Madhu.pdf.

Berndt, M. (2002), *Global Differences in Corporate Governance Systems*, Wiesbaden: Deutscher Universitätsverlag.

Bhagat, S. and Romano, R. (2007), 'Empirical studies of corporate law', in A. M. Polinsky and S. Shavell, *Handbook of Law and Economics*, Amsterdam: Elsevier, 945–1012.

Braendle, U. C. (2006), 'Shareholder protection in the USA and Germany:– "Law and Finance" revisited', *German Law Journal*, **7**, 257–78.

Branson, D. M. (2001), 'The very uncertain prospect of "global" convergence in corporate governance', *Cornell International Law Journal*, **34**, 321–62.

Cadbury Committee (1992, applied since 1993), *Code of Best Practice*. London: Burgess Science Press.

Calaba, V. F. (2001), 'The insiders: a look at the comprehensive and potentially unnecessary regulatory approaches to insider trading in Germany and the United States', *Loyola of Los Angeles International and Comparative Law Journal*, **23**, 457–85.

Cary, W. L. (1974),'Federalism and corporate law: reflections upon Delaware', *Yale Law Journal*, **83**, 663–707.

Chakrabarti, R. (2005), 'Corporate governance in India: evolution and challenges', http://ssrn.com/abstract=649857.

Cheffins, B. R. (2001), 'Does law matter? The separation of ownership and control in the United Kingdom', *Journal of Legal Studies*, **30**, 459–84.

Coffee, J. C. (2001), 'The rise of dispersed ownership: the role of law in the separation of ownership and control', *Yale Law Journal*, **111**, 1–82.

Cools, S. (2005),'The real difference in corporate law between the United States and continental Europe: distribution of powers', *Delaware Journal of Corporate Law*, **30**, 697–766.

Cooter, R. D. and T. Ginsburg (2003), 'Leximetrics: why the same laws are longer in some countries than others', http://ssrn.com/abstract=456520.

De Cruz, P. (1999), *Comparative Law in a Changing World*, 2nd edn, London: Cavendish.

Delaware (2006), 'Sub-division of corporations', http://www.delaware.gov/.

Djankov, S., R. La Porta, F. Lopez-de-Silanes and A. Shleifer (2008), 'The law and economics of self-dealing', *Journal of Financial Economics*, **88**, 430–65.

Dyck, A. and L. Zingales (2004), 'Private benefits of control: an international comparison', *Journal of Finance*, **59**, 537–600.

Easterbrook, F. and D. Fischel (1991), *The Economic Structure of Corporate Law*, Cambridge MA: Harvard University Press.

Enriques, L. (2004), 'The mandatory bid rule in the takeover directive: harmonization without foundation?' *European Company and Financial Law Review*, **1**, 440–57.

EU (2007), Directive 2007/36/EC of the European Parliament and of the Council of 11 July 2007 on the exercise of certain rights of shareholders in listed companies, *Official Journal of the European Union*, L184, 17–24, available at http://eur-lex.europa.eu/lexUriServe.do?uri=OJ:L:2007:184:0017:0024:EN:PDF

Gilson, R. J. (2001), 'Globalizing corporate governance: convergence of form or function', *American Journal of Comparative Law*, **49**, 329–59.

Glenn, H. P. (2004), *Legal Traditions of the World*, 2nd edn. London: Oxford Univeristy Press.

Gordon, J. N. (1989), 'The mandatory structure of corporate law', *Columbia Law Review*; **89**, 1549–98.

Gordon, J. N. (1994), 'Relational investors: a new look at cumulative voting', *Columbia Law Review*, **94**, 124–92.

Gordon, J. N. and M. J. Roe (eds) (2004), *Convergence and Persistence in Corporate Governance*, Cambridge: Cambridge University Press.

Goswami, O. (2003), 'India: the tide gradually rises', in C. Oman (ed.) *Corporate Governance in Development*, Paris: OECD, 105–60.

Greenbury Committee (1995, applied since 1996), *Code of Best Practice*, London: Gee Publishing.

Hampel Committee (1998, applied since June 1998), *Combined Code of Best Practice*, London: Gee Publishing.

Hansmann, H. and R. Kraakman (2001), 'The end of history for corporate law' *Georgetown Law Journal*, **88**, 439–68.

Hebert, S. (2004), 'Corporate governance French style', *Journal of Business Law*, **47**, 656–71.

Hüffer, U. (2004), *Aktiengesetz*, 6th edn, Munich: Beck.

Khanna, T. (2000), 'Business groups and social welfare in emerging markets: existing evidence and unanswered questions', *European Economic Review*, **44**, 748–61.

La Porta, R., F. López de Silanes and A. Shleifer (2006), 'What works in securities law?', *Journal of Finance*, **61**, 1–32.

La Porta, R., F. López de Silanes, A. Shleifer and R. W. Vishny (1998), 'Law and finance', *Journal of Political Economy*, **106**, 1113–55.

Lele, P. and M. Siems (2007), Shareholder protection index for the UK, the US, Germany, France and India, http://www.cbr.cam.ac.uk/pdf/Lele-Siems-Shareholder-Index-Final1.pdf.

Licht, A. N., C. Goldschmidt and S. Schwartz (2005), 'Culture, law, and corporate governance', *International Review of Law and Economics*, **25**, 229–55.

Manne, H. (1966), *Insider Trading and the Stock Market*, New York: Free Press.

Markesinis, B. (1997), *Foreign Law and Comparative Methodology: a Subject and a Thesis*, Oxford: Hart.

Markesinis, B. (2001) *Always on the Same Path: Essays on Foreign Law and Comparative Methodology*, Volume 2, Oxford: Hart.

McDonnell, B. H. (2002), 'Convergence in corporate governance: possible, but not desirable', *Villanova Law Review*, **47**, 341–85.

OECD (2004), 'Principles on corporate governance', http://www.oecd.org/dataoecd/32/18/31557724.pdf.

Pagano, M. and P. Volpin (2005), 'The political economy of corporate governance', *American Economic Review*, **95**, 1005–30.

Pistor, K. (2000), 'Patterns of legal change: shareholder protection and creditor rights in transition economies', *European Business Organization Law Review*, **1**, 59–110.

Pistor, K., M. Raiser and S. Gelfer (2000), 'Law and finance in transition economies', *Economics of Transition*, **8**, 325–68.

Powell, J. L. (1988), *Issues and Offers of Company Securities: the New Regime* London: Sweet and Maxwell.

Roe, M. J. (2002), Corporate law's limits, *Journal of Legal Studies*, **31**, 233–71.

Romano, R. (1993), *The Genius of American Corporate Law*. Washington DC: AEI Press.

Romano, R. (2005), 'The Sarbanes-Oxley Act and the making of quack corporate governance' *Yale Law Journal*, **114**, 1521–611.

Schmidt, K. (1997), *Gesellschaftsrecht*, 3rd edn, Cologne: Heymanns.

Siems, M. M. (2005a), 'Numerical comparative law: do we need statistical evidence in order to reduce complexity?', *Cardozo Journal of International and Comparative Law*, **13**, 521–40.

Siems, M. M. (2005b), 'The case against harmonisation of shareholder rights', *European Business Organization Law Review*, **6**, 539–52.

Siems, M. M. (2005c), 'What does not work in comparing securities law', *International Company and Commercial Law Review*, **2005**, 300–5.

Siems, M. M. (2006), 'Legal adaptability in Elbonia', *International Journal of Law in Context*, **2**, 393–408.

Siems, M. M. (2008a), *Convergence in Shareholder Law*, Cambridge: Cambridge University Press.

Siems, M. M. (2008b), 'Shareholder protection around the world ("Leximetric II")' *Delaware Journal of Corporate Law*, **33**, 111–47.

Singh, A., A. Singh, and B. Weisse (2002), 'Corporate governance, competition, the new international financial architecture and large corporations in emerging markets', http://www.cbr.cam.ac.uk/pdf/WP250.pdf.

Spamann, H. (2006),'On the insignificance and/or endogeneity of La Porta *et al.*'s *Anti-Director Rights Index* under consistent coding', http://ssrn.com/abstract=894301.

Stout, L. A. (2002), 'Do antitakeover defenses decrease shareholder wealth? The *ex post/ex ante* valuation problem', *Stanford Law Review*, **55**, 834–61.

Van den Berghe, L. (2002), *Corporate Governance in a Globalising World: Convergence or Divergence? A European Perspective*, Boston: Kluwer Academic Publishers.

Varma, J. R. (1997), 'Corporate governance in India: disciplining the dominant shareholder', *IIMB Management Review*, **9**, 5–18.

Werder, A. von, T. Talaulicar and G. L. Kolat (2005), 'Compliance with the German Corporate Governance Code: an empirical analysis of the compliance statements by German listed companies', *Corporate Governance*, **13**, 178–87.

Zetzsche, D. (2004), 'Explicit and implicit system of corporate control: a convergence theory of shareholder rights', http://ssrn.com/abstract=600722.

11. Legal aspects of UK bank corporate governance

Dalvinder Singh

INTRODUCTION

A complex nexus of corporate law, public regulation and supervision resides over the activities banks are allowed to undertake, such as the business of deposit taking. The traditional focus of corporate law is essentially the relationship between the corporation and its directors and shareholders. Indeed, the corporate legal framework as set out in s. 172 of the Companies Act 2006 places a legal obligation on directors to maximize shareholder wealth, albeit presupposing an 'enlightened shareholder' appreciative of the interests of other corporate stakeholders. However, the interests of others are only considered, if at all, to a limited extent; in the case of creditors, for instance, only if problems arise. The mechanisms to protect depositor interests involve compliance with statutory provisions and rules put in place by the regulator responsible for overseeing the business of banking to protect financial stability, market confidence, and depositor and investor interests. These statutory requirements can transcend the business operations of banks over non-bank business, and also transnationally through consolidated supervision. The regulatory framework places a responsibility on the firm, its directors and its senior management, and indeed to some extent on the shareholder controllers, to be mindful of the interests of depositors (as unsecured creditors) both legally and morally over and above the expectations of the traditional corporate governance paradigm.

This chapter will focus on the UK Financial Services Authority (FSA), which is responsible for the regulation and supervision of banking, investment and insurance businesses as set out in the Financial Services and Markets Act 2000 (FSMA 2000). The first section will consider the scope of corporate governance and its importance, highlighting that the corporate legal framework simply focuses on the interests of the company and shareholders as a whole. The second section analyses the position of depositors as stakeholders in banks, and delineates the duty the bank has towards them as unsecured creditors and the limited powers depositors have to respond collectively. The third section will focus on the wider stakeholder ideas incorporated in the FSMA 2000 by examining the FSA's work to meet its objectives. The fourth section outlines the FSA's powers governing authorization and supervision, paying particular attention to the additional responsibilities placed on shareholders to safeguard the interests of depositors. The FSA's regulatory regime formally refers to the interests of a whole host of stakeholders – consumers, regulators and financial intermediaries – not just depositors, in the pursuit of its objectives of regulation. These outweigh the interests of shareholders. The fifth section will examine the 'Principles for Businesses' and the 'Approved Person' and 'Fit and Proper' criteria. Here the regulatory provisions pertaining to the legal duty of directors and management of regulated firms are analysed, as are recent Financial Markets Tribunal decisions, to show how other interests are protected. Finally, some brief observations will be offered regarding the problems experienced with Northern Rock plc and the interplay of corporate law and financial regulation. The general question that needs consideration is whose interests in the final endgame does the state want to protect? The interests of those who seek to capitalize on the fortunes of corporations such as Northern Rock, or the 'benign' depositors who think their money is safe when it is deposited in a bank?

CORPORATE GOVERNANCE

'Corporate governance' is an ambiguous term that embraces both the internal and the external operations of a company (Cadbury Report, 1992; Parkinson, 1993; Sheikh and Rees, 1995; Cheffin, 1997; Hampel Report, 1998). In the UK the corporate governance debate has generally focused on internal operations as they relate to the direction and control of the company. The idea of direction and control consists of numerous issues: the effectiveness of the board of directors, non-executive directors, shareholder involvement, external auditor independence, the robustness of the internal controls, the audit committee and the internal audit function, to name just a few. In the context of direction and control, specific emphasis has been placed on maintaining a sustainable entrepreneurial spirit of profit maximization (Hampel Report, 1998: para. 1.1). This refers to the company ensuring that it takes informed decisions to minimize adverse risks and maximize its performance. The fundamental concern is that the processes of accountability do not hinder or undermine the entrepreneurial spirit of a corporation by placing layers of bureaucracy on its decision making to reduce its performance in terms of taking risks and profit maximization. This is reaffirmed in the Hampel Report on corporate governance, which states that governance and accountability should not override the objective of improving shareholder returns. Notwithstanding the importance of an 'entrepreneurial spirit', providing the degree of accountability required to ensure that directors do not have unfettered discretion in the way shareholders' interests are steered remains the main challenge. Indeed, the possibility of a company taking on more risk to improve investment returns needs to be kept in check, given that such decisions may turn out to be imprudent.[1]

The Anglo-American legal framework of corporate governance places the interests of the company and shareholders at its centre. The board of directors and managers are required to direct and control the company on behalf of its shareholders; this is generally referred to as the principle of separation of ownership and control (Berle and Means, 1997 [1932]). It provides that the company through its board of directors has a primary duty to the interests of the company (*Percival v. Wright* [1902]),[2] which equates to satisfying the interests of shareholders (*Heron International v. Lord Grade* [1983]).[3] While boards of directors are responsible for relations with a broad range of stakeholders, they are accountable only to shareholders as a whole (*West Mercia Safetywear Ltd v. Dodd* [1988]).[4] As such, the appointment of external auditors on behalf of the shareholders is designed to ascertain whether the stewardship of the company is satisfactory and void of any irregularities (*Barings plc v. Coopers & Lybrand* [1997]: 435; see also *Bank of Credit and Commerce International (Overseas) Ltd (in liquidation) and Others v. Price Waterhouse and Another (No. 3)*; *Berg & Sons v. Adams* [1993]). The shareholders are then able to gauge whether the company is being governed in an appropriate way.

THE POSITION OF DEPOSITOR CREDITORS

The common law position on the status of bank customers gives a useful basis to delineate the limited protection that corporate law provides for their interests (Campbell and Singh, 2007: 40–70). In general, unsecured creditors, such as depositors of a bank, will have very little redress to recover their debts if a company is put into liquidation (Keay, 2001, 2003; Prentice, 1990; Sappideen, 1991). The courts will not deal with the question of which class of creditor should have priority over other classes in such circumstances (*Space Investments Ltd v. Canadian Imperial Bank of Commerce Trust Co. (Bahamas) Ltd and others* [1986]).[5] In the case of banking, it indicates the limited responsibility of a bank towards depositors once the bank has the money put into its account. The principle illustrates that the relationship between the depositor and the bank is not one of principal and agent, where the bank as agent acts on behalf of principals in their interests. The money deposited in an account is no longer deemed as belonging to the principal, but rather to the bank. In this relationship the bank is only contractually accountable for the sum of money paid in. This is the sum of money the bank is required to give back, including any interest accrued. According to Cottenham LC in *Foley v. Hill (Edward Thomas Foley v. Thomas Hill* [1848]: 1005–6),

> The money paid into the banker's is money known by the principal to be placed there for the purpose of being under the control of the banker; it is then the banker's money; he is known to deal with it as his own; he makes what profit of it he can, which profit he retains to himself . . . The money placed in the custody of a banker is, to all intents and purposes, the money of the banker, to do with it as he pleases; he is guilty of no breach of trust in employing it; he is not answerable to the principal if he puts it into jeopardy, if he engages in a hazardous speculation.

The decision in *Foley* set to rest the ambiguous idea that the relationship between bank and customer is one of agent and principal. According to Smart (1990: 2), the fiduciary obligation was regarded as too onerous a burden for the bank and its business, as it would have placed a continuous responsibility on the bank to account for its decisions. The bank does not have to advise customers on how it uses its 'reservoir' of deposited funds and the risks at which it places them once the money is in its accounts. By contrast, if an investment product is being bought by a customer, a whole host of common law fiduciary rules govern the sale of such products. Some have advocated the adoption of a fiduciary duty on directors to safeguard the interests of depositors (Macey and O'Hara, 2003). However, the adoption of such a rule has not been articulated with the practical relationship of banker and depositor as being one of debtor and creditor in mind, as the obligation would strike at the heart of the universal principle on which banking law is based. The business of banking would then need to be undertaken in the interests of depositors as beneficiaries. The implications of this would be very burdensome for the banking industry in terms of the compliance costs it would incur and the cost of reconfiguring the way banks undertake their business. The cost implications for depositors would also be a significant issue to consider in the light of the way banking would need to be administered.

The principle also highlights the large degree of discretion the bank has in the way it can use other people's money. The obligation on the bank to pay on demand the sum placed in an account is obviously a curb on its discretion. Furthermore, depositor activism could prove a force to contend with if the bank went off on a frolic of its own: depositors can wield influence over the decisions of bank management because they have the power to withdraw their deposits on demand. This gives them some leverage in the affairs of the business, to make sure their interests are not undermined. However, this leverage is limited, considering the fact that informational asymmetry regarding the bank's business makes the timing of the decision to withdraw deposits very difficult,[6] thus the question of whether depositors can actually wield any influence on bank management is open to debate. According to Garten (1986: 134), the position of a bank depositor is distinguishable from that of an investor. In the case of depositors the reasons for opening an account with a particular bank are more practical in nature than the reasons of investors, for whom the return associated with the account is more important. Thus the desire of depositors to monitor bank risk is generally low, even though a real risk exists of a bank failing and depositors potentially losing their money. Garten contends that depositors have a unique perspective of risk in comparison with investors, giving rise to little incentive to monitor the activities of banks. The limited involvement regarding deposits produces a large group of 'involuntary investors' with relatively inert interest in what the bank is actually doing with their money.

In addition to these general factors, the asymmetry of information surrounding the business of banking places depositors in a vulnerable position. For example, depositors will not know whether their bank has a high or low propensity towards taking risk. This is exacerbated by the fact that banks have no obligation to inform depositors about the risks they are pursuing. The principle governing the bank-customer relationship illustrates the importance of formal prudential regulation to protect the interests of small depositors. It also indicates the unfettered autonomy of the banks, which could threaten the overall stability of the banking system. The conclusion can therefore be inferred from the common law that the interests of the depositor, as a creditor, are secondary to the interests of shareholders as a whole. This inequality of treatment is one reason for some kind of public regulation to mitigate the risks to which depositors are exposed. These risks are different from those associated with investment business, hence bank regulation focuses on the business of accepting deposits and prohibits illegal deposit-taking (FSMA 2000: s. 19).

THE FINANCIAL SERVICES AND MARKETS ACT 2000

The FSA is required to undertake its responsibilities in accordance with the objectives and principles set out in the FSMA 2000: market confidence, public awareness, protection of consumers and reduction of financial crime (FSMA 2000: s. 2(2)). These are fleshed out by the FSA in a complex system of handbooks[7] that set out detailed guidance and rules with which regulated firms and approved persons are required to comply in order to protect the interests associated with financial regulation. These are called the Principles for Businesses; Senior Management Arrangements, Systems and Controls; and Statements of Principles and Code of Practice for Approved Persons.

The objectives of the FSMA 2000 are not listed in order of priority. Nevertheless, it is fitting that market confidence is first, as it captures a broad range of macroeconomic and microeconomic factors to do with the financial system that directly or indirectly relate to the other listed objectives. These objectives and principles provide a foundation for the decisions the FSA takes to fulfil its responsibilities. The financial services industry needs to be mindful of them as being the underlying rationale behind the rules and guidance, governing, *inter alia*, authorization, supervision and enforcement. The objectives thus provide not only an external but also an internal mechanism to safeguard other stakeholder interests. For example, the second objective (consumer awareness) provides an obligation on the financial services industry as a whole to raise the public's understanding of the industry and its products (FSA, 1998: 17). The third objective (consumer protection) provides an obligation on regulated firms and approved persons to exercise the appropriate level of care when dealing with customers. The inclusion of the interests of other stakeholders into the broader corporate decision-making process is said to give rise to a more ethical approach to business, which subsequently enhances a company's reputation. The ramifications of failing to take into account the interests of other stakeholders are suggested to be much wider than simply damaging the reputation of the firm: it can also undermine the overall reputation of the financial system (FSA, 2002a). Thus the interests of the firm and the market are not mutually exclusive but are interdependent, giving rise to a responsibility to undertake business without undermining investor or depositor confidence.

FSA SUPERVISION

The FSA exercises its supervision over regulated firms and individuals on a continuous basis to ensure compliance with the FSMA 2000 and its handbook rules that make up the regulatory regime. The FSA has adopted a risk-based approach in its supervision: it attempts to assess the degree of risk each kind of regulated firm poses and its compliance with the regulatory objectives. The FSA administers its resources according to the principle that the higher the risk a regulated firm poses to the FSA in achieving its regulatory objectives, the more resources are needed to mitigate the risk. The risk-based approach is said to enhance the efficiency and effectiveness of supervision for both the regulated and the regulator because it allows both parties to focus their attention on the areas of greatest concern. The FSA identifies changes in the areas of 'consumer confidence', 'developments in the industry' and 'regulated institutions' as posing the greatest obstacles in achieving its objectives.

The risk-based operating framework sets out the FSA's approach to its risk-based system of regulation. It outlines the processes the FSA goes through in identifying the risks the sector and a regulated firm pose to its objectives. The FSA embarks on several steps to create a risk map: environmental assessment; firm and non-firm regulatory risk analysis; new responsibilities; strategic aims; strategic outcomes; prioritization and resource allocation; regulatory response; performance evaluation; and reporting on performance against objectives. The impact of a risk on the regulatory objectives determines the 'intensity' of the action the FSA takes to mitigate that risk. Once the process is complete, the regulated firm is given an individualized risk assessment in the category of high, medium-high, medium-low or low impact. However, this banding of regulated firms does not necessarily mean these firms are risky institutions. A firm could be placed in the high band but pose a low risk: it is the potential of a risk 'crystallizing' which determines the category. The high-impact band gives rise to a high probability of a risk adversely affecting the regulatory objectives if it 'crystallizes'. The FSA determines the response to the risk by assessing whether it is firm or non-firm specific and industry-wide. A regulatory tools matrix sets out the possible responses the FSA can take. This matrix is categorized according to whether tools are monitoring (to monitor risks), diagnostic (to identify and measure risk), preventive (to mitigate risks) or remedial (to address crystallized risks).

THE SHAREHOLDERS' OBLIGATIONS TO DEPOSITOR CREDITORS

Authorization to undertake deposit-taking business requires shareholder 'controllers' of a bank to be 'fit and proper' before they are allowed to operate (FSMA 2000: s. 49). The obligation of shareholder controllers extends beyond simply contributing towards the capital of the company in consideration for the shares issued. The policy of monitoring the controlling interests of a bank was first introduced under the Banking Act 1979, but it was limited to recognized banks and did not apply to licensed institutions; it was extended to all authorized institutions with the repeal of the 1979 Act by the Banking Act 1987 (HM Treasury, 1985: 27).

The FSA monitors very closely the shareholders who constitute 'control' of an authorized body (FSMA 2000: Part XII, ss. 178–92). A person who is proposing to acquire a significant holding is required to notify the FSA of this intention (SUP 11.2G). The FSMA 2000 provides that a person acquires control if, *inter alia*, s/he holds 10 per cent or more of the shares in an authorized body and is able to exercise significant influence over its management by virtue of powers such as shareholding or voting rights. Shareholders can wield a considerable amount of influence on management to pursue business in a more aggressive manner. While the entrepreneurialism of a bank is not to be dampened down by taking a cautious approach to business and profitability, it certainly needs to be mindful that it must take decisions prudently in the interests of its depositors as well.

The regulator will first require shareholder controllers to be assessed, to gauge whether they are fit and proper to have such a holding in a bank (SUP 11.7.5G(1)–(2)). This ascertains the financial status of the acquiring person, to determine whether the acquisition could put the bank in jeopardy if those buying it are in a relatively weak financial position. A change in control, whether associated with the parent company or another entity within the group, may require the submission of a 'comfort letter' regardless of the number of controllers that exist (IPRU Section 1, 22). In the case of a bank a comfort letter giving assurances that the acquiring person is fit and proper and the interests of consumers are not threatened is required if the person acquires 15 per cent of the bank's voting power. This is to ensure that the shareholder controllers are aware of their obligation to stand behind the bank if concerns regarding its liquidity or solvency arise. The UK position is that a comfort letter is not legally binding like a guarantee or warranty, but does in financial regulation have considerable moral weight attached to it: it is a representation of a moral responsibility extending the obligations of shareholders beyond the return on their investment (*Kleinwort Benson v. MMC Metals Ltd* [1989]; *Banque Brussels Lambert v. Australian National Industries* (1989)).[8] As will be highlighted in the final section on Northern Rock, whether or not the shareholders do assist (which is not entirely clear in that case), it will not be sufficient to prevent a bank run, which can only really be avoided by intervention from the central bank backed up by the government with emergency liquidity support. Moreover, the authorities may consider it politically inappropriate to ask for further assistance from shareholder controllers, as this could damage the investment climate.

THE PRINCIPLES FOR BUSINESSES

The Principles for Businesses provide a set of 'fundamental obligations' to which a regulated firm is required to adhere, and build on the FSA's regulatory objectives. The interests of consumers, regulators and other financial intermediaries figure largely. The Principles for Businesses apply not just to the regulated firm but also across a group and its worldwide activities (PRIN 1.1.3G, 1.1.5G and 1.1.6G). These principles provide the context within which regulated business must be undertaken; the consequences of a breach could be intensive supervision, enforcement actions or, in the worst-case scenario, withdrawal of permission to undertake regulated activities (PRIN 1.1.7G–9G).

A breach of the principles arises on the basis of an objective 'reasonable care' test (PRIN 1.1.7G). The FSA must assess a number of factors on the basis of the reasonable care standard before liability is successfully established. It has to consider whether the act or omission departs from general practice. 'General practice' is interpreted to mean the typical behaviour of a skilled person. The individual is not required to have a high level of skill: the act or omission needs to be judged on whether it departs from 'general practice'. In addition, the FSA will need to determine the probability of loss or damage. It has been held that the mere predictability of harm is not sufficient to identify a breach of duty; one needs to establish whether an act or omission was unreasonable. The FSA also has to consider the likelihood of the risk occurring: this is to determine whether a reasonable person would have attempted to avoid creating the risk in the first place. The FSA must take into account the precautionary measures that a reasonable and prudent person would take in the circumstances, to determine whether the possible precautionary measures would have been apparent to a person of that level of skill. It is also important to assess whether the precautionary steps would have averted the damaging consequences of the acts or omissions. Finally, to establish a breach a balance needs to be struck between taking the necessary precautions and the cost of not taking them.

Principles 1 and 2 govern the way regulated business is undertaken with 'integrity' and 'skill, care and diligence', respectively (PRIN 2.1.1R). For example, Abbey National Asset Managers was fined £320 000 (FSA, 2003) for, *inter alia*, its breach of Principle 2 in not exercising the appropriate level of 'care, skill and diligence' in addressing concerns about the effectiveness of its systems and controls reported by its compliance department (PRIN 2.1.1R). Principle 3 requires a firm to take 'reasonable care' with its management and control (PRIN 2.1.1R). The FSA (2005c) fined City Index for a breach of Principle 3 because its risk management controls failed to spot that the risk warnings were too small on its financial pro-motions, thereby preventing customers from fully appreciating the risks associated with its products. Citigroup Global Markets was required by the FSA (2005b) to give up profits in the region of £9 million and pay a fine of £4 million for its failure to adhere to Principles 2 and 3 as a result of executing a trading strategy in the bond market that manipulated the trading system within which bonds are bought and sold. The FSA decided that the firm failed to take due care in its strategy. Principle 4 requires a firm to 'maintain adequate financial resources' (PRIN 2.1.1R). Principle 5 requires a firm to maintain 'proper standards of market conduct' (PRIN 2.1.1R). Principles 6, 7 and 8 respectively require a firm to safeguard the interests of its customers by treating them fairly; 'pay due regard to their communication' needs and avoid misleading them; and 'manage conflicts of interest fairly' (PRIN 2.1.1R). The FSA (2005a) imposed a fine of £800 000 on Abbey National for failing to treat customers fairly in its mishandling of the complaints process emanating from endowment mortgage mis-selling. It considered that Abbey National breached Principle 6 as a result of its failure to comply with the regulatory requirements at the time to assess the complaints made by its customers. Principles 9 and 10 require the firm to ensure that the advice it gives to customers is suitable and their assets are adequately protected (PRIN 2.1.1R). Principle 11 requires the regulated firm to 'deal with its regulators in an open and cooperative way' (PRIN 2.1.1R; PRIN 3.3.1R and Table: 4–5). A firm can breach Principle 11 by persistently failing to submit annual accounts despite being asked to do so (FSA, 2005d). The UK FSA (2002b) fined Credit Suisse First Boston £4 million for deliberately misleading its regulatory counterparts in Japan about its derivatives business. According to Carol Sergeant, former man-aging director at the FSA, the fine was imposed as a signal to others that misleading regulators was considered a very serious offence which under-mines the credibility of the financial markets (FSA, 2002c).

THE FSMA 2000 APPROVED PERSON REGIME

In its statutory provisions and handbooks the FSA has built on the common law principles that govern directors', senior management's and indeed employees' responsibilities with additional rules to address the idiosyncratic features of the financial services industry. The common law provisions prescribe not only what standard of care is expected of directors and senior management, but also the kinds of acts or omissions that have resulted in liability; they also prescribe how the acts or omissions of direc-tors, senior management and employees can give rise to liability through the principle of attribution of knowledge (*Tesco Supermarkets Ltd v. Nattrass* [1972]; *Meridian Global Funds Management Asia Ltd v. Securities Commission* [1995]; *Dubai Aluminium v. Salaam* [2002]). The FSA has extended those ideas beyond the jurisdiction of incorporation to take into account the way business operations are undertaken and managed by organizations, as highlighted in the Barings case. The decision in *Barings* (*Barings plc v. Coopers & Lybrand* [2003]: para. 945) outlines how in a matrix management system of control and direction the 'directing mind and will' could be located in a sister company in another jurisdiction. In this instance the matrix management system overseeing parts of Barings' business included activities in other jurisdictions, namely Japan, London and Singapore where rogue trader Nick Leeson undertook trading activities on behalf of Barings Group in the UK.

The FSA has articulated the principles emanating from the common law into rules specifically designed for regulating and supervising activities within the financial system. For instance, the standard of care expected is that of reasonable care. In addition the FSA has extended the scope of its rules so that the interests of consumers and regulators are given equal prominence, beyond the interests of the company *per se*. Indeed, there is a common thread running through the FSA guidelines that mirrors the common law.

The FSA regime not only governs who can undertake regulated activities at an institutional level, but also those who are responsible for discharging a firm's responsibilities on its behalf. Whether or not an individual requires approval by the FSA depends on the role they perform; that is, whether they perform a 'controlled function' (SUP 10.4.5R). The functions designated as controlled are those that 'add value' to the regulatory process and assist the FSA to fulfil its objectives (APER 4.4.1G–9E). No person can exercise a controlled function unless the individual is approved by the FSA under s. 59 of the FSMA 2000 (SUP 10.2.1G). In accordance with the FSMA 2000 those approved have to meet the FSA's 'fit and proper' criteria before they can take up their positions. It is the responsibility of the regulated firm to exercise reasonable care when appointing individuals to undertake a controlled function to ensure they are appropriate for the position. The FSA has responsibility for establishing whether a breach of the rules has occurred. An individual who is refused approval on the basis that s/he is not 'fit and proper' does have a right to have the case heard by the Financial Services and Markets Tribunal. Indeed, a number of cases have been heard which have shed further light on the decision as to whether someone is fit and proper to undertake a controlled function. The role of the tribunal in these matters is to consider the case 'afresh in the light of all the evidence made available', which includes evidence that was not previously available to the FSA. The tribunal acts as a court of first instance rather than an appeal court. Therefore a decision by the FSA to withdraw approval on the basis that the individual is not fit and proper would have to be reviewed in the light of the tribunal's decision (FSMA 2000: s. 133(5)).

The idea of a controlled function is not simply confined to the higher levels of directors and senior management of a regulated firm, but includes those with positions at the customer interface (SUP 10.4.5R): employees who have contact with customers, whether in an advisory capacity or to organize or undertake transactions on their behalf. A function is 'controlled' when it fulfils the general conditions of s. 59(5)–(7) of the FSMA 2000. The controlled functions are separated into three categories: s. 59(5), where the individual has significant influence over the conduct of the approved person; s. 59(6), where the individual deals with customers; and s. 59(7), where the individual deals with the property of customers. The FSA has listed the functions that require prior approval: there are currently 27 controlled functions. The first 20 are deemed functions of significant influence: 1–7 relate to the governing body (directors, chief executive officer and non-executive directors); 8–12 govern 'required functions' (money-laundering officer); 13–15 govern systems and control functions; and 16–20 govern significant management functions (internal auditor). Items 21–27 govern customer functions.

THE FIT AND PROPER TEST FOR APPROVED PERSONS

Any individual performing a controlled function is required to be a fit and proper person (FIT 1.1.2G). The FSA sets out a number of factors that need to be considered, such as 'honesty', 'integrity', 'reputation', 'competence', 'capability' and 'financial soundness' (FIT 1.3.1G). In general terms, to be 'fit and proper' a person must be suitable to 'hold a licence' and undertake the business of the licence holder (*R v. Hyde* JJ [1912] 158). This requires an assessment of the individual's character and the nature and complexity of the business undertaken by the regulated firm. In this respect it is the responsibility of the individual to satisfy the FSA that they are 'fit and proper' to undertake a controlled function rather than for the FSA to show that they are not. The FSA has the authority to withdraw approval if it considers a person not to be fit and proper for the controlled function for which they have sought approval (FIT 1.2.3G). The FSA takes a cumulative as well as an individual approach towards regulatory failures, rather than taking action against individual incidents of minor indiscretion that would not necessarily always lead to holding a person unfit. This policy concurs with the views of Nicholls V-C in *Re Swift 736 Ltd*, where he strongly emphasized the importance of condemning a blatant disregard of not fulfilling reporting requirements. The V-C suggested that attitudes such as these need to be corrected (*Secretary of State v. Ettinger, Re Swift 736 Ltd* [1993] 900). The essential ingredient in this form of non-compliance is blatant disregard of such requirements rather than an element of dishonesty. Provisions like these ensure accountability; thus an accumulation of 'administrative' failures suggests a lack of rigour or discipline. For example, the FSA (2005d) took action against India Buildings Friendly Society for repeated failure to submit annual accounts, which called into question its compliance with the threshold conditions and its willingness to cooperate with the regulator.

The probity of an individual is very important for the purposes of the FSA. Probity refers to an individual's uprightness and honesty. For example, the FSA (2004) prohibited John Edward Rourke from performing any function in relation to a regulated activity because he had been convicted on several counts of illegal deposit-taking, resulting in a custodial sentence. The evidence in the case went to the very core of his honesty and integrity, demonstrating he was not fit and proper. A person's probity is an important characteristic; this is called into question whatever position an individual holds in a regulated firm when breach of trust and level of culpability need to be ascertained. Gowan J generally interprets honesty as equating to acting in good faith (*Marchesi v. Barnes* [1970]: 438). The FSA takes into account a person's reputation and whether the person has a criminal record or has contravened any regulatory requirements, and also non-compliance with non-statutory codes of conduct governing the capital markets. According to Mayo J, reputation is a summation of all the beliefs popularly held about the individual in a community, whether positive or negative (*Dias v. O'Sullivan* [1949]: 591). Consequently, the FSA has the discretion in many respects to delve further than formal records about the individual.

The competency of an individual is also important when judging whether a person is fit and proper. It is generally interpreted by Winn J to mean that a person, on a fair assessment, is able to perform a particular function in the light of the problems involved and the degree of risk associated with the task (*Brazier v. Skipton Rock Co., Ltd* [1962]: 957). This interpretation of 'competency' can be complemented by the definition provided by Cantley J, who suggests that it is the virtue of a practical and reasonable man who can look and recognize what to look for (*Gibson v. Skibs A/S Marina and Orkla Grobe A/B and Smith Coggins, Ltd* [1966]: 478). These interpretations focus on an individual's experience and knowledge in identifying relevant issues and dealing with them accordingly to contain the possible adverse consequences that may arise.

In the standard of care required of an individual, skill is referred to widely. The traditional approach adopted by the English courts is that a director needs no special qualifications for that office (*Re Brazilian Rubber Plantations and Estates Ltd* [1911]: 437). However, this is based on the proviso that if a director does have specialist knowledge then he is bound to bring that knowledge to his office. According to Clarke and Sheller JJA, skill is a special level of competency that is distinct from that possessed by a reasonable man, is gained by special training and experience and is determined by the level of care reasonably expected of a person undertaking particular work (*Daniels v. Anderson* [1995]: 667). This definition clearly highlights that particular qualities are required, additional to those an 'ordinary man' would profess to have. The FSA recognizes that a director's responsibilities are relative to the department and the position held. According to the FSA, a person could be fit and proper for one position but not for another because it involves different responsibilities and duties (SUP 10.13.1G).

WITHDRAWAL OF APPROVAL

The FSA has the authority to withdraw approval if it considers an individual not fit and proper to take up the controlled function indicated with a regulated firm. The reason for withdrawal would be a failure to satisfy the criteria set out for approval to be granted. In respect to an approval decision, it is important to assess whether the individual poses a significant risk to consumers and confidence in the financial system. However, whatever decision the FSA reaches it must be proportionate to the risks an individual poses.

The most important factors to be taken into account are the honesty, integrity, competence and capability of an individual. The withdrawal of approval needs to comply with the enforcement guidelines which refer, *inter alia*, to issues of honesty, integrity and reputation; the individual's openness in dealing with the industry, consumers and regulators (present and past); competence and capability to carry out the controlled function; whether the individual has failed to comply with the Statement of Principles; the relevance and nature of the incident and the time that has elapsed since it occurred; the severity of the risk the individual poses to consumers and confidence in the financial system; and finally the individual's previous disciplinary record. In deciding whether an individual is not fit and proper, the standard of proof required is one of a balance of probabilities. A decision to reject an application for approval for a controlled function has to be based on material significance.

In the decision of *Cox v. the FSA* (*Ian Douglas Cox v. Financial Services Authority*, 2003) an application for approval was refused on the basis of Cox's previous conduct in trying dishonestly to surrender a pension, which resulted in two insurance companies and the Inland Revenue being defrauded. The tribunal's decision was to dismiss his application on the grounds that while it was a one-off incident, the matter was not completely resolved as the Inland Revenue was not given the opportunity to seek reparations and hold him to account for the dishonesty he had perpetrated. The decision highlights the fact that an individual could be considered fit and proper to hold a controlled function if a sufficient length of time has elapsed between an incident and seeking approval, and if approval were granted the individual would be appropriately supervised. However, in this instance Cox did not satisfy the tribunal that that was the case.

In *Hoodless and Blackwell v. the FSA* (*Geoffrey Alan Hoodless and Sean Michael Blackwell v. Financial Services Authority*, 2003), the issue was an incorrect announcement relating to the placement of a share issue. In this case the tribunal rejected the FSA's decision simply to withdraw approval on the basis that the individuals were not fit and proper. Indeed, it rejected the FSA's claims that their behaviour was dishonest, and that they failed to cooperate with regulators and put in detriment the interests of consumers and confidence in the financial system. Here it was said an individual was dishonest if he must have realized that what he was doing was dishonest by the ordinary standards of reasonable and honest people. In this case the evidence pointed to limited failures rather than a general failure: for instance, a lack of volunteering information to regulators was not evidence of improper motive or lack of integrity. Moreover, an isolated lack of candour did not automatically amount to evidence of dishonesty. Therefore, in the case of Hoodless the tribunal considered him to be fit and proper as it did not consider him to pose any threat to consumers or to confidence in the financial system.

THE ASSESSMENT CRITERIA

The approved persons regime is governed by a number of principles that delineate the standards expected of persons who undertake controlled functions. In line with the obligation to provide principles, the FSA also provides a code of practice to assist in their interpretation. The code highlights the kinds of acts or omissions that may give rise to an approval being called into question because it fails to comply with the principles (APER

1). To ascertain whether a person has breached the principles, the FSA will look at the person's acts or omissions to try to assess the degree of culpability (APER 2.1.2; APER 3.1.4G (1); APER 4).

Principle 1 focuses on carrying out approved functions with 'integrity' (APER 4.1.1G). Principle 2 requires that those exercising such functions should act with due skill, care and diligence (APER 4.2.1G). Principle 3 requires observation of proper standards of market conduct (APER 4.3.1G). Principle 4 requires the approved person to cooperate with the FSA openly (APER 4.4.1G). Principles 5–7 relate specifically to those in senior management and performing controlled functions; they are not necessarily more draconian than the other principles, but recognize that those in senior management have an additional responsibility regarding the affairs of the business. Principle 5 requires senior management to organize the business so that it can be controlled effectively with reasonable care (APER 4.5.1G). Principle 6 requires an approved person to exercise due skill, care and diligence in their management responsibility (APER 4.6.1G). Principle 7 requires an approved person to ensure that the firm for which they are responsible complies with the regulatory requirements (APER 4.7.1G).

The code of practice highlights the kind of acts or omissions that can result in a breach of the principles. It not only articulates conduct that could be deemed negligent, but also highlights acts that could give rise to criminal charges. In addition to these kinds of serious offences there are other offences which, although less serious, would entail a breach of the principles. In relation to Principle 1, acts or omissions that evidence, *inter alia*, falsifying information and misleading clients or a firm can give rise to serious questions about an individual's integrity. These acts and omissions are of a very serious nature and could lead to criminal charges; they are at the least evidence of gross negligence. A failure to inform a client about the nature of a financial product or risks associated with it could call into question Principle 2: whether an approved person has exercised the appropriate level of skill, care and diligence in carrying out their functions. A failure to comply with the necessary market conduct rules could result in evidence that the approved person has breached Principle 3. In relation to Principle 4, failure to cooperate with the regulator, or failing to disclose to the FSA information the approved person holds that may be of material significance, could amount to a breach.

Principles 5–7 specifically relate to those individuals who are approved to undertake controlled functions which are of significant influence. A breach of Principle 5 can arise if, for instance, an approved person fails to organize the business with reasonable care so that responsibilities within the organization are not apportioned or delegated properly. An approved person could breach Principle 6 if they fail to exercise due skill, care and diligence in managing the business of the firm. This could arise were they to fail to take reasonable care to inform themselves adequately about the affairs and/or risks associated with the business they are undertaking. Failure to take reasonable care to ensure that the firm undertakes its business in accordance with the relevant requirements and standards of the regulatory system could amount to a breach of Principle 7.

The FSA (2005e) prohibited Michael Harding from performing a controlled function on the basis that it was not satisfied he was fit and proper after he had failed to undertake a review of the pensions sold by his firm as required by the Personal Investment Authority. Harding had failed to be 'fit and proper' by not acting with the necessary level of honesty, integrity and competence. The FSA held that he breached Principle 1 by falsifying information about the firm's pensions review quarterly returns; providing inaccurate information to the firm; submitting misleading information to the FSA; and failing to treat his customers fairly. A breach of Principle 2 was also evidenced by the fact that he failed to inform his partner correctly about the progress of the pensions review. The FSA considered Harding to be in breach of Principle 4 as a result of his failure to report accurately the actual progress made with the review.

NORTHERN ROCK: SOME BRIEF OBSERVATIONS ON THE DEPOSITOR AND SHAREHOLDER INTERESTS

Northern Rock's request on 14 September 2007 for emergency liquidity support from the Bank of England via the Tripartite Committee (HM Treasury, the Bank of England and the Financial Services Authority) exposed in many ways the Achilles heel of the UK system of financial regulation and supervision: its inadequate approach to dealing with banks in distress (Bank of England, HM Treasury and FSA, 2008). For example, the risk depositors are exposed to as unsecured creditors in corporate insolvency is unsatisfactory and could lead to a bank run (Campbell and Singh, 2007: 50). The central reason for the authorities to intervene and subsequently put in place a blanket guarantee to support Northern Rock was to protect the interests of the depositors and the financial system as a whole rather than the interests of shareholders, who saw the value of their shares plummet. In this light Northern Rock plc is an interesting case, as it illustrates the competing interests of shareholder and depositor creditors, and indeed the intervention of the state financially to protect the latter to prevent a bank run. The authorities' lack of power to intervene constructively exposed the competing interests of shareholders and depositors: the former were aware of the business model and sought returns on the back of it; and the latter had only a benign interest in the business strategy and misguidedly believed that their savings were safe and they bore no risk if the bank failed.

Northern Rock no longer had access to its normal sources of funds due to the fall-out of the credit crisis that arose in August 2007 (European Parliament, Economic and Scientific Policy Department, 2007). It therefore did not have the money to support its business operations. As Philip Aldridge (2007) highlights, Northern Rock was three times more exposed from its wholesale funds to deposits than its next rival, revealing quite explicitly the extent to which it was relying on the liquidity of the wholesale market for funds to do business. To all intents and purposes this put it in a position of insolvency regardless of the fact that it continued to fulfil the regulatory capital requirements, which meant it was technically solvent. It did not, however, have the appropriate level of liquidity to continue to support its business when the wholesale markets closed their doors on it; so it turned to the Bank of England as lender of last resort. The FSA response at the time was very strong, but had little effect on reducing the queues outside Northern Rock branches: 'To be absolutely clear, if we believed that Northern Rock was not solvent, we would not have allowed it to remain open for business' (FSA, 2007).

During this period the tension between the shareholders, Northern Rock and the interests of creditors was very much played out publicly, which was very damaging to the UK's reputation of being a premier regulated financial centre. Depositors sought to fly to safe havens by withdrawing their money from Northern Rock and putting it in perceived safer banks, albeit that the government intervened to put in place a blanket guarantee to protect depositors and raise the level of compensation if the bank were to be judged in default and a payout was necessary. In addition, the government was essentially one of Northern Rock's main creditors, supporting it until a private sector deal to buy it, and so was eager to protect taxpayers' money used to support the bank. In the light of this it was keen to secure the most appropriate solution to ensure the funds were paid back as speedily as possible.

The terms of any sale to secure this outcome would very much influence whether or not it got shareholder approval. A lack of confidence in the matter of ensuring sufficient shareholder value led two of Northern Rock's shareholders to seek *inter alia* to restrict the authority of the board directors, to prevent the bank from disposing of its assets without shareholder approval. These shareholders, SRM Global Master Fund and RAB Special Situations (Master) Fund, called an extraordinary general meeting to achieve this aim and raise funds by amending the article of association. This was successfully curbed by the Northern Rock directors at the meeting, explicitly highlighting the duty of the company 'as a matter of law, to consider the interests of a number of categories of stakeholder in the Company as well as the interests of shareholders . . . it must have regard to the position and interests of the Company's creditors, and to take action to avoid or minimize their loss, if there is a serious risk of the Company's failure' (Northern Rock plc, Extraordinary General Meeting, 2008: 5). This highlights the directors' duty in general corporate law to Northern Rock plc to take into account the interests of the company's creditors over and above those of the shareholders when a company gets to a point near to insolvency (Keay, 2001, 2003).

The UK regulator could have avoided this spectacle if it had in place powers to deal with banks that are not technically insolvent but are experiencing considerable levels of financial distress. In addition to its extensive powers to supervise and take enforcement action against a bank failing to comply with the regulatory requirements noted above (Singh, 2007: 113), it needed to have in place a crisis management strategy that recognized the implications of corporate transparency and disclosure, and also a strategy to manage the media reaction. In the light of the publicity about the FSA's inadequacy, it not only failed to buy time to resolve Northern Rock's problems, but in fact aggravated them. Second the UK's lack of a coherent strategy to restructure a bank in distress prevented the FSA from resolving the issues as efficiently as possible. Third, the last obstacle and in many ways the most difficult was the lack of mechanisms to restructure the bank and its balance sheet, either to turn its fortunes around or to liquidate it and have it wound up. In this case, mechanisms used in the USA, such as bridge banks and purchase and assumption regimes, could have enabled the authorities to deal with the problems efficiently; this would have protected depositors and financial stability by enabling customers to get access to their funds as quickly as possible (Bliss and Kaufman, 2006; Mayes and Liuksila, 2003). More specifically, the FSA needs formal mechanisms to intervene before insolvency ensues; to take full control of a bank; to take control of the management of a bank and set to one side the interests of shareholders and creditors at the earliest opportunity; to assist in a merger or sale without getting shareholder approval; to seek a timely recapitalization of a bank with shareholders' assistance; and to restructure a bank and allow other institutions to take on critical banking functions. In addition, the authorities needed to be able to deal with the individual directors and senior management of Northern Rock if they thought its demise was the result of mismanagement, rather than unforeseeable events outside the control of its management (Hupkes, 2000; Campbell and Cartwright, 2002).

CONCLUSION

This chapter has sought to analyse the interplay between general corporate law and banking regulation and supervision. It is important to highlight how corporate law provides limited safeguards to protect the interests of depositors, giving rise to the necessity for some form of public regulation. In general terms corporate law is designed to maximize shareholder wealth; the interests of creditors are only considered to a limited extent during the existence of a company. Reports on corporate governance have preserved the importance of 'entrepreneurial spirit', and have avoided putting in place layers of accountability that may hinder this.

In the banking context the interests of depositors and shareholders can compete with one another, depending on whether one is looking at it from a corporate law or a bank regulation perspective. From a bank regulation perspective, for the purposes of depositor protection additional responsibilities are placed on shareholders to ensure they are fit and proper to hold a controlling position in a bank. The criteria require shareholder controllers to be mindful of the interests of depositors and to stand behind a bank if need arises, as a possible last resort. While bank regulation and supervision do not advocate pulling back the 'entrepreneurial spirit', they have certainly reconfigured the general corporate law position so that banks are mindful of the interests of other stakeholders in their decision-making processes. Regulators have thus mirrored commercial practice, and enshrined the idea that 'entrepreneurial spirit' is secure provided it satisfies supervisory objectives.

The FSA has brought to the fore the interests of a number of other stakeholders of which banks need to be mindful, including regulators. In addition, the importance of maintaining market confidence, integrity and reputation gives rise to the possibility of the FSA taking enforcement action if these are undermined or damaged by a bank's actions. The FSA has formalized rules and principles to govern regulated firms at institutional and individual levels. These principles and rules have a number of features in common with the standard of care expected in common law. The standard of care is, however, fleshed out with additional rules and guidance to ensure more certainty and precision in its application. The way in which the principles have been enforced at institutional and individual levels indicates that the FSA has tried to realign the interests of consumers and practitioners through their enforcement. However, when a bank in the UK experiences distress, like Northern Rock, the system at the moment does not have the appropriate mechanisms to deal with the situation as efficiently as possible. As a consequence the authorities were forced to take the extreme measure of putting in place a blanket guarantee to prop up Northern Rock. What this demonstrates is that banks need not only a separate system of regulation but also a separate system of insolvency and liquidation procedures to protect financial stability and depositor interests. The authorities will have the difficult task of weighing up these as well as a host of other competing interests which is not easy at all, as none of the possible measures highlighted above will really be a panacea for dealing with banks in distress.

ACKNOWLEDGEMENTS

I would like to thank Dr Eva Hupkes, Head of Regulation, Swiss Federal Banking Commission for comments.

NOTES

1. It is the accountability of the company and its management which is the primary issue examined in this chapter.
2. See also *Dawson International plc v. Coats Paton plc* [1989], where Lord Cullen interpreted the position as directors having only 'one master, the company'; *Howard Smith Ltd v. Ampol Petrol Ltd* [1974], in particular where 'in the interests of the company as whole is interpreted to mean in the interests of the company as a commercial entity', at p. 824; and *Brady v. Brady* [1988], where Nourse LJ referred to 'the interests of the company' as having a meaning relative to the principles which are being considered, at p. 23.
3. Where the decisions taken by directors needed to only take into account present rather than future shareholders, at p. 244.
4. See also Hampel Report (1998: para. 1.17). It cautions against expanding directors' obligations to other stakeholders with an interest in the company. See also s. 172 of the Companies Act 2006.
5. Lord Templeman: 'If the bank becomes insolvent the customer can only prove in the liquidation of the bank as unsecured creditor for the amount which was, or ought to have been, credited to the account at the date when the bank went into liquidation', at p. 1074.
6. A bank is exposed to the risk of a bank run if it experiences a large number of depositors simultaneously seeking to withdraw the money in their accounts.
7. Available online. The URLs are listed in the References under the sub-heading *FSA handbooks*.
8. In the *Banque Brussels* case, where there was a similar set of circumstances, a contractual promise was said to exist. But the decision in *Kleinwort Benson* was reaffirmed by the Court of Appeal in *Re Atlantic Computers plc* [1995].

REFERENCES

Cases

Bank of Credit and Commerce International (Overseas) Ltd (in liquidation) and Others v. Price Waterhouse and Another (No. 3), *The Times*, 2 April 1998.

Banque Brussels Lambert v. Australian National Industries (1989) 21 NSWLR 502.
Barings plc v. Coopers & Lybrand [1997] 1 BCLC 427.
Barings plc v. Coopers & Lybrand [2003] EWHC 1319 (Ch) 11 June 2003 (unreported).
Berg & Sons v. Adams [1993] BCLC 1045, 1055.
Brady v. Brady [1988] BCLC 20.
Brazier v. Skipton Rock Co., Ltd [1962] 1 All ER 955.
Daniels v. Anderson 16 ACSR [1995] 607, 667.
Dawson International plc v. Coats Paton plc [1989] BCLC 233.
Dias v. O'Sullivan [1949] ALR 586.
Dubai Aluminium v. Salaam [2002] 3 WLR 1913.
Edward Thomas Foley v. Thomas Hill [1848] II HLC 1002.
Geoffrey Alan Hoodless & Sean Michael Blackwell v. Financial Services Authority, 3 October 2003, www.financeandtaxtribunals.gov.uk/decisions/seldecisions/financialservices.htm, 8 June 2006.
Gibson v. Skibs A/S Marina and Orkla Grobe A/B and Smith Coggins, Ltd [1966] 2 All ER 476.
Heron International v. Lord Grade [1983] BCLC 244.
Howard Smith Ltd v. Ampol Petrol Ltd [1974] AC 821.
Ian Douglas Cox v. Financial Services Authority, 12 May 2003, www.financeandtaxtribunals.gov.uk/decisions/seldecisions/financialservices.htm, 8 June 2006.
Kleinwort Benson v. MMC Metals Ltd [1989] 1 WLR 379.
Marchesi v. Barnes [1970] VR 434.
Meridian Global Funds Management Asia Ltd v. Securities Commission [1995] BCC 942.
Percival v. Wright [1902] 2 Ch 421.
Re Atlantic Computers plc [1995] BCC 696.
Re Brazilian Rubber Plantations and Estates Ltd [1911] 1 Ch 425.
R v. Hyde JJ (1912) *The Times Law Reports*, **106**, 152.
Secretary of State v. Ettinger, Re Swift 736 Ltd [1993] BCLC 896.
Space Investments Ltd v. Canadian Imperial Bank of Commerce Trust Co. (Bahamas) Ltd and others [1986] 1 WLR 1072.
Tesco Supermarkets Ltd v. Nattrass [1972] AC 153.
West Mercia Safetywear Ltd v. Dodd [1988] BCLC 250.

FSA Handbooks

APER *Statements of Principle and Code of Practice for Approved Persons*, http://fsahandbook.info/FSA/html/handbook/APER.
AUTH *Authorisation*, http://fsahandbook.info/FSA/html/handbook/AUTH.
COND *Threshold Conditions*, http://fsahandbook.info/FSA/html/handbook/COND.
ENF *Enforcement*, http://fsahandbook.info/FSA/html/handbook/ENF.
FIT *The Fit and Proper Test for Approved Persons*, http://fsahandbook.info/FSA/html/handbook/FIT.
IPRU *Interim Prudential Sourcebook for Banks*, http://fsahandbook.info/FSA/html/handbook/IPRU-Bank.
PRIN *Principles for Businesses*, http://fsahandbook.info/FSA/html/handbook/PRIN.

SUP   *Supervision*, http://fsahandbook.info/FSA/html/handbook/SUP.
SYSC   *Senior Management Arrangements, Systems and Controls*, http://fsahand-book.info/FSA/html/handbook/SYSC.

Literature

Aldridge, P. (2007), 'Who's next? Financial stocks dive on contagion fear', *The Times*, 15 September, p. 29.

Bank of England, HM Treasury and FSA (2008), *Financial Stability and Depositor Protection: Strengthening the Framework*, Cm 7308, January.

Berle, A. A. and G. C. Means (1997 [1932]), *The Modern Corporation and Private Property*, New Brunswick NJ: Transaction Publishers.

Bliss, R. R. and G. G. Kaufman (2006), 'A comparison of US corporate and bank insolvency resolution', *Federal Reserve Bank of Chicago, Economic Perspectives*, **44**.

Cadbury Report (1992), *Report of the Committee on the Financial Aspects of Corporate Governance*, London: Gee Publishing.

Campbell, A. and P. Cartwright (2002), *Banks in Crisis: The Legal Response*, Aldershot: Ashgate.

Campbell, A. and D. Singh (2007) 'Legal aspects of the interests of depositor creditors: the case for deposit protection systems', in A. Campbell, J. R. LaBrosse, D. G. Mayes and D. Singh (eds), *Deposit Insurance*, Basingstoke: Palgrave, 40–70.

Cheffin, B. (1997), *Company Law: Theory, Structure, and Operation*, Oxford: Clarendon Press.

European Parliament, Economic and Scientific Policy Department (2007), *Financial Supervision and Crisis Management in the EU* (IP/A/ECON/IC/2007-069).

FSA (1998), *Meeting Our Responsibilities*, August.

FSA (2002a), 'An ethical framework for financial services', *Discussion Paper 18*, October.

FSA (2002b), *Final Notice: Credit Suisse First Boston International*, 11 December.

FSA (2002c), FSA/PN/124, 19 December.

FSA (2003), 'FSA fines Abbey National companies 2,320,000', 10 December FSA/PN/132/2003, http://www.fsa.gov.uk/Pages/Library/Communication/PR/2003/132.shtml

FSA (2004), *Final Notice: John Edward Rouke*, 18 November.

FSA (2005a), *Final Notice: Abbey National plc*, 25 May.

FSA (2005b), *Final Notice: Citigroup Global Markets Ltd*, 28 June.

FSA (2005c), *Final Notice: City Index Ltd*, 22 March.

FSA (2005d), *Final Notice: India Buildings Friendly Society*, 7 October.

FSA (2005e), *Final Notice: Michael Harding*, 21 January.

FSA (2007), *Statement for depositors: Northern Rock*, 15 September.

Garten, H. A. (1986), 'Banking on the market: relying on depositors to control bank risk', *Yale Journal on Regulation*, **4**, 129–72.

Hampel Report (1998), *Report of the Committee on Corporate Governance*, London: Gee Publishing.

HM Treasury (1985), *Banking Supervision*, white paper, Cmnd 9695, HMSO.

Hupkes, E. (2000), *Legal Aspects of Bank Insolvency*, The Hague: Kluwer Law Publishing.

Keay, A. (2001), 'The director's duty to take into account the interests of company creditors: when is it triggered?', *Melbourne University Law Review*, **25**, 315–39.

Keay, A. (2003), 'Directors taking into account creditors' interests', *Company Lawyer*, **24**, 300–6.

Macey, J. R. and M. O'Hara (2003), 'Corporate governance of banks', *Federal Reserve Bank of New York Economic Policy Review*, April, 93 http://www.newyorkfed.org/research/epr/03v09n1/0304mace.pdf, 5 July 2005.

Mayes, D. G. and A. Liuksila (2003), *Who Pays for Bank Insolvency?*, Basingstoke: Palgrave Macmillan.

Northern Rock plc (2008), 'Notice of extraordinary general meeting and unanimous recommendation of the directors to vote against resolutions 1, 2, 3 & 4 and for resolutions 5, 6, 7, 8 & 9', Newcastle: Northern Rock plc.

Parkinson, J. (1993), *Corporate Power and Responsibility: Issues in the Theory of Company Law*, Oxford: Clarendon Press.

Prentice, D. D. (1990), 'Creditors' interests and directors' duties', *Oxford Journal of Legal Studies*, **10**, 265–77.

Sappideen, R. (1991), 'Fiduciary obligations to corporate creditors', *Journal of Business Law*, July, 365–97.

Sheikh, S. and W. Rees (1995), *Corporate Governance and Corporate Control*, London: Cavendish.

Singh, D. (2007), *Banking Regulation of UK and US Financial Markets*, Aldershot: Ashgate Publishing.

Smart, P. E. (1990), *Leading Cases in the Law of Banking*, London: Sweet and Maxwell.

Index